FortCollins
Yesterdays

by

Evadene Burris Swanson

Fort Collins.

D. Van Lennep's Sketch of Fort Collins dated 1866.
The original is in the Special Collections Department of the Colorado State
University Libraries.

Copyright © 1975 Evadene Burris Swanson
Library of Congress Catalog Card Number 74-83114
International Standard Book Numbers: Paperback ISBN 0-9600862-2-6
                                          Hardbound ISBN 0-9600862-1-8
Composition and printing by Don-Art Printers, Inc.
Publisher Evadene Burris Swanson, 620 Mathews #115, Fort Collins, Colo.
   80521
Endorsed by Colorado Centennial-Bicentennial Commission

Contents

Acknowledgments

The long term residents who have graciously shared their reminiscences and advice for this study have made the work a friendly and inspiring experience. They make far too long a list to be cited individually, but special thanks are due for their good humor, patience, and encouragement to Richard S. Baker, Mildred Payson Beatty, Nedra Dils, Wesley Swan, the staff of the Pioneer Museum, and friends in the Western History Interest Group of the Colorado State University Women's Association. Much of the material was assembled during field trips sponsored by this group.

Picture Credits:

Fort Collins
    Christine Schlitt Amen, page 55
    Richard S. Baker, 89
    Mildred Payson Beatty, 117
    Colorado State University, 10, 15, 16, 43, 45, 48, 50, 97, 118 top
    Carrie Williams Darnell, 28
    Fort Collins Public Library, 198, 199 top
    John Hartman, 125
    Home Federal Savings and Loan Association, 163
    B.B. Marshall, 207 top
    Eva Martinez, 67
    Frank McConnell, 201
    Nelson McGraw, 211, 212
    Lydia Hoffman Morrison, 109
    Bill Moseley, 92, 93
    H.S. and Irene McClelland Norlin, 158
    Pioneer Museum, 14, 53, 54, 87, 95, 117 bottom, 118 bottom, 185
    Roy and Margaret Ross Portner, 127, 201
    Doris Rust, 7, 81, 194
    William C. Stover, 183
    Martha Trimble, 168 bottom
    Jack Wagar, 88

Denver
    Colorado Historical Society, 90, 91, 118, 160
    Public Library Western History Collection, 41, 107, 111, 116, 119, 122
    Kenneth Fuller, 166 top, 167
    Great Western Sugar Company, 52, 58

Elsewhere
    Greeley, Colorado Museum, 151
    Nevada State Museum, 75
    Sara Overholt, Mattituck, N.Y., 29
    Charles Scribners' Sons, 31
    Smithsonian Institution, National Anthropological Archives, 8, 82, 83, 84

Fort Collins
Yesterdays

There is an aura of mystery and romance about the beginning of a city. Just why was a cluster of houses built at one particular spot at a certain time, and were the lives of the people shaped in a special way because they chose that location? The history of the formation of a western city is particularly exciting because the pioneer epic was barely history when it began to be re-enacted in vivid fiction, wild west shows, and cowboy movies. These all had dramatic settings, magnificent scenery with open prairies and backdrops of rugged mountains. There was tenseness because of the clash between whites and Indians. Both sides had heroes and villains. Finally the settlers won out over many adversities. The little town lived through a rough period of adjustment and grew into a typical American city, racing to catch up with the amenities and culture of older areas.

Can we apply the techniques of historical scholarship to one city, Fort Collins, and sift fact from fiction to test the pattern? Many of the people moving into the city in the 1970's are eager to try. They are amazed to find how young the city is and how many relics there still are from early days. The Pioneer Museum is crammed with them. They include a lacy jabot that adorned the neck of one lady at Christmas, 1866, a soldier's rusted sword abandoned in a stable at the fort, and trade beads that some Indian once carried found a few miles north of the city. One entire cabin from the fort itself survived many uses and was moved to an honored spot in the modern city's park. A second cabin, slightly older, now placed next to it, belonged to a French Canadian trader. He married a Sioux, learned that language, and served as interpreter and guide for the soldiers.

In the surrounding countryside scattered through foothills and canyons are traces of early occupants. There are square nails, old wheels and bottles, logs from miners' cabins and sawmills, paths from toll roads, and a stage coach stop once run by a notorious desperado who was later hanged by vigilantes in Montana. Even Mark Twain considered meeting the wicked Jack Slade a highlight of his western journey in 1861. There are many official documents, surveyors' records and maps, land titles, water records, and government reports with clues to specific incidents related to Fort Collins. There are still a few people who can recall first hand some of the dramatic changes and many, a generation or two removed, who cherish stories, pictures, and heirlooms associated with their relatives.

The centennial of Colorado and the bicentennial of the country strongly spotlight the search for knowledge about problems and people at the grass roots level. It is not that Fort Collins was so different in its development from other areas, but perhaps by studying it in depth we will discover a pattern and a meaning for life in America. Residents were real people, not characters in a novel. Few were famous beyond the county border, yet living here added a zest to their existence, and their lives add zest to ours. Newcomers, through historical tours, can see where they lived, worked, worshipped, and played, and can value living here more than ever.

Ansel Watrous, a young carpenter, arrived in Fort Collins in late December, 1877, having come by train from Wisconsin to Cheyenne. The Colorado Central to Denver had engine, tender, baggage car, and one coach. The passengers were all men, mostly stock growers or traveling salesmen. W.B. Miner (later mayor of Fort Collins) and Hugh Barton, another sheep raiser, got off at Bristol Station (north of present Wellington) to go to their ranches. Between that stop and the bluff north of Fort Collins there was no house, cabin, or tree! Lights in three homes twinkled as Watrous approached. One belonged to P.G. Terry whose property later became the site of the Larimer and Weld Reservoir. Another was P.P. Black's at the north end of the present Terry Lake. Augustine Mason's, south of Willox Lane near the river, was the third. Ansel's uncle, William Watrous, met him at the station and took him in a spring wagon to the family home on College and Myrtle. Ansel thought he'd never seen so dreary a town when he woke Sunday to explore, yet he grew to love every inch of it and to appreciate the people. Best of all, he meticulously wrote up all that he learned.(1)

Watrous relied on the files of the newspaper he founded but went far beyond that to produce his monumental **History of Larimer County** in 1911. It was a labor of love, not a finanial success, and finally many unsold copies were destroyed to save storage costs. But by 1972 the library volumes were so tattered and the book so rare that the local DAR chapter somewhat hesitantly issued a reprint of the book. This time there was no question of finding storage space for unsold copies. There was an immediate and continuing rush of buyers at Juliana Miller's dance studio office on Shields Street when the books became available. Many purchasers bought a personal copy and one for each child in the family or for interested relatives and friends.

The notes assembled in this study are intended as a supplement to Watrous' tremendous achievement. They are offered as an interpretation for newcomers to orient those unfamiliar with the locale and landmarks which have changed from those Watrous described in 1911.

The first part is an overview of the town. It introduces the people who came and shows how the geography of the area dictated drastic changes in their life styles.

The second section is a personal sampling of people, places, and problems. Every house has a story to tell. Each individual's life is of value. The material presented in this section cannot cover the wealth of available stories. It does not even limit itself to the most powerful or influential citizens of the fledgling community. These are just the people who emerged as real persons to me. Those who study any of the topics may revise the picture. Since each section in Part II is to be read as a unit, there is some repetition of essential facts to make each sketch independent.

Part I: The Overview

The decade of the 1830's was a busy one for fur traders on the South Platte. Between the modern cities of Greeley and Denver there were four adobe forts in operation. Traders, French Canadians from St. Louis, mountain men, and Indians followed the tributaries into the mountains and northwest along the branch which came to be known as the Cache la Poudre.(1) The river curved and bent and formed oxbows as the current cut new channels. It encouraged the growth of a few cottonwoods and willows, and served as a point of location for the travelers along the foothills. The lush grasses of the flood plains attracted game needed by both whites and Indians.

There are many authentic records for this period of the fur trade at Fort St. Vrain, the most northern of the four posts. It was located near modern Greeley. Little was written about the Cache la Poudre, the banks of which were used by prairie dog colonies rarely disturbed. The plains were treeless, and the river gave little promise for future town building. More recent boosters of Larimer County insisted that the mountain men would not have neglected the trapping and hunting in their canyons and foothills. On the weakest of sources, (2) they have adopted the colorful Kit Carson. Most newcomers today on their first trip up the canyon of the Big Thompson or the Cache la Poudre will be told that Kit trapped the headwaters. The story is possible but not verified.

Carson knew the trail well along the foothills northwest to Wyoming's Laramie Plains. He and Thomas Fitzpatrick, another experienced mountain man, had crossed Colorado many times traveling between Taos and Santa Fe in Mexican territory, Bent's Fort on the Arkansas, and Fort Laramie in present day Wyoming. The last was at the junction of the Laramie and North Platte Rivers. Bent's Fort and Fort Laramie were strategic points in the fur trade of the late 1830's. John Charles Fremont used Fort St. Vrain in 1843 for preparations, outfitting his exploring expedition into the far west. He was lucky to have both Carson and Fitzpatrick as guides. While they were in that area they encountered Friday, the Arapaho friend of Fitzpatrick, who later became a well-known figure at Fort Collins. Part of Fremont's party went northwest along the Poudre crossing it a number of times. On the return journey from the west Fremont entered Colorado in the large mountain parks now called North, Middle and South Park. This was all then part of either Mexican or Texan territory, but claims were vague and unimportant since the area was unoccupied.

The late '40's brought many changes to the region because of the Mexican War, the settlement of Oregon, the Mormon trek to Utah, and the gold rush to California. Even the political conflicts over slavery had repercussions on the Rocky Mountain west. The picturesque days of the fur trade were over. In 1849 Fort Laramie was made a military post, part of a chain to protect the travelers in covered wagons. The organization of Nebraska Territory including northern Colorado and the present site of Fort Collins under the Kansas-Nebraska Act of 1854 made legal apparatus for land claims a little more definite for the area. All these developments encouraged some individuals to settle near the trails where they furnished hay and stock to the soldiers and immigrants and shared in what few amenities these rough outposts provided.

In 1858 when gold was discovered near modern Denver, Antoine Janis left Fort Laramie, became a guide for prospectors and in 1859 built his log cabin on the north side of the Cache la Poudre.(3) He was joined by other French Canadians, many with Indian wives, and the town site of Colona, later Laporte, was laid out. The whole area along the foothills north of Pike's Peak was explored by excited miners and the little cluster of cabins around that of Janis grew with the flurry of the "rush." One of these hopeful individuals in 1859 was Dr. A.F. Peck known to history through his advertisement on the first page of the first issue of the **Rocky Mountain News.** The doctor expected to open an office at Cache-a-la-Poudre, Nebraska Territory, where he promised to be found "when not professionally engaged or digging gold." The paper was set up in Omaha before he and William N. Byers left there to go west, one to practice medicine and pan gold, the other to start a newspaper. The doctor performed an autopsy on a lynched horse thief in Omaha. Examining the victim's clothes, he found three hundred dollars which he appropriated to outfit himself and Byers for the trip west. He abandoned Laporte for Denver in 1860.(4)

Horace Greeley came west in 1859 and went from Denver to Fort Laramie where he took the Overland Stage to California. He, like Dr. Peck, refered to the little settlement (later Laporte) as Cache la Poudre and he heard that encouraging signs of gold had been found.

Miners and freighters were shadowy figures on the frontier moving casually from place to place. They were not overly concerned about founding cities, but several, around 1860, seemed ready to settle down and were attracted by the natural beauty of the Poudre valley. Ebenezer Davis from Wales tried his luck mining and trading with the Indians, then settled southwest of present Fort Collins near the river. George Robert Strauss, a young man of twenty-seven seasoned by the border wars of the '50's in Kansas, took an oxteam to Utah in 1858 with supplies for Albert Sidney Johnston's army. The soldiers were sent there because the federal government was uneasy about the Mormon activity in Utah. There was a basic dislike of their philosophy and suspicion that they were inciting the Indians to unite. The Mormons and Indians seemed to help one another as minorities on the defensive. Strauss planned to go on to California after completing his mission,

Strauss Cabin on the Poudre near Horsetooth Road

but he contracted pneumonia, was robbed by Mormons, and finally in six weeks walked back east as far as the Cache la Poudre valley, arriving in May, 1860. He hunted game for the Denver market, raised vegetables north of the river to sell to immigrants, and after the flood of 1864 built a cabin south of the river which is still standing on the original site.(5)

The election of Lincoln and the outbreak of the Civil War made the military posts along the western trails and the carrying of mail even more essential to defense. Indian unrest in Wyoming caused the Overland Stage to change its route to northern Colorado in 1862. The line ran generally east-west across the northern plains, with a loop down to Denver for those who chose it. Laporte became a "home" station for coaches from Denver and from Latham, south of modern Greeley. The Sherwood brothers' ranch on the river between present day Drake and Horsetooth Roads was a coach stop.

Fifteen different station sites have been identified in Larimer County though not all were used at one time. Some were simply for change of horses, not providing inn facilities, meals, and a real "rest stop" like the "home" stations. Since Laporte was quite a distance from Fort Laramie by horseback or coach, troops were stationed there, first from Denver in 1863, and then cavalry units from Fort Laramie in the spring of 1864.

The 1864 flood that damaged Strauss' garden did even more damage to the soldiers' rude cabins and tents at Laporte so that summer the commander at Fort Laramie ordered that a better location be chosen. It must be on higher and more

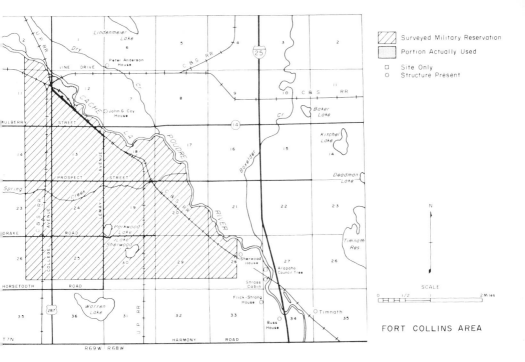

FORT COLLINS AREA

open ground to defend it against approaching Indians. Unfortunately, since the new site was selected in July when the waters had subsided, the soldiers were unaware that they were moving from one flood plain to another.

Affairs were going well for the Union forces when these western soldiers moved to the new site. Lincoln had been reelected and Sherman was planning his victorious march to the sea after his victory in Atlanta. Both the camp at Laporte and the new location received the name of William O. Collins, commander at Fort Laramie, who supervised the activities. The quartermaster for the army advertised for hay for "Camp Collins" in 1866, and the officials called the election precinct on the new site "Camp Collins" in 1868, so the moment when it ceased to be a "camp" and became a "fort" is uncertain. In fact, one pioneer recalled:

It was not much of a fort after all. There were no embattled walls.....not even a stockade to keep out the moaning wind and the whistling arrow. It was a plain, every day, very western fort, consisting largely of parade ground and flagpole with a trio of log huts on one side for the officers quarters, and on the east and west sides, extending toward the river, the log barracks for the men. Under the bluff in dugouts were stationed the horses of the command. The enclosed space, falling off gently to the river, formed the parade grounds.(6)

7

Friday, right, at Cheyenne Agency c.1860. American Philosophical Society Transactions XII, 1863.

Most of the fur traders' forts had adobe walls or log stockades as a boundary, but the little group of cavalry on the Poudre lacked even this protection. Why was this fort made in such a casual fashion? Perhaps the Colorado route was considered less dangerous because of the friendly Arapahoes. The cavalry of the Eleventh Ohio from Fort Laramie built Fort Mitchell in a more substantial way near Scott's Bluff, Nebraska Territory, in 1864 and this was used until 1867, exactly the period of Fort Collins. It was of adobe and port-holed with sentinel towers at the corners. It never developed into a town and the remains are completely plowed up now.

The new site of Camp Collins was occupied in October, 1864, just before one of the most important Indian encounters of western history, the Battle or "Massacre" at Sand Creek in November in southeastern Colorado. This slaughter of Indians spread the desire for revenge through the tribes and made overland travel dangerous for isolated parties. The soldiers and settlers along the Poudre were fortunate, however, in having as neighbors Chief Friday and friendly Arapahoes, who stole horses but apparently never threatened lives.

Another bit of good fortune for the cavalry was having Auntie Stone, a vigorous woman in her sixties, who cooked for the officers in her log cabin. This is the only building which has survived from the days of the fort. She got the soldiers to put in a garden across the river and the celery she planted was the first raised in the valley. Besides improving the diet she added to the fun. Her stepson, Lew Stone, lived north of the fort in a canyon that still bears his name. He called square dances at Auntie's parties. Her widowed niece, Elizabeth Keays, came west in June, 1866, with her young son and quickly found a new husband in the area short of women. She recalled that there was only one inspection of the troops after her arrival and the men struggled to pass it.(7) General Sherman came to look over the fort in 1866, and found the soldiers poorly armed for Indian warfare though he did praise the storage houses. He recommended the abandonment of the post. Many of the soldiers had already been discharged in 1866 and the fort was closed in March, 1867, having existed less than two and a half years.

Primitive though the accommodations at the fort were, the needs of the soldiers attracted some civilians and brought profits to those already living along the river. Besides Auntie Stone and her relatives there were Henry Clay Peterson, a gunsmith, and his brother, Fountain, a photographer. Peter Anderson, an immigrant from Norway, moved from Wisconsin to the fort in 1865. E.W. Whitcomb, from Massachusetts, and Benjamin Whedbee, from North Carolina, were engaged in cattle business in the neighborhood. John G. Coy, a New Yorker, traveling west by covered wagon in 1862, stopped to winter in the Poudre valley and settled permanently across the river from the fort. By far the most prosperous of the area residents however was the French Canadian, Joseph Mason. He combined stock raising which was just beginning in the region, with the profitable job of running the sutler's store at the fort.

Mason had several partners in his various enterprises. He and one of the Sherwood brothers supplied horses to this post and others along the army's line of defense. Mason's older brother, Augustine, moved west to join him at the fort in 1866. Joseph hired him to drive a mule team east to Fort Leavenworth taking soldiers at thirty dollars a man to be mustered out. Mason had recommended the site for Fort Collins when it was moved from Laporte and the official military reservation lay between his claim and Sherwoods'. His taxes, paid at Laporte, the county seat, in 1866 were almost two hundred dollars higher than those of the other

FIRST STORE IN FORT COLLINS.

Drawing from Das-
tarac's map, 1884.

residents. Whitcomb, Whedbee, Loomis and the Sherwood brothers shared a tax bracket between fifty-five and eighty-five dollars, Strauss paid sixteen, Auntie Stone fifteen, and the Petersons, Coy, Anderson, and Dr. Smith, the civilian physician for the soldiers, all under ten.(8)

As the fort dwindled in importance in 1866 Mason had much to lose by the decline of the trading center which had begun at the post. The first transcontinental railroad was pushing across the country, and in 1867, Cheyenne, a new city, was born at "end of track," the construction point reached by the eastern extension. Fort Laramie, stranded north of the railroad, declined, and "Laramie City," as the present town of Laramie was known to distinguish it from the fort with the same name, grew up west of Cheyenne. It hoped to be the Pittsburgh of the west since the railroad repair and supply center was located there. Some people sold their Denver property and moved to Laramie in anticipation of a boom. But a town to the south of either Laramie or Cheyenne on the way to Denver had good prospects.

To boost Fort Collins' prosperity, Mason took the lead in persuading the legislature to transfer the county seat from Laporte to Fort Collins. This push was successful in 1868 and the county records were moved into "Old Grout," Mason's store. This building served as courthouse, church, theatre, community center, post office and heart of the little settlement. Henry Clay Peterson and Auntie Stone built a flour mill in 1869. A brick kiln was another new industry and a few brick houses were constructed. The soldiers had opened a road up the nearest canyon to the north to bring in timber. The Mason brothers built a bridge on that Rist canyon trail. Sawmills were begun near the river. In the 1870's there was one owned by Fred and Henry Smith on the Lone Pine Creek far in the mountains near the present Red Feather Lakes.(9) The road to Smith's mill had been built by tie crews bringing lodgepole pines down for the construction of the Union Pacific Railroad.

Other soldiers stationed at the fort really liked the area, claimed land, and brought families west when the Civil War ended and their military service was over. Two of these were John Mandeville and George Buss who both predicted a bright future for the Poudre valley. Buss bought a house in 1866 not far from Strauss' cabin on the river. The grove of cottonwoods at an oxbow on the Poudre north of his farm was a popular picnic area for pioneers. Mandeville and Buss helped preserve memories of the fort by sketching its appearance in 1865. Because the drawings differ in detail they form interesting sources for speculation today.

Another momentous decision of the territorial legislature was selecting Fort Collins as the site of a future agricultural college. This action in 1870 elevated the status of the little community in northern Colorado. The Land Grant College Act of 1862 had established a national pattern, and those interested in promoting the area counted on this prize. The period between the end of the fort in 1867 and the aggressive development of the town by the Agricultural Colony in 1873 was a shaky one for the few residents. Having the territorial government select Fort Collins as the site for a future land grant college was a tremendous boost to the morale.

Settlement as a joint enterprise of like-minded individuals was a principle as American as the Pilgrims and the Puritans, but it got new force in the post-Civil War development of Colorado Territory. A group from Mercer, Pennsylvania, tried Laporte and Fort Collins in 1869, calling themselves the New Mercer Colony. They built an irrigation ditch from the river, part of which is still used. Greeley was started by the Union Colony in 1870. The crusade against alcohol as the social evil of the century was upheld by Nathaniel Meeker and other founders. Longmont was a colony town of 1871. Immigrants from the little town of Ryssby, Sweden, chose a spot southwest of Longmont around 1870 to start Ryssby, Colorado.

Some of the leaders at Greeley had barely launched that town when they decided to sponsor another one upstream and the Agricultural Colony at Fort Collins was organized. The fort itself had used only a tiny part of the four square miles reserved for military needs and closed to settlement. The opening of this land for private titles gave the special incentive. The new business men had to conciliate the residents already settled in the neighborhood, some of whom were made trustees and were recognized in the new street names.

The river ran southeast by the fort and the first streets

View toward south at College and Mountain. Whedbee's store, white, in left foreground.

were parallel to its course. In the survey of the new town the direction of the streets was governed by compass points instead. Because of the system of rectangular land surveys, main roads developed a mile apart at the borders of each section. Vine, Mulberry, Prospect, and Drake are section boundaries as are College and Shields. The value of a few diagonals was recognized in nineteenth century city planning and Canyon Avenue was one, following an old trail to the mountains. Roads which clung to natural courses were called "gun barrel roads" and Riverside is an example of this type.

The first drawing for lots in December, 1872, on what was bravely designated as "College Avenue," brought a choice site into the hands of a lawyer, Jay H. Bouton, who represented a profession much needed on the frontier. Bouton had been admitted to the bar in Binghamton, New York, in 1870. He served as secretary of the Agricultural Colony. His frame office with false front, typical western town construction, was the first business structure on the new main street. Benjamin Whedbee had taken over some of Joseph Mason's mercantile interests since the latter had bought the flour mill, ran a livery stable and served as sheriff. Whedbee moved his building from Jefferson Street, the old Denver road in times of the fort, to the southeast corner of the intersection of Mountain and College avenues. Bouton and the newcomers were using lots on the northwest corner. Whedbee's cooperation with the development of New Town helped swing sentiment and land values in that direction though loyalties were strongly divided between the two contiguous sections for the next forty years.

New ideas were coming to the West. When people went to Whedbee's store for drugs or general merchandise or mail in the rear section which served as post office, they studied a poster of an ape pouring liniment on his leg and read the ditty:

If I am Darwin's grandpapa
It follows don't you see
That what is good for man and beast
Is doubly good for me(10)

Darwin's theories appearing in the 1860's were expanded in his publication, **THE DESCENT OF MAN**, in 1871. No better place to be introduced to new concepts existed on the frontier than the general store and post office. The public reading room was still one decade in the future and the public library three.

The next few years after the new streets were laid out were times of real testing and decision-making for many individuals in the Poudre valley. Would the town grow and prosper and make a pleasant setting for a home or were chances better in one of the communities popping up elsewhere in the Rocky Mountains? In 1875 the population of Fort Collins was estimated at five hundred. It boasted a drugstore, newspaper, livery stable, bank, three hotels, three sawmills nearby, one church with a building and three or four other congregations, and a flourmill. The mill, powered by water through its millrace nearly a mile long, was valued at fourteen thousand dollars. This was the bright side. The town had also suffered severe setbacks. The first bank, founded by the son of a Greeley colonist in 1873, failed in the national panic. Plagues of grasshoppers destroyed the crops for several seasons.

The shops, frame buildings with gables toward the street like Whedbee's, or with false fronts like Bouton's law office, opened on board sidewalks dotted with hitching posts along the dusty roads. That intrepid world traveler, Isabella Bird, stressed the drab qualities of the whole crop of new western towns in 1873. Cheyenne was "an ill-arranged set of frame houses and shanties." The odor of the offal from recently-butchered antelope and deer contaminated the air. Her hotel room in Greeley came complete with bedbugs and flies. The one in Fort Collins had fewer bugs and more flies. The tone of Fort Collins was characterized by "coarse speech, coarse food, coarse everything, nothing wherewith to satisfy the higher cravings if they exist." The lack of trees and the sandy ground dotted with prairie dog holes repelled those

Scotch pioneers celebrating Robert Burns' birthday.

accustomed to more luxuriant natural growth in areas of greater rainfall.

In spite of the drawbacks, representatives of countries all over the world came to seek their fortunes, establish temporary or permanent homes, and participate in town building. They provide an international flavor which has endured as a characteristic of the community.

There were many skilled craftsmen with confidence that they could pursue their trades anywhere. Vincenz Demmel, a shoemaker from Germany, came in 1873. His wife and children came later, planning to meet him in Denver. Somehow the appointment was missed and they arrived in Fort Collins by stage to spend the anxious first night buried in their feather ticks and expecting an Indian attack. Auntie Stone called the next day to welcome and reassure Mrs. Demmel. Though she spoke no German and the newcomer no English, Mrs. Stone hired Mrs. Demmel to help out in the hotel kitchen.(11)

Louis Dauth, a German veteran of the Franco-Prussian war, opened a bakery on Linden in 1877. After a few years he retired to Denver with sufficient funds to invest in real estate there and enjoy a comfortable old age. Albert Damm, born in Magdeburg, Germany, started another bakery on Linden Street in 1889, and later another on College. His family continued to operate the business a few years after his death in 1929. There was also A. Thoss, a watchmaker who had learned his trade in Germany, working in Fort Collins in 1882. Trautman, a glovemaker, leased ground north of the millrace to build a tannery in 1884. William Schueler, a blacksmith on Mountain Avenue in 1906, had thirty-eight years previous experience and held licenses from Cologne and Berlin. His father and grandfather had had similar licenses and some of the family had carried on that trade since 1736.(12)

Scotch farmers settled both north and south of the tiny town and by February 2, 1882, were celebrating the one-hundred and twenty-third anniversary of the birth of Robert Burns. They had a piper in kilts to add to the fun of their affairs. The Cuthbertson brothers, the Strachans, and the Strangs all lived south of town. James Strang bought a log cabin (now sided over) which stands on the road south of the Strauss cabin.

North of town was another Scotch community. William O'Brien, Charles Willox, and James and John Fraser settled on Willox Lane. The Willox family bought out Augustine Mason and moved his old house from the river northward, closer to the road where it still stands as a comfortable home for his descendants. Jane Fraser came from Scotland to marry O'Brien and Watrous noted that "she never had occasion to regret the voyage across the Atlantic."

Though Captain Josiah McIntyre, the blind Civil War veteran, was born in America, he gave his son, Clyde, a treasured heirloom from Scotland, a slate used by his great-grandfather.(13)

The three Davis brothers locating on farms southeast of Fort Collins were from Wales. So was William Morgan, a blacksmith with a shop on Chestnut, north of Jefferson. The railroad offered half fare for anyone wishing to go to Denver in 1896 for the "Eisteddfod." That celebration of old Welsh customs and dances was a happy gathering for new "westerners" from the old country.(14)

There were glamorous natives of France who added a special note of elegance and sophistication to many western towns. Georgetown had Louis Dupuy, who opened the Hotel

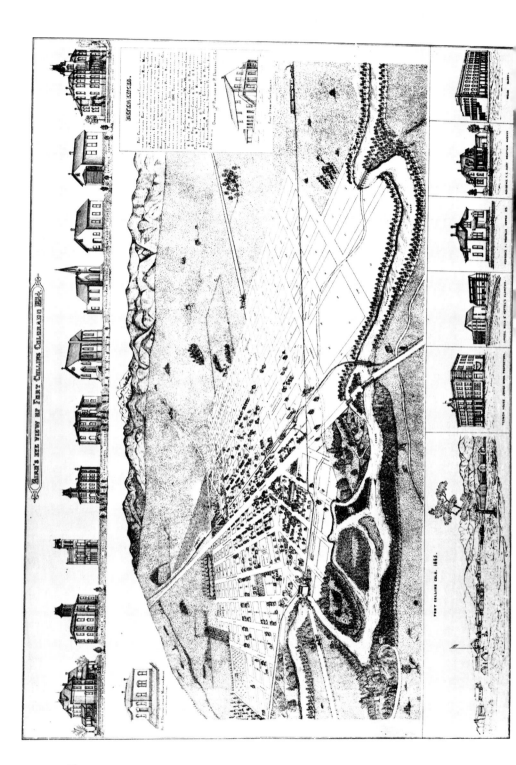

BIRD'S EYE VIEW OF FORT COLLINS COLORADO 1865.

FORT COLLINS COLO. 1865.

de Paris in 1875, and gained fame all over the Rockies for his gourmet food served in fashionable surroundings. Fort Collins had Frank or Pierre Dastarac, who painted houses and signs in the '80's and '90's. He had a gift for drawing and he worked for several years making a bird's eye view map of his adopted city which is one of the rare sources for the town's history. For its border, he sketched some of the homes of the out-standing citizens, Franklin Avery, James Arthur, and Benjamin Hottel. With these, he included the modest dwelling he oc-cupied, and the cottage of a compatriot, Madame Mary Roucolle, dressmaker lately of Paris, who guaranteed satisfaction in the cutting and fitting of garments. The Roucolle family contributed articles on the Franco-Prussian war from the French viewpoint to the local paper.(15)

Besides bonafide Frenchmen from Paris, there were French-Canadians holding claims on the river from Laporte to Tim-nath. They were a seasoned and hardy bunch who laughed at the difficulties of the wilderness. Fremont, whose father was a French tutor from the Caribbean, appreciated the bra-very of the French-Canadians on his 1843 expedition. Basil Lejeunesse swam the swollen Platte with a rope in his teeth to help pull the heavily-laden boats to the other side. On an earlier trip he refused to shorten the explorations for lack of food: "We'll eat the mules," he informed Fremont.

Some of these men were ready to settle down in the '50's and '60's. Many of them had Indian wives. Some are known only by their names on the transfer of claim titles. Jesse Sherwood described his land title near Drake road in 1863 as the Baptiste claim. Joe Mason bought his place near Vine and Shields on the south side of the river from the Indian widow of a French-Canadian, Gangros. Phillip Lariviere settled north of the river near College, the present location of Jax Surplus store. Joseph Lariviere was farther west. Desjardins was another oldtimer.

Most of the French-Canadian names are easy to recognize, but some are overlooked because they were anglicized. Joe Mason and his three brothers, Augustine, Frank, and Godfrey had the surname, Messieur, but changed it. Augustine spoke only French until he was twenty-one. Joe was the organizer of the family, running freight trains and hiring the others. A descendant of Augustine noted however "Augustine's contri-bution was populating the prairie. He had eleven children and over fifty grandchildren, several of whom still live in Fort Collins or close by."

Frank Mason's daughter, Caroline, married Pete Dion who

Arilla Dion McQuain, second from right at Wellington Hotel c.1916.

came to the Laporte area in the 1860's. Their cabin still stands, stuccoed over, in Bender's Trailer Court on North Shields off Highway 287. Their daughter, Arilla, born in 1881, kept the homestead papers made out in 1887, and her son has them now. She married Walter McQuain, a wellknown auctioneer. She was a dainty waitress in a hotel in Wellington in her youth. Later she was a popular and active member of the Daughters of Colorado Pioneers Club till her death in 1967.

Phillip Lariviere was a freighter and wagonmaster working for Joe Mason between Fort Laramie and Fort Hallock in the '60's. He was with A.H. Patterson running a bull train to Julesburg in 1866. He married Mary Harris, then went back to Canada. In 1878, hearing about the booming prosperity of Fort Collins after it had a railroad, he came back.

Louis Orleans, a veteran of Sand Creek, operated a store in Laporte for a while.

The moment of decision came for many of these families in the late '70's when pressure was put on the men with Indian wives to send or go with them to reservations. Antoine Janis went with his Sioux. Claymore and Morissette from the Laporte area also chose reservation life. John Provost stayed in Laporte while his wife went. Caroline Frazer Taft reminisced in 1911 about the Indian wives: "I liked them much and recall their dusky faces with pleasure and hoped they called me friend. They were kindly and cordial and loved sociability." She remembered particularly a granddaughter of Antoine Janis who was a neighbor.(16)

Not all shared her attitude as Fort Collins grew more settled with churches, good stores, and schools. Ansel Watrous disapproved so strongly of these alliances, he listed only the offspring of Rock Bush's second wife, Johanna Forbes, though his Indian wife died young and Johanna raised the step-children, Antoine and Joe. Grandchildren of both wives keep up family contacts today in spite of Watrous' deletion of part-Indian descendants in the family tree. Bush's name was originally Bousquet.

Far away China also contributed citizens to the area. All through the west wandered Chinese willing to do the menial work that others avoided. Three teen-agers came from Cheyenne in April, 1880—George Gowy, Chong Lay, and Chiong Ling. They ran a laundry and lived in a cabin back of the Tedmon House. Their arrival brought some expression of hostility for stones were thrown through the only window into the room where they were sleeping. They fired in response and Frank P. Stover reported bullets hitting his roof across the street. They did not give up though, and the laundries filled a much needed niche in Fort Collins society. George Gowy started a shop opposite the Commercial Hotel in November. In June, 1881 he had a storeroom in a building at the rear of the police court, and had a stock of teas and Chinese notions, including silk handkerchiefs and fans. Sam Lung had a laundry in the rear of Bernard's shoe store. In 1889 there were two competing Chinese wash houses, one on College, and another, run by George Along, on Cooler Alley. They once got into a fight and had to appear before Judge Bailey.

An expression of race relations quite in contrast to the stoning was evidenced in February, 1883. The Chinaman whose laundry was on College Avenue missed the train departing for Denver. He ran after it, skidded on Pine Street which was glazed with ice and collapsed. "Wooden sandals, clutching hands, and pigtail, made an amusing appearance." The conductor stopped the train; the man finally reached it, but was too exhausted to get on. Bolivar S. Tedmon, hotel builder and rancher, on the rear platform, pulled him aboard.(17)

In 1885 there was sharp censure for the killing of Chinese at Rock Springs, Wyoming: "A disgrace and lasting reproach to humanity." The territorial legislature had encouraged Chinese immigration in 1870, but national legislation stopped this movement in 1882. On the Colorado frontier, however, these newcomers were still needed and were appreciated. By 1890 there were about 1400 Chinese in the state.

The English, of course, were everywhere in the west in the late nineteenth century. It was the favorite place for the investment of capital and the placement of restless young men. In the foothills northwest of Fort Collins near the Poudre canyon was one of the "cowboy schools" where English families paid to have young men work on ranches. Catherine Lawder, an Irish barmaid at the Elkhorn Hotel nearby, divorced her miner husband and married Cecil Moon. When he inherited a title in 1898, it gave Fort Collins a sense of nearness to aristocracy to have Lady Moon living in the back country on a ranch. Even if she did not quite measure up to the image envisioned for Victorian or Edwardian England, she was a conspicuous figure when she appeared in town, generally wearing a plumed hat though the rest of her outfit was often somewhat disheveled. Silver, engraved with the coat of arms of the Moon family, is still used today by some Fort Collins' families.

Another treasure that suggested Britain and Empire was a camphorwood chest made in India for Leslie Horsley's father. He used it for desk and chest during thirty-five years of service with the British army. It was designed with removable legs so it formed a chest during travel. This heirloom found its way to the son's Livermore ranch and then to the town home of the Horsleys at 1001 Remington.

Most of these people came to Fort Collins by choice. One British subject who called the rough little town home between 1875 and 1882 was assigned to the region as missionary for the Episcopal church. Father Francis Byrne was sixty-eight when he arrived in Fort Collins and borrowed the Methodist church to hold an Episcopal service. In 1879 he preached in the Livermore hotel for the English scattered on ranches in that area. In 1880 he performed the service for the marriage of his daughter to a Fort Collins citizen. Later that year he helped in the Fourth of July celebration with the Rev. E.E. Edwards, president of the Agricultural College, who gave the oration. In February, 1881, he conducted the graveside service for Joseph Mason, whose funeral was in the Methodist church.(18)

After years in the mission field and the discouragement of working with miners, Father Byrne was delighted to build up the little congregation at St. Luke's in Fort Collins. He had the support of a few people like Jay Bouton and Benjamin Hottel who were firmly committed to the town. Then just as his parishioners were ready to build their own church the bishop abruptly transferred him to a mining community again.

He wanted badly to remain. He baptized his new grandchild just before leaving. In his new assignment he found his only support was the Sunday offering and a missionary stipend, an arrangement of the bishop of which he knew nothing till arrival, and he had to set about again making habitable a dilapidated old residence with leaky roof. "The Lord will provide," he wrote in his diary. He returned to Fort Collins in 1884 and 1885 for visits with his daughter and to deliver an address in the Methodist church. After four men had succeeded him he was invited to give a sermon at St. Luke's church on St. Luke's Day, October, 1887. His contribution to the pioneer community was commemorated by a stained glass window. This was incorporated in the chapel of the new church when the old building was dismantled in 1965.

Father Byrne had seen much of the world before he reached the western frontier. He had joined the British army to escape a stern Scotch father in Ireland, was ordained in Jamaica, and sent west from Boston. The Reverend Henry Martyn Richardson, Presbyterian minister for a time in Timnath, matched Father Byrne with his memories of distant places. He was born to missionary parents in Broussa, Turkey, in 1866, educated at Roberts College in Constantinople, at Beloit College in Wisconsin, and at a seminary in Chicago before his assignment to various Colorado churches towards the end of the century.

Religious services were held in other languages than English. Father Robinett was preaching in French at one hour and in German at another in 1885. A minister from Denver held Lutheran services in Norwegian and Danish the same year. In 1896 John Knutson preached in Swedish at the Christian Tabernacle.(19)

Those rugged characters who brought religion to the west shared in the hardships but loved the adventures and challenges. The American story has been jokingly summarized by the modes of travel employed. The Methodists came by horseback, the Presbyterians by train, and the Episcopalians waited for the Pullman. This fits Fort Collins only for Sheldon Jackson, that fiery little Presbyterian missionary. In Iowa he saw the Union Pacific heading west in 1869 and chose to follow it to a mission field in the Rockies in the '70's. He did not live in Fort Collins but helped organize its First Presbyterian Church in 1872. After founding many churches in Colorado, Wyoming and Montana, he took on the challenge of a new frontier in Alaska in the '80's. There while preaching the gospel, he accumulated a valuable collection of Indian and Eskimo art treasured today in a Sitka museum and displayed in Washington, D.C., at the National Gallery in 1973.(20)

Though the instruction at the college was rudimentary in the 1880's, a visitor came from Australia to inspect the campus and report to a Melbourne, Victoria paper. He found eighty students at the school. He summed up the work of the four faculty members under the categories botany, chemistry and physics, planting and plowing, and designing farm houses. He thought the professors poorly paid, getting but three hundred pounds a year, but he admired the practical approach in the classroom. They actually worked at the lathe, anvil, laboratory, and conservatory, or in the garden.(21)

Another man with experience in Australia was Hugh Barton. He came to work with sheep first on the Bachelder ranch at Spring Canyon, then on the Bristol ranch north of Fort Collins in 1879. He was born in Ireland, worked in Australia and New Zealand from 1857 to 1874, and then landed in California. Bachelder encouraged him to come to Larimer County. Barton compared ranching in the various areas and was quoted in the Fort Collins paper: "I wish you to say the American shearers are much better than those I have known in Australia and New Zealand. They are usually an intelligent set of men and do their work well." He opposed the introduction of the Cotswold breed into Larimer County, preferring grades worked up from Mexican ewes and Spanish Merino rams.(22)

Not only was Fort Collins a crossroad for people of the world, but settlers in the town were often taking off for foreign parts. Jerry DeCelle, a popular blacksmith, went to Australia in 1874. After his return to Kansas City, he was enticed by F.W. Sherwood and others to return permanently to Fort Collins. They sent him a one-way ticket in 1879. They wanted his expert work on their horses for the races at the county fair. He ran a shop on College Avenue till after the turn of the century.(23)

Joseph Murray, born in Ireland in 1843 and a veteran of the American Civil War, was a member of the Greeley Colony in 1870. He moved to a farm in Larimer County near Harmony Road where the homestead still stands. He was active in early labor movements in the state, particularly the Knights of Labor. He organized the quarry workers at Stout west of Fort Collins in the '80's. In 1889 he took a federal government assignment in Alaska where he spent the next decade working for the protection of Alaskan seals. His family remained in Fort Collins. Murray was commissioned by the college in 1895 to collect such exotic fauna as walruses, polar bears, musk ox, fur seals, and sea birds for the zoology department. George Makepeace, a Fort Collins butcher, married Mrs. Murray's sister in 1887 at the family home. Their daughter, Laura, had an active career teaching in a country school, serving as librarian at the college, traveling to other continents and lovingly studying the history of her home town.(24)

Helen White, later Mrs. John Rigden, was another whose life in the Poudre valley included years spiced with travel. She was born in Scotland in 1862, moved with her parents to Larimer County in 1881, and graduated from the Agricultural College in 1885. In 1889 she enjoyed a tour back to Scotland and other points in Europe.(25) Dr. P.J. McHugh, already trained in medicine, came to Fort Collins in 1890 and married Auntie Stone's great niece, a graduate of the Agricultural College. In 1904 he went for advanced study in Vienna where Freud was expounding his revolutionary ideas in psychology. Dr. W.A. Kickland, a resident of Fort Collins after 1895, studied in Vienna in 1907 and in 1919. Pioneer women like Mrs. F.W. Sherwood and Mrs. James Arthur took European tours in 1911, and Caroline Taft had many goodies packed by oldtime friends to enjoy on the train in old Mexico when she traveled south of the border in 1920.(26)

Many of the prime movers in the colony were temperance men who approved of the ideals Greeley was trying to maintain. The clash of the ideal with the practical on this theme divided the town as it did the nation for almost a century. Sheldon Jackson, the Presbyterian missionary, wrote in 1874:

The saloonist is in the advance of our civilization in the West. He has time to ruin scores of men before the advance guards of the Church arrive.(27)

Even if Greeley was dry, nearby Evans, Colorado, was very wet. Similarly, no saloons in Fort Collins only meant more prosperity for those in Laporte. The idea of a saloonless year in 1874 was supported by William Stover, Billy Patterson, and Henry Clay Peterson on a trial basis. This was opposed by the owner of the Agricultural Hotel, Marcus Coon. Finally in 1875, Fort Collins yielded to the practical and eventually tried to limit the number and character of such establishments by charging a high fee.(28)

Not all was lost by this policy. The treasury of the city gained and T.J. Wilson who got the first license made enough money to provide a good building for his saloon on Jefferson with a hall on the second floor that served as an auditorium. The Presbyterian ladies gave benefits there and the famous

Hutchinson family put on a performance in 1879 which was well received and gave "real solid pleasure and enjoyment." Compromise on social issues was inevitable and the Hutchinsons from New Hampshire, whose ballads supported temperance, accepted the necessity of performing above a saloon. They had been popular before the Civil War for their humorous country-style songs agitating for abolition and temperance. They sang for Lincoln in the White House, toured England, and trained new recruits as part of the "family" when some members of the troupe married or died.

In the late 1870's, Asa Hutchinson, still holding fast to his ideals, ran a hotel in Leadville where he served Negroes in the dining room and had the courage to campaign for temperance in a mining town! They were making a last grand tour and were a trifle old-fashioned, but to an audience with many Civil War veterans, they must have had some appeal.(29)

Wilson even added a skating rink to his establishment in 1885. Maudie Place, child champion, waltzed, schottisched, and danced the polka on ice. Skaters had a masquerade on the rink.

William Lindenmeier, German immigrant and one of Chivington's soldiers at Sand Creek, ran what Fort Collins people called a "sample room" rather than a "saloon" on College Avenue. The official name was "Board of Trade." Joe Mason and other men were gathered there when the Welch Block fire broke out nearby in 1880. Then, in 1884, a vote within the city council led to another experiment with total prohibition. This gave liquor dealers and saloon keepers two options, to operate illegally and pay penalties if arrested, or to run saloons elsewhere. William Lindenmeier did both. He had a saloon in Cheyenne called the "Stock Exchange." He installed the newly available electricity. It sounded up-to-date and attractive. Then he, Frank Miller, and others operated as before in Fort Collins and paid fines when taken to court. These were so much less than the previous license fee of one thousand dollars, they found prohibition profitable.

Meanwhile the city council calculated that prohibition meant higher taxes. One-third of the city budget of $16,500 in 1885 could be covered by high license fees. They saw prohibition as a fiscal error. After eleven months they rescinded the ordinance. Saloons were accepted as a necessary if undesirable feature for the next ten years.(30) In 1890 there were only four. Then in 1895 the temperance forces recovered strength, elected an anti-saloon mayor, and Fort Collins went dry until 1969.

Fort Collins was much too small a town to have a "red light" section. The scattered locations of brothels through the main business districts and the outskirts of the settlement were well known to residents, and ignored as much as possible unless court action was necessary. A raid of the houses of ill fame was even announced in advance in the newspaper in October, 1881. In June of that year a black prostitute named "Liz" had her "dive" on Meldrum two blocks west of the Colorado and Southern depot in a low, frame building, the property of Isaac Catlin. A white man found there was given twenty-four hours to leave town. The place received even more publicity in December when a black dishwasher from the Tedmon House was killed in a dispute there.

In June, 1882, "the women of the town paid the penalty of their mode of life" in police court. People complained in July of the goings-on. "The conduct of inmates wouldn't be tolerated among barbarians in Africa." In 1884 along with the push to close the saloons, the officials clamped down on the brothels. Judge Gunn fined several women. One Minnie Johnson, the paper reported with a possible effort at humor, was tried "for running a house of ill fame, a house of prostitution, and a disorderly house and found guilty of all three counts." She went to jail instead of paying the fine. A Negro prostitute, Belle Walters, whose house was across the millrace, was fined thirty dollars and the two white men taken in the raid only seven dollars and fifty cents in 1887.(31)

Most conspicuous in court was Madame Marie Lafitte on Jefferson who was in trouble with the authorities many times in the early 1900's. A headline in 1905, "Marie Still in the Ring," introduced an article noting that she had been selling liquor for many years. The case was appealed from county to appellate court. There was a note of grudging admiration for the tough old days in the comment: "Marie is a sure enough fighter." Most of these pathetic characters existed on marginal incomes and disappeared unnoticed. Madame Lafitte, however, came into possession of several thousand dollars because she sold her establishment to the Union Pacific Railroad when the track was laid along Jefferson in 1911. Her death left the disposition of some funds to be settled, the county expecting a part for "caring for her in her last years on earth." The hope that such spots would vanish entirely when the saloons went was clearly wishful thinking. The Courier **commented** in a brief paragraph in 1903: "Jefferson Street's disorderly houses are like prayer meetings compared with those uptown."(32)

Interspersed with such places were respectable shops like Mrs. Bolivar Tedmon's millinery and trimming store on Linden. She advertised in 1879 "Hats and bonnets trimmed to order at short notice in the latest styles and at reasonable rates." She also took orders for goods, patterns, and magazines from any of the eastern cities. In 1880 ladies' headgear in Fort Collins was bedecked with heads, breasts, and wings of hummingbirds. Further choice included ostrich plumes, laces, and plush and chenille flowers. The camel's hair hat was something new in the west though it had been worn in the east the year before. Even the men were not deprived of colorful apparel for at Frank Chaffee's store also on Linden in 1890 the necktie case was "a flower garden in silks and satins." The store also offered "Stetsons, Fedoras, or Tigers."(33)

Fort Collins looked like a haven of coziness and sociability to the wives on the ranches in the county and many, after the hard work and isolation in their youth, aspired to a snug little cottage in the town for the vintage years. An amazing number achieved this dream. In Indiana, pretty Mary Hackard, not yet eighteen, married Martin Calloway, a soldier back from the war in 1868. The next year they came with their new baby to Cheyenne by train and then down to the Boxelder Creek. At first she lived in a log cabin and the only other woman she saw for six months was an Indian married to O.P. Goodwin who lived a mile away. She helped Mrs. Goodwin cut bolts of material, usually red plaid, into dresses for her six girls, receiving in turn moccasins and driving gloves, tanned, cut and beaded by her new friend. The Calloways converted an abandoned stage station into a two-room home to replace the cabin. Mary learned to handle a gun but she feared wandering Mexicans for their roughness and stealing more than she feared Indians. She sold butter in Cheyenne. They had hired shearers for their sheep, got a good price on wool, and Martin was one of the first day depositors in the new Poudre Valley bank in 1878.

When Martin died in 1879, she took a quick trip back to Indiana but decided that her future was in the west. She returned to Fort Collins, and put her children in the new Remington school. Two years later she married her widowed brother-in-law, William Calloway, and returned to ranch life, this time in the Livermore area. William died in 1891 and Mary ran the ranch with the help of five children and stepchildren. She lost the little house in a fire in 1894, saved her piano, and later built a large two-story home. Then in 1897 she sold the ranch to move to town again. She lived in a pleasant cottage at 400 Meldrum when she celebrated her eighty-first birthday in 1932. She wore a lavender dress with a filmy soft fichu at the throat and received pink and lavender sweet peas from the Presbyterian ladies.(34)

Another neighbor of the Martin Calloways in the '70's near the Boxelder was E.W. Whitcomb from Massachusetts. The various homes he occupied illustrate the rapidity with which some individuals adapted to opportunities in the west. He lived in a tepee near the fort in 1865. Within three or four years he owned a substantial log ranch home on the Boxelder which boasted a room one hundred feet long. Still later he enjoyed an elegant town house in Cheyenne with hand-carved staircase, parquet floors, and high ceilings. For a boy who freighted along the western trails in the '50's and walked a thousand miles barefoot, much of the way through prickly pear cactus, because he had lost his only boots, this was quite an achievement. His Indian wife apparently made a successful adjustment to these changes too.(35)

Whitcomb was one of the first to deal in Texas cattle, beginning in 1865 on the Cache la Poudre. He acquired a substantial ranch which was a stopping point for people traveling to Fort Collins from Cheyenne, and his parties there were highlights of the social life in the county. Most of the men had Indian partners. Whitcomb bought whiskey to keep the fiddler and other musicians playing. These men were seated on a temporary platform on one end of the large room. They played all night and till noon the next day. People who had traveled forty miles by horse and buggy for a party wanted it to last.(36)

Though the Agricultural Colony named the street on the western boundary of Fort Collins, as platted in 1873, for Whitcomb, he sold the ranch in the '70's to the Bristol family, one of whose members became Fort Collins mayor in 1885. Whitcomb concentrated on business interests in Cheyenne and on ranching in Wyoming. Since the cattle industry of Larimer County and of Wyoming were so intertwined economically, Fort Collins residents were confused about the news of the Johnson County War in Wyoming and Whitcomb's arrest in 1892.

People have been puzzled about this episode ever since, and the missing chunks of evidence from the original reports encourage historians and descendants alike to re-hash the happenings and quarrel over the interpretation. Whitcomb had misgivings about the venture, but once having promised to support it, went along with an elite group of cattlemen who aimed to rid northern Wyoming of rustlers and bothersome small ranchers. Their extra-legal activity, including a couple of murders, involved the authorities of the town of Buffalo, the Wyoming governor, and eventually President Benjamin Harrison. Whitcomb and the others were discharged after a trial in Cheyenne. The Texas gunmen they had hired held a champagne party and went home. Johnson County refused to cover any legal expenses and the Wyoming legislature had to meet these. The ranchers who had dreamed up the plot had to pay for the six-car special train they had chartered. It cost them, according to one report, one thousand dollars each.

The fiasco represented poor judgment at best, but the Fort Collins paper probably expressed public sentiment when it loyally concluded: "It would be extremely hard to convince the people of this county that they were activated by unworthy motives when they set out upon that unfortunate expedition."(37) Peter Anderson of Fort Collins had been a partner of Charles Campbell, another arrested rancher. There was naturally a belief that the major objective, scaring the rustlers, was justified even if the method of achieving it was not.

In the '70's the Calloways, Whitcombs and others were living northeast of Fort Collins and their cattle and sheep were ranging east toward Nebraska. Men were selecting land or buying claims from earlier settlers ready to quit in the area northwest in the foothills. Clerin Woods, playing the fiddle at Whitcomb's party, was offered help by Bill Calloway who guided him to a favorable site at Trail Creek. William Watrous' son, Frank, bought it from Woods and tried country life there for a while in the '90's, and David Watrous spent a few years

Williams ranch home c.1890 on present Roosevelt Forest.

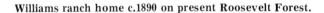

Frances Amelia
B u s s, daughter
Varah, and hus-
band, George Buss
c.1866.

of childhood there before the Watrous family moved back to town.

John S. Williams tried the Livermore area, pushing farther west to the junction of North and South Lone Pine Creek, tributaries of the north fork of the Poudre in 1890. There he built a two-story house which is still standing today on land which is part of the Roosevelt National Forest. Mrs. Williams had a pleasant bay window with many blooming plants.(38) The red of fuchsia and geraniums attracted hummingbirds. She missed the companionship of other women however and begged her husband for news of what a friend was wearing when he returned from a neighbor's home. He finally ended the inquiry by stating: "Mattie, she was wearing a dress. I am sure I would have noticed had she not been."(39)

The loneliness of country life for women was the theme of Amelia Buss' diary which she kept in 1866-67 in her home still standing near the Strauss cabin. Mrs. Jesse Sherwood came to call and said: "I really pity you in coming here." The latter did give up on western life and left Sherwood to take her children east. Amelia, however, dried her tears, thanked her husband for making an outhouse after living five months without one, and made him buckskin pants.

Amelia accepted the farm on the Poudre as her permanent home by September, 1867. She bought two cows for a hundred dollars. She wrote:

29

Buss family country house near Strauss cabin.

Buss city home at 209 West Olive.

My prospects look brighter today than they did one year ago. We have raised enough for our own use and some besides and very slowly we are gaining a little of this world's goods.(40)

The Busses celebrated their silver wedding anniversary in April, 1879. Friends came from up and down the valley with silverware, a silver castor set, and silver money. After Amelia's death in 1884, Buss married a Wisconsin girl who made such good cheese she competed with a new creamery in Fort Collins in 1887. They moved into town in the '90's and lived in the small home still standing at 209 W. Olive.

Ambitious individuals among the freighters and mule train drivers opened up the ranching industry in northern Colorado. Some got ideas from cattlemen in Old and New Mexico, but no one knew what adaptions were needed for the northern plains. The Goodnight-Loving Trail for driving Texas cattle north was used from 1865 to around 1890. Among the drovers was the father of Will James, cowboy artist. He later sketched the scene familiar to his father and many Colorado pioneers. The route lay parallel to modern Interstate Highway 25 and a few miles east. Neither drovers nor cattle however observed strict traffic rules by keeping to that trail and they spilled over all the way to the foothills. Children in Timnath were taught to take refuge from the wild longhorns. The McClelland farm on Fossil Creek where Joseph was beginning his famous orchards was sometimes invaded by wild steers in the '70's, even though it was fenced. Joseph, noted for his fiery red hair and temper, took his shot gun to frighten the invaders.

An incident illustrating cattle drives north which occurred in 1878 involved shooting a buffalo on land which later became the college campus. William Schenck saw a buffalo cow grazing with cattle there, and quickly shot it. Then two cowboys, herding the drive, appeared and denounced the marksman for killing the pet buffalo of the Boulder man for whom they worked.(41)

The whole future of agriculture in the new region and with new technology was a gamble. Should the new settlers

turn to fruit culture as McClelland had? Charles Pennock near Bellvue was experimenting with fruit too. Were bees the best way to make a fortune? Nathaniel Alford, raising them on Rabbit Creek and helping in a state organization for their culture, claimed they worked harder in the dry climate! Would wheat be the best product? The early settlers of Timnath named their district "Wheatland" and concentrated on that crop. Should one select sheep, cattle, or horses, or a combination? What breeds would be best here? These were all momentous questions facing newcomers from many countries and various climates.

Fremont's notes in 1843 had reported observations of abandoned oxen feeding with buffalo and looking amazingly healthy after a long, hard Wyoming winter. Many suspected that grazing might be the best possible use of western grassland but everything was yet to be tested in the area around Fort Collins in the '70's. For many people the rest of the century was simply a period of trial and error. Most of the land was open country unfenced, and the system of branding and roundups made stock raising necessarily a communal enterprise.

The schedule for the roundup points was occasionally announced. On June 27, 1882, the cowboys were approaching Fort Collins from the south intending to meet at Bill Brandeth's ranch at the mouth of the Boxelder. On June 29, they were in town! Bristol Station was the spot for the next day, then Jack Springs, both north toward Wyoming.(42)

The Livermore and Boxelder ranchers, all near the tributaries of the Cache la Poudre, shopped in Fort Collins for their supplies. Many of them had land in Wyoming as part of their livestock operations. Charles and Horace Emerson on the Lone Pine bought land near Chugwater in 1877 for summer grazing. By owning only a small piece of land, with water, they had access to a large grazing area. The Williams family had a Wyoming ranch near Tie Siding and a Colorado farm at Williams lake, now Parkwood lake, a Fort Collins sub-division today. John Coy, whose farm was in the floodplain near the fort but north of the river, had a Wyoming ranch which he had developed from a desert claim by 1886.

The Wyoming border really meant nothing and some people buying up railroad land grants were not even sure until after some period of ranching in which geographical unit their land was. The Livermore ranchers were a closely knit group who cooperated well with one another. They dominated the Larimer County Stock Growers' Association which was formed in 1884. The Association held most of its meetings in Livermore with the occasional one in Fort Collins to encourage broader membership in the county.

Living right in Fort Collins were many individuals active in livestock who had allied businesses which made town residence preferable. W.B. Miner in 1878 owned eight ranches with F.B. Warren of Wyoming as a partner. Miner sheared 20,000 sheep in 1880, and 8,000 in 1887. He kept one of his ranches east of Owl Canyon until 1909 when it was sold to the Ripple family for $32,500. The site of Park Station, a stop on the Overland Stage, was on the Miner Ranch. Miner built an attractive brick house on the southwest corner of Mathews and Myrtle in 1884.

Another sheep raiser, Sewall Adams, reported shearing 2,200 sheep in 1879, having a clip of 9,060 pounds, and getting 21c a pound.

In August, 1878, Abner Loomis returned from inspecting his ranch at the mouth of Bates Creek on the Platte. He had 5000 head of cattle, 3250 of his own, and the rest belonging to his wife's sister, Kate Trimble, recently widowed, and to his herders. His home in the '70's was on the west side of Linden near the present location of the Salvation Army. W.C. Stover, store owner and banker, bought the Yeager cattle ranch near Steamboat Rock and gave notice of this purchase in 1879. That same year Benjamin Franklin Hottel, the miller, was on his stock range in Wyoming. He and Joe Mason owned over 4000 head of cattle together in 1881 as well as the mill.(43)

Peter Anderson who had a harness shop in Fort Collins in 1866 was actively dealing in cattle in the '70's and '80's. He purchased 5,135 head of Texas cattle in Ogallala and took them to Cheyenne in 1880. In 1881 when he returned from a trip inspecting his cattle, he reported seeing buffalo and Arapahoes fifty miles north of Fort Fetterman. Anderson participated in the Wyoming Stock Growers' Association from its early days. He was prominent in Wyoming and northern Colorado in the cattle trade. He had a hardware and agricultural implements store on Walnut. In 1893 he was vice president of the First National Bank of Fort Collins and also director of a bank in Columbus, Nebraska. His old farm and homestead northeast of Fort Collins gave the name "Andersonville" to the area when it was platted. His comfortable town home was at 300 S. Howes.(44)

Another member of the Wyoming Stock Growers' Association from Fort Collins was William Lindenmeier. Besides dealing in cattle he was a successful saloon keeper. He had a farm house south of the lake which bears the family name, but also vast holdings on the Wyoming border. Artifacts of prehistoric man, the so-called Folsom points of spears, were found on this area in 1924, and the Lindenmeier site is better known today for this discovery than for the old ranch.

Edgar Trimble bought two hundred head of cattle in Missouri in 1885. He made arrangements in Denver to take them fifty miles north of Grand Junction. Abner Loomis and Charles Andrews had a ranch on the Belle Fourche and they were such a successful team that they joined the founders of the Poudre Valley bank to increase its capital from six to fifty thousand dollars. To house the bank they built the Loomis Building in the early '80's on the northwest corner of Linden and Walnut. This structure, now known as the Linden Hotel, is one of Fort Collins' historic landmarks. A new set of Loomis and Andrews partners in the cattle business, but on the Green River in 1885, included Lon, the son of Abner, and R.J., the brother of Charles. In that same year Charles Andrews purchased Henry Clay Peterson's mountain ranch on the Poudre above Rustic and fitted it up as a summer residence. There he raised Shetland ponies for the eastern market.

Franklin and W.H. Avery had their cousin bring one hundred head of fine Merino sheep from Vermont in 1884. The Bristol family had pioneered in bringing pure bred Merinos into Colorado, reporting that they had three Colorado-raised pure bred Spanish Merinos by 1880.(45)

Some people switched from country to city or city to country. Bolivar Tedmon built a hotel on Jefferson in 1880, then sold it and went to ranching near the Cherokee Park Road. J.G. Hoyt moved into town to take over the harness shop in 1885 and his brother, Jack, moved to the ranch.

In June, 1893, E.R. Barkley traded a ranch of 640 acres with stock near Steamboat Springs to J.S. Sloan for Fort Collins property. "This lets Barkley out of the cattle business and Sloan in." Barkley's hardware store on Linden was begun in 1882.(46)

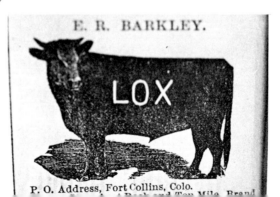

E. R. BARKLEY.

LOX

P. O. Address, Fort Collins, Colo.

Another successful cattleman who always lived in town was James A. Brown who came to Fort Collins in 1868 from Canada. He and his brother, John R. Brown, started as blacksmiths and wagon makers. Brown had cattle on the Powder River in Wyoming and in Nebraska in the '80's. He built more than a dozen houses in Fort Collins, including the first frame house. He was alderman in the early 1900's, and was active in getting the sugar beet factory started.

T.H. Robertson opened a hardware store on Linden in the '80's and built a handsome brick house on Mountain in 1893. Along with the other big cattlemen he had a cattle brand pictured in the local paper in 1890. Jay Bouton had a big farm on Prospect west of Taft Hill Road. Today this is developed under the name of the "Brown Farm" but the land once was part of Bouton's holdings. Alexander Barry bought land from Joe Mason north of the river and east of College Avenue and lived there till 1902 when he moved to a large brick house on the northwest corner of Laurel and Mathews. Though he lived in town, he managed a farm hear Windsor he had acquired in the '80's. All professions were represented in agriculture. Dr. Ethan Allen Lee bought the H.P. Handy ranch in 1885. Even the priest at St. Joseph, Father LaJeunesse, was going to Kelim in April, 1915, to oversee spring planting on his large farm.(47)

The ups and downs of cattle for beef and sheep for wool were important to the town's prosperity in the '80's and the diversified interests of the business men dealing in livestock protected them in bad years. There was no sharp crisis in Larimer County like the blizzard of '87 in Montana with the dramatic losses portrayed so vividly in Charles Russell's painting, "The Last of Five Thousand," or "Waiting for the Chinook."

Still, it was a speculative business for everyone. Prominent Wyoming cattlemen organized an exclusive club in 1880 and built an elaborate clubhouse the following year in Cheyenne but they could not maintain it after 1887. Fort Collins ranchers shared the same economic problems. The county escaped the bitter wars between sheep and cattle raisers which were notorious elsewhere in the west. The big operators may have avoided this friction because they were using grazing land in Wyoming for cattle and because they shifted to sheep for meat instead of for wool in the '90's. Outside interest in the Larimer County beef industry is illustrated by the purchase of a North Park ranch by Swift Cattle Company of Chicago in 1887. Even while the open range was the general pattern, feeding cattle on a lot was tried. John G. Coy had sixty steers he was feeding for himself and others in February, 1879.(48)

An innovation of the '80's was the recently-invented barbed wire. It had been patented in Illinois in 1874. It then cost twenty dollars a hundred pounds, dropping to one dollar and eighty cents in 1897. The price itself confirms the assessment of oldtimers that it was not common until around 1900. L.W. Welch advertised "the celebrated Glidden barbed wire" in 1879. In the '80's it was unusual enough in Larimer County for accidents involving it to be newsworthy. A fine three-year-old stallion colt belonging to Jesse Harris was severely cut on a wire fence near Livermore in 1885. Squire Mathews walking home from Laporte to his boarding house on Linden in 1881 walked into a barbed wire fence near an irrigation ditch when he lost his way in the dark.(49)

Another helpful mechanical aid was the windmill. They had been manufactured in the 1850's in the east and a decade later on a large scale in Illinois. They were much more essential in the western arid plains. Peter Anderson advertised this item in Fort Collins for his store in the '90's. The pictures of prosperous ranch and farm homes around the city in the early 1900's all show windmills in the background.

Farmers coming into town were nearly all identified by their teams. The small bronco type was common. The Schuttler and the Studebaker spring wagons were popular. There were few buggies. Most people used regulation farm or mountain wagons and big horses were appearing in 1883. That was the Fort Collins that met the eye of J.W. Lawrence arriving fresh from Cambridge and Massachusetts Institute of Technology to teach at the Aggie College.(50)

Barbed wire made possible the improvement of quality in livestock through control of breeding, but it was a long, slow process and extremely difficult to regulate in western range conditions. As late as 1919 the Larimer County Stockgrowers Association was just adopting a rule that all bulls run on the Roosevelt National Forest must be registered or eligible for registration. In the '80's and '90's many of the intelligent ranchers living in Fort Collins welcomed scientific information but the practical problems they faced seemed insurmountable.

First of all, there were wild horses running about the prairie. The explorers like Fremont, the trappers, and the Indians had known them long before settlement. Zane Grey popularized a picturesque myth of these animals as noble stallions untouched by rope or bridle, epitomizing the wilderness primeval. This was in direct contrast to reality in Larimer County in the '70's, as one oldtimer described the animals on the open range: "Wild horses were runty specimens of the genus, horse.....a wild unmanageable breed that gave outlaws to rodeos and wildwest shows."(51) The Northern Colorado and Southern Wyoming Horsebreeders Association, formed in Fort Collins in February, 1877, had the responsibility of covering the range, shooting wild horses, and picking up strays.

Then there was the problem of getting horses to supply the growing demand as settlers came in. The livery stable served as the local source. There were work horses, the cowboys' riding horses, spirited race horses for the tracks, and fancy matched teams for drawing carriages as some individuals prospered and sought this evidence of their elevated status. Running a livery stable was really a prestige occupation. Joe Mason built his on Jefferson in 1874. A bad wind caused one grout wall to collapse and destroy a new Schuttler wagon on the street. He sold that stable to Billy Patterson who had an elk confined in it for awhile awaiting shipment to Buffalo Bill Cody for his wild west show. Patterson sold the business to Jesse Harris in 1880, and though Harris moved to more modern quarters, the Grout Livery stable survived until 1911 when the Union Pacific Railroad cleared out north Jefferson Avenue for its new tracks. Thus Joe Mason's livery stable lasted almost forty years while his sutler's store built at the time of the fort endured for only sixteen.(52)

Some of the activities going on in the simple old frame barn on Mountain Avenue where Tom Earnest and Todd Branner had their livery in the early '80's typified the early phase of the horse industry in Fort Collins. The partners made a big purchase of animals in Texas in 1882, and Branner was delegated to be with them during the drive north while Earnest kept the business going at home. In May, he heard that they had been badly scattered by a storm. In June they arrived, and a ripple of excitement went over the town. They were "Andalusian breed." Most sold in a range from forty-five to eighty-five dollars, but bidding was competitive. One Greeley man paid one hundred and fifty dollars for his. He justified his extravagance on the claim that the horse had been ridden by Santa Anna in the war for Texan independence. Though such a steed would certainly have deserved greener pastures by the 1880's than those in Greeley, the buyer boasted that money was no object when his children could connect with such interesting historical remembrances!(53)

Later in the month at Rogers' old sheep ranch the partners branded some twenty-five or thirty horses that had escaped the iron in Texas. Earnest sewed up a mule seriously cut by a pitch fork. He had a fine reputation for knowing what to do with sick or injured horses. Even in 1867 he had worked all one night to save Dr. Timothy Smith's horse, thus paying off the cost of his wife's confinement by his own skill. In 1882 Earnest and Branner took advantage of the newly available water in the city by having a hydrant installed on Mountain Avenue to pump water for their stock. Perhaps the biggest bit of evidence of just how important these men were was the news that a San Antonio visitor gave them a gold quartz watch and chain and a diamond stud. This Texan spent five hundred and eighty-six dollars on one shopping trip, which was not everyday business for the jewelry trade in Fort Collins.(54)

The two men divided up the company later; Branner took the unsold Texas horses to North Park near the Grizzly River and Earnest left for the Niobrara where he had a cattle ranch. The Mountain Avenue stable went into other hands. Incomplete though the tidbits of information are, they reveal the industry's importance and also the public's interest in it.

There was considerable competition and turnover in the horse trade. William Campton came to Fort Collins in 1885 and ran a livery stable before going northwest of the city to develop one of the first dude ranches at St. Cloud, later called "Cherokee Park." John Currie from Canada had a livery stable and his friend, J.A.C. Kissock, grazed cattle and horses in the mountain parks on the Little South, tributary of the Poudre, even in the '70's. Currie's location was on Mountain Avenue in 1887. Kissock was pasturing cattle on the Bouton farm in 1880. Both Kissock and Bouton are remembered more as business men than ranchers, but the problems of livestock permeated the growing business community.

The display of skill in handling horses was another attraction at the Fort Collins stables. In 1882 Will Torrens was working with Joseph Graham of Greeley. The two promised to break anything that ever wore hair. "Will and Joe can be found anywhere on the street or at any of the livery stables. Bring on your colts and get them back horses."(55)

While Earnest and Branner's company fitted into the Hollywood image of the old west there was developing in the same decade just a couple blocks away on Jefferson another company conducted in quite different ways, and satisfying different tastes in the Fort Collins market. Jesse Harris, with several changes of partners throughout the years, imported horses from Great Britain. When N.C. Alford sold his ranch to H.T. Miller in 1880 he included a Norman stallion valued

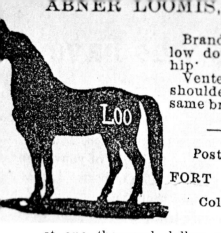
at one thousand dollars and one hundred forty-five brood
mares. It was animals like this that interested Harris. The
old Grout livery stable which he bought from Billy Patterson
in August, 1880 was not modern enough and he built a new
one on the southwest corner of Jefferson and Chestnut which
was the showplace of the city. It was two stories high and
twenty feet wide on two sides and across the end of the
corner facing the street. There was a central court, sixty-five
by one hundred and fifty-five feet. Another building twenty
feet wide, two stories high in the center of the court, extended
back one hundred feet from the front. There were eighty large
double stalls, iron mangers, feed boxes, and other modern
conveniences.(56)

A half interest in the company sold for thirteen thousand
dollars in 1885. In that year Harris sold J.R. Napier, an energetic young Englishman representing Captain Roxby's ranch
near the Elkhorn, a neat single footer for three hundred and
seventy-five dollars. Napier also bought thirty grade mares,
one pair of work horses, and one fine stallion. The total bill
was three thousand dollars. Imported that same season from

Famous stable at Inverness, site of present Jax Surplus.

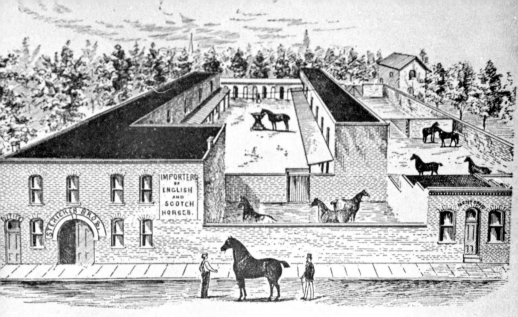

STERICKER BROS.' STABLES.

Scotland via Quebec were twenty-five Iceland ponies, Cleveland Bay stallions and Clydesdale stallions. He went to Europe again in 1888 and 1889 arranging importation. In 1889 he and Myron Akin were in California selling horses, so his sales were not limited to northern Colorado.

In 1890 Harris sold the Jefferson street stable and moved his headquarters to Inverness, a farm north of Fort Collins with a most favorable location on the low flat meadows near the river. One of the stables Harris used there still stands behind the old barn and is used for storage by Jax Surplus.

The new owners of the Jefferson Street stable were the Stericker Brothers of Pickering, England. They were in horse-exporting on a substantial scale, and had a branch in Springfield, Illinois, as well as the stable in Fort Collins. Arthur Stericker managed the firm here. He sent two horses to the World's Fair in Chicago, having them receive their final grooming in Springfield before showing. Stericker was elected an alderman of the Fort Collins city council.(57)

Part of the excitement in the horse business was gambling at the races. Tom Earnest's course southeast of Fort Collins on the Poudre had five entries in 1874. He outwitted Denver sharpies' effort to "fix" a race on his track by riding behind his horse and jockey, armed with a .45 revolver and threatening to kill the boy if he didn't win. It was said afterwards that he was almost first over the line himself, he was so angry after hearing about the plot.

College and Mountain with horse fountain.

A race scheduled in November, 1880, at the fair grounds got a poor turnout because of the cold, blustering wind. The weather was most favorable for the event in December. W.F. Scribner was running "Jim Broadwell." Cross & Harris had "Mollie." The hackmen were making money and one man came away with all pockets filled with watches he had won. In July, 1885, Jacob Flowers' horses were matched against those of James Evarts at the fair grounds with stakes $200.00 as a side bet.(58)

A tribute to the horses and their importance in the life of the town was the erection of a water fountain for them at the intersection of College Avenue and Mountain, the heart of the city. The city council gave permission in May, 1897. Mr. C.R. Welch and others paid for it. Its honored place was usurped in 1908 by the street cars, and a spot for the relic was eventually found in Lincoln Park where it can still be seen, back of the Pioneer Museum, near the cabins. The scars and nicks on its sides were made when thirsty horses jostled the tongues of their wagons against it.(59)

The town's prosperity depended upon agriculture-related industries. Education was one of them. The Agricultural College showed signs of being some help in the 1880's though it got off to a slow start. The school was the pioneers' own prize, fought for in the territorial legislature and kept from Greeley competitors by the erection of a "claim" building long before there was any provision for faculty or classes. A.K. Yount, founder of an early bank, drew the sketch for this little structure. A.H. Patterson, John Mathews, Henry Clay Peterson, and Joseph Mason were among the settlers who donated land for the campus. Patterson planted trees to line the road that led from the tiny town past his land to the site then out in the country.

In 1875, one year after the "claim building" was erected, the newly-organized grange decided to plow up the land and raise a crop to start a local fund for college support. Alexander Barry, John G. Coy, Andrew Ames, Harris Stratton, A. R. Chaffee, and Peter Green Terry were all in on the project. Chaffee had a span of broncos weighing under a thousand pounds each. They pulled a ten-inch breaking plow through the virgin soil. One observer recalled:

We knew the first furrow was the toughest to break so we said: "Chaffee, head up to the foothills." Twenty others followed. Terry later harvested the crop with his McCormick reaper, the grain was threshed and put in the brick shack, and later sold to the mill.(60)

Fort Collins leaders not only gave the land for the campus and plowed and planted for a crop, but they lobbied in Denver for appropriations and served on the Board of Agriculture created in 1877 to govern the college. N.C. Alford in the House in 1877 worked long into the night persuading a representative from Pueblo to support a college appropriation. The weary man finally agreed, but retorted: "I feel as if it is throwing money away, for you never can make Colorado an agricultural state. It is only fit for a cow pasture and for mining."

The first real school building, "Old Main," was a solid two-story brick structure with a tower. The cornerstone was laid in 1878 and construction completed in 1879. It was a landmark on the south as was the Hottel mill on the north. People could easily walk from the country campus to the city near the river. On muddy days, many chose the path of the railroad which ran behind Old Main and brought much excitement and encouragement for business after its completion in 1877. "The grounds look beautiful, a mass of living green" ran the report in August, 1880. Apple trees given by a New York tree farm were planted in front of the building, and the boys were working hard keeping up the flowers, stock, balsam, pansies, and pinks.

The first president of the Agricultural College was E.E. Edwards, a preacher who also filled the pulpit of either Methodist or Presbyterian churches on occasional Sundays. Since he failed to grasp the purpose of the college, the practical town leaders got busy themselves. In 1880 they decided the

L HALL.
CHEMICAL LABORATORY.
MAIN COLLEGE BUILDING. CIVIL & IRRIGATION ENGINEERING BUILDING.
DOMESTIC SCIENCE BUILDING.
LAUREL ST.
COLLEGE AVE.
COMMERCIAL DEPARTMENT.
MECHANICAL ENGINEERING LABORATORY.
HORTICULTURAL HALL. MECHANICAL

Artist's view of Agricultural College Campus c.1895.

college should offer a Farmers' Institute. C.C. Hawley and George E. Buss, both old soldiers from the days of the fort, with A.L. Emigh, W.F. Watrous, John G. Coy, and John Sheldon formed the committee for that project.

George Glover was only fifteen when he enrolled in November, 1879 and even though the class was small he suffered the usual panic of the freshman student. He thought Lelia Loomis and Elizabeth Coy, coeds he saw outside his window, looked so much more sophisticated, though he had come to college in his first ready-made suit of clothes, that he stayed in his room for two days. Then President Edwards came down searching for him and insisted he join the others. He graduated in 1884 in the first class. Just before Commencement, J.W. Lawrence, who married Elizabeth Coy, also one of the four graduates, came to Glover's room. Plans for advanced study for the promising young man were simple:

"I've heard you would like to take a course in veterinary at Ames, Iowa, but are unable to do so because of financial matters. I thought I'd take a chance on you and loan you the money. Would you care to go?" Glover took advantage of the offer, received the training, and returned in time to serve as inspector of Texas cattle being trailed north. He soon paid off the loan. In 1899 he joined the faculty and in 1907 he organized a division of veterinary science.(61)

Supporters of the college were patient and optimistic during the early years of its development. In 1886 several declared firmly: "The Agricultural College is a success" when they

43

were interviewed by H.H. Bancroft's staff visiting the Tedmon House to collect data for his history of Colorado.(62) In 1888 the students were invited to bring specimens of grain, grass seed, and fruit to the Opera House for a study session. President Charles L. Ingersoll addressed them.

There was great pride in the practical emphasis. In 1890 the seventy or so students were required to work two hours every day on the farm or in the garden or shop. "They do not sit with Plato in their hands or mumbling over logarithms and conic sections with a piece of chalk all day." In 1894 the goal was clearly stated: "To promote liberal and practical education of the industrial classes in the several pursuits and professions of life." The five courses of study included "agricultural, mechanical, chemical, irrigation engineering, and ladies", though all classes were open to both sexes. Since the tuition was free, the annual yearly expense would not exceed two hundred dollars and it was stressed: "This included everything."(63)

When Justin Morrill died in Washington, D.C. in 1898, his bust in Old Main in Fort Collins was draped in mourning. His philosophy, embodied in the Land Grant College Act at the time of the Civil War, had initiated the program which made the college possible.

A subject of constant dispute in the faculty was the curriculum. Just how much general education and how much depth in science could and should be provided? In 1906 President Barton O. Aylesworth mediated in a debate between Professor Carpenter and an opponent. Carpenter supported the necessity of book learning, and his opponent wanted the college to turn out "tillers of the soil and raisers of livestock." In a general way Carpenter's influence predominated. In 1907 tuberculosis was found prevalent in the college herd and in local dairies as well, and a city ordinance followed requiring inspection. Typhoid epidemics occurred occasionally. Jesse Harris gave the students a drinking fountain in 1902 when he was on the Board of Agriculture. At one period those living nearby went to the campus with buckets for their drinking supply because of fear of contaminated city water.(64)

The college pioneered in two developments which revolutionized life in the county and the town—irrigation and sugar beet culture. In matters of irrigation, the town leaders had quite a head start on the college since water was the first thing people needed. It was only in the late 1890's and the early 1900's that engineering knowledge and ingenuity emerged in the tiny faculty to help solve practical problems for the region. The town itself had several ditches for sources of

Left, Jesse Harris Fountain and shelter early 1900's.
Right, Harris fountain in 1975.

water that were important from its very beginnings. The millrace laid out by Henry Clay Peterson in 1866-67 ran southeast from the south bank of the river beginning at a point north of modern Loomis. It crossed College between Sycamore and Cherry, and continued southeast through the area the fort was then occupying to the mill on Lincoln. Its course is clearly delineated on Dastarac's birdseye view of the city in 1884. While its purpose was to supply energy to operate the water wheel, people living near it dipped into it for supplemental water used in the homes.

The town ditch or Fort Collins Irrigating Canal was another source of water in the '70's. It came out of the river somewhat west of the millrace headgate and looped its way south near the western boundary of the early town. It crossed Whitcomb several times, and entered the area later used for the campus near Meldrum and Howes. Later the Sherwood lateral ditch carried water east to an outlet in Williams (now Parkwood) Lake.

There were three other important ditches which ran south parallel to the town ditch and west of it. Eventually, as the city expanded west, all four came to be partly within the boundaries. The town ditch was not really owned by the town but by a corporation formed by some individuals who planned the colony in 1873. When the city developed its waterworks in 1882, building the plant near Laporte, there was a more efficient source for the growing town and the laterals to the town ditch were sometimes neglected and left clogged. In March, 1887 James Arthur, along with William Stover, Jay Bouton, Charles Mantz, and F.W. Sherwood, formed a new company to buy the ditch and from then on it was generally known as the "Arthur Ditch," though he was only one of the owners. Bouton was also a director of the Highline Reservoir and Canal Company in 1885 so he was well situated for investment in water, the most important resource in the county.

This ownership of water by private corporations was a new phenomenon of the Rocky Mountain states and a puzzling feature of western law for people whose background has been shaped by water law recognizing riparian rights. The latter system, as implied by the name referring to the river bank, associated the water with the land through which the river flowed. This was traditional in the eastern United States and in English law. The arid west developed quite a contrary viewpoint. Water needed for mining in the days of the California gold rush supported an industry far distant at times from the course of the river. Colorado miners and ranchers in territorial days seized upon this doctrine of prior appropriation and water became a commodity to buy and sell, independent of land.

Since Greeley was somewhat older and was downstream from Fort Collins, the founding of the latter city and removal of water from the Cache la Poudre on which both depended made a lively controversy in the '70's. The problems have needed specialists in water law forever after. The amount of river available has never satisfied the growing demands and even in the '80's reservoirs and ditches were built in the high country as well as in the area near the town. Storage of water at higher altitudes with cooler summer temperatures meant less evaporation and more control of this essential resource.

The establishment of priorities for the Arthur ditch is an excellent historical example of the procedures involved in early water law. It was dug in 1873 when Colorado was still a territory. In 1876 the new state provided that four points must be considered in owning water: the date it was taken, the amount diverted, the continued use and type of use, and the acceptance of the legality of these first three by a court. In 1879 in court even before Arthur and the others had gained complete control of the ditch, they were reaching back in history to make the date the earliest they could possibly claim. There was a neat chain of events which satisfied the court and carried Arthur ditch priority back to a period even before it was dug!(65)

The town ditch in construction had cut across an older one known as the Watrous, Whedbee, and Secord ditch. In 1873 the owners of this ditch had agreed to let their water run into the town ditch, and abandon the lower part of theirs, so thereafter they would draw water from the town ditch. Thus it became most important to know when, how much and why the water was diverted for the older ditch. F.W. Sherwood, Abner Loomis, and Joseph Mason all appeared in court in 1879 to testify on their knowledge of the earlier ditch.

The vagueness of the statements and the conflicts in stories reveal the poor evidence which was used to establish claims. Sherwood thought it was a small ditch in 1861, about two plowed furrows, with no headgate, from which a Mr. Lewis irrigated a few onions, and he had not seen any irrigation there after 1861. Loomis recalled that the ditch came out of the Poudre in 1867 one and one-half miles below Laporte on land then owned by Zach Thomerson, Charles Hilton, and J. Bailey, later owned by John R. Brown. (In 1879 Secord had just purchased some of the land.) Joe Mason felt there was no survey, that the water was thrown into the ditch by means of a dam across a slough.

All three men were asked if they were talking about the same ditch, and under oath, Sherwood could answer only: "I do not know." Mason replied: "I am not certain, I believe so."

In 1882, the case was back in court again. The Watrous ditch decree was set at 10.1 cubic feet of water all antedating 1868. In 1884 when a flood changed the river course, the Watrous ditch was abandoned entirely. The town ditch one-half mile downstream from the other diversion took in the Watrous, Whedbee, and Secord water, which it felt it owned, through its own channel directly from the river. The city further complicated the situation by selling part of its water. On April 16, 1885 Young and Desjardins purchased water from the old town ditch to operate their shop near Hottel's Mill.

In 1899, old timer Charles C. Hawley, veteran from the days of the fort, and ordnance officer for the army at Sand Creek, was water commissioner for District 3 which included Fort Collins. He challenged the Arthur ditch claim to the Watrous, Whedbee, and Secord water. Greeley lawyers, sensing a possible loophole in the chain, argued that the Watrous appropriation had been abandoned and the water belonged to the river, not the Arthur ditch. The court upheld the claims of the Arthur ditch owners in 1902.

The Fort Collins paper announced authoritatively: "The decision is universally approved because it is based upon justice and right." The chance that Greeley would gain and Fort Collins would lose no doubt influenced the high praise for the decision. It was advantageous for "the welfare of the city, the experimental grounds at the Agricultural College, the poor farm, and the rights of water users on several farms

Stereopticon view from top of Old Main, Spruce Hall in foreground.

adjacent to the city." This is by no means the end of the litigation for this one ditch, but the story to 1902 reveals the marvelous opportunities opened up for the legal profession on the frontier by Colorado's water law.

The pioneers were attached to the system that upheld their investments, despite its intricacies. Sherwood, giving testimony in 1879, was part owner of the Arthur ditch in 1887. Alfred Howes, pioneer in the 1860's, helped Andrew Ames build a ditch near his farm and that of John Coy's, north of the river. When he was elected to the state senate in 1890, his campaign promise included a "scrutinizing revision of our irrigation laws, keeping in view no infringement of the priority principle."

The pioneers needed engineers as well as lawyers. The practical aspects of the college research led to the invention of the Parshall flume to measure diverted water. Ralph Parshall, a member of the faculty, had worked out the main features of this device by 1920. In 1932 there were more than 1500 installed in Colorado ditches. A special branch known as civil and irrigation engineering had been evolving since the '80's and Professor Carpenter traveled in Europe and Asia

Minor studying irrigation practices. The staff for a while had the old dormitory, built in 1881, later called "Spruce Hall." In the early 1900's there was progress towards a new building. Money was appropriated in 1903. Parshall and Horace Hubbell surveyed the site on the southwest side of the present Oval Drive and the basement holes were dug in 1904. In 1906 the walls and roof went up. In 1909 more money was appropriated. In 1910 it was completed except for any arrangement for heating. The date, 1909, was chosen to set in mosaic tile in the vestibule.

The Colorado Agricultural Experiment Station, established in Fort Collins in 1888, concentrated on sugar beet culture. There was a test planting of one-fourth of an acre in the college garden. Dr. Ingersoll, president of the college, was director of the station. He visited the sugar beet factory in Grand Island, Nebraska. A progress report on the research in 1891 compared the yield per acre of the college, twenty-two to twenty-nine tons, with that of Germany, fourteen. Another factor noted was that land cost ten times as much in Germany as in Colorado. Tests were reported in 1892 even more glowingly.

The success attained at Fort Collins in sugar beet culture last year has never been equalled in the United States. The Department of Agriculture is getting out a new sugar beet bulletin in which Larimer County is put ahead of the world.(66)

William Watrous' son, Frank, left the college before receiving a degree, because he was offered a job at Rocky Ford supervising sugar beet testing. Local opinion was sampled to get ideas on the attitudes toward beet sugar instead of cane.

Added to the excitement over this new prospect for Colorado agriculture was the realization that feeding sheep was a new occupation which would be integrated with the culture of beets. The accidental stranding of some Mexican lambs in Colorado and the necessity of feeding them near Fort Collins in the winter of 1889-90, together with their successful spring sale brought a totally new emphasis to local agriculture. Both the sugar beet tops in the field and the by-products in the factory supplied feed for the lambs. Unfortunately just when the experiments made future prospects look good, financial panic and depression hit the country in 1893. There were several years of hard times, and Loveland beat Fort Collins in getting capital for a factory, which began slicing beets in October, 1901. Local farmers began raising beets. In July 1902 wagon loads of German-Russians were brought up from Loveland to work in the fields. The fall crop of beets was sent by

Loading sugar beets for train to Loveland, 1901.

wagon, then train to Loveland. Frank Michaud of a pioneer family north of town was one of those loading the first beets for the short train ride south.

To let the new industry go to the rival town permanently was unthinkable. Benjamin Franklin Hottel, James Arthur, Peter Anderson, Joseph McClelland, Jesse Harris, and others worked at the problem. Jacob Welch and his sons had been prominent in the department store field in Fort Collins since the '70's. C.R. Welch built a handsome house on the northwest corner of College and Mulberry in 1899 and was called a "merchant prince" of Fort Collins. He too was drawn into the circle chartering the Fort Collins Sugar Manufacturing Company.

Building began on Vine Avenue north of the river in November, 1902, and the first beets were sliced in January, 1904. Assurances were given farmers that field labor would be plentiful. German-Russian immigrants from Kansas and Nebraska were willing to come. The Great Western Sugar Company was formed to handle the processing of the beets on a large scale with many factories. The new company bought the factories at Loveland and Fort Collins in the summer of 1904, but the groundwork for the industry in this locality had been laid by Fort Collins men. Much of the town's prosperity for the next forty years revolved around the cultivation of beets and the feeding of lambs. Local business hinged on the program. Dr. Peter J. McHugh, having served as mayor in 1903 and 1904, continued to be prominent in local politics. He represented the beetgrowers in Washington, D.C. in 1913, lobbying against a cut in the sugar tariff. Then he continued travel to Baltimore for surgical training.

Just how profitable the new agriculture—raising sugar beets and feeding lambs—really was for those who went into it aggressively is hard to measure but the **Courier** reported in 1902 that former Governor Eaton had gone from moderate wealth to millionaire status in the previous two years because of the new crop. There were fields of sugar beets from Mulberry to Laurel and from Whitcomb to Shields for this space was not built up. Sacks and improvised cover were arranged on the fences to shade babies while their mothers worked with the fathers and older children. All of the tillable area north of town near the factory was put into beets.

In 1903 a Harvest Festival was prepared at Douglas Grove, a tract of boxelder and cottonwoods. Tables with a total length of 300 feet encircled the barbeque pit, which was 35 feet long, 5 feet wide, and 7 feet deep. Oxen, sheep, and hogs were roasted by experts. Business houses closed. There was room for a thousand wagons. The thick growth of short clean grass kept down the dust. Excitement in the crowds and pride in the town were all part of the affair.

In 1909 the specialty was lamb. The aim was to let the world know that "Fort Collins was the center of one of the largest lamb-fattening districts in America. Two hundred lambs

Welch-Evans house at College and Mulberry.

Above - Great Western Sugar Beet Factory—north facade.
Below - view of Great Western factory from south.

Public barbecue—early 1900's.

Henry T. Miller feed lot near Dixon Canyon.

were sacrificed on the altar of publicity." The crowd for the free barbeque was estimated at eight to ten thousand. Excursion trains brought people from neighboring towns. Everyone was involved. Butchers carved; Agricultural College students waited table. It was all served right on Oak Street near the business district. People milled about on the courthouse lawn, on private grounds, and all over the downtown area. Senator William A. Drake and other lamb feeders helped the merchants on the expenses.

A similar event in 1910 was not as spectacular and the merchants were quoted: "It is enough; we have let America know where to come for lamb chops." In 1911 Mayor Jesse Harris pled: "Let's have Lamb Day if we have only one lamb," but the merchants hesitated. The lamb-feeding industry was clearly so profitable that it no longer needed special publicity.(67)

The railroad helped by bringing German-Russian families packed in box cars from Nebraska to Fort Collins where they were assigned farms on which to work. The German-Russians had come from the Volga and the Black Sea area of Russia, some directly from Europe, but most after a stop-over in Nebraska or Kansas. Their ancestors had been German immigrants to Russia in the eighteenth century, invited by the Czarina, Catherine, who was German herself, to settle there. The Spanish-Americans were from southern Colorado and New Mexico and from old Mexico, many recruited by the immigration agents of Great Western Sugar Company.

The German-Russians were of mixed religious background, and not solidly Lutheran. The religious wars after the Re-

Children of German-Russian immigrants: Schlitt sisters Catherine, Lydia, and Christine.

formation had ended with a settlement for the German states leaving the decision on religion to the local noble for his area. The ones who migrated to Russia included Catholics, Lutherans, Mennonites, and other sects. Those of one religion clustered together in one village in Russia and many moved in groups forming new towns in Nebraska predominantly of one religion. This solidarity was completely lost when they filtered into the Fort Collins area. The Catholics went to St. Joseph which had just completed a new church on Mountain Avenue. Some formed religious connections without reference to the old family background. Christina Schlitt, later Mrs. John Amen, chose Seventh Day Adventist. She was born in Russia in 1892 and her parents moved to Nebraska where her sisters, Katherine and Lydia, were born in 1893 and 1896. In 1903 they moved to Fort Collins, attracted here by the work in the sugar beet fields.

The church was so important in the lives of the immigrants that having one where German was spoken was essential. By June, 1904, the Fort Collins architect, Montezuma Fuller, was receiving bids for the construction of the German Congregational church on the southwest corner of Whedbee and Oak. The foundation was red stone, the walls were Fort Collins pressed brick with red stone trimming. The tower was fifty feet high. The auditorium had a bowled floor with circular seating in tiers. The style was called "pointed Gothic." The cost was $6,000.(68)

The sincere determination of the German-Russians to become Americans by building this beautiful church so soon after their arrival when their homes were barely established must have impressed other congregations. It was certainly a help in time of war when anti-German sentiment flared up. One German-Russian near Severance was forcibly required to buy a $500 Liberty bond, and to take an oath of allegiance, in April, 1918. Mathew Auld, whose tenor voice contributed to musical performances at the First Presbyterian Church, led the singing at the German-Russian Congregational church in June, 1918 and reported that there was no disloyalty. The audience sang patriotic songs with fervor. Many old people did not understand English.

Propaganda slipped into the entertainment field when Ringling Brothers' circus advertised in local papers against a competing show owned by a man with a German name. War tensions had emotional repercussions which kindly interdenominational contacts calmed.(69)

German-Russian Congregational Church, early 1900's.

NOTHER SPICY STATEMENT

ingling Brothers' Circus

has a punch left and one that will jolt all true Americans into a realization of the outrageous falsehoods being perpetrated upon them by the Carl Hagenbeck Circus

Will Mr. CARL HAGENBECK, the "FAMOUS GERMAN SHOWMAN," deny the following charges?

That up until the time the United States actually declared war on Germany there was painted upon each and every wagon and railroad car belonging to the Carl Hagenbeck circus, the COAT OF ARMS of THE IMPERIAL GERMAN GOVERNMENT.

Furthermore, this deliberate exploitation of the German name and German propaganda was begun or flaunted in the faces of American citizens for only two years after the beginning of the war, in spite the fact that the Hagenbeck show now claims that it is an American owned circus.

Why, Mr. Hagenbeck? Why, Mr. Ballard?

WHY NOT COME OUT IN THE OPEN, MR. HAGENBECK?

If you are seeking American dollars why not be frank with Americans?

WHY didn't you take your AMERICAN OWNED CIRCUS THROUGH THE EASTERN STATES THIS SEASON?

Was it not because you were afraid that all good Americans in the East would remember about the GERMAN COAT OF ARMS on all your wagons and cars?

Will what is known in the Circus World as

The Big Gray Car

be in evidence Friday, with its crew ready to intimidate peaceful citizens and visitors from out of town who refuse to fall for the high-handed methods practiced by the Hagenbeck show?

OF COURSE, the big gray car won't have the German coat of arms on it in Fort Collins, as it did all last season, but will it again try to do the same things it has done during the past?

The cornerstone for another German church was laid in 1914, a block south from the first, on the southeast corner of Whedbee and Olive. It was engraved "Evangelical Lutheran Bethlehem Kirche." The church was dedicated in March, 1915. Gray sandstone quarried west of Fort Collins was used for the structure, which was described as "severely Gothic." The builder was Ernest Wycott of Fort Collins; decorations were done by M. Pfeffer.

Some of the homes for the German-Russian immigrants were shacks on particular farms to which they were assigned. Others lived in new houses built north of the river in the flood plain at Buckingham Place. This location was within walking distance of the factory and many fields. In December, 1902, there were thirteen little box houses, twenty by twelve, each with four little windows, going up at Buckingham. There were sheds for horses and cows. "The houses while small seem comfortable and new ones are being built daily."(70)

The news of the Russian-Japanese war seemed close to Fort Collins in February, 1904. The proposal was made that the Cache la Poudre be fortified to protect the Russian settlement here from any Japanese warship. Construction was going on at "Andersonville" too, Peter Anderson's old farm east of the first settlement. Buckingham Place had received its name from one land owner, Charles Buckingham, a wealthy

Flood of 1904 at Lincoln Avenue Bridge looking north. Sugar factory in background.

Below - view from the millrace.

Boulder banker who owned property scattered all over northern Colorado. He gave money and his name for a library at the University of Colorado, a distinguished memorial. The area in Fort Collins which retains the Buckingham name was less prestigious. In the early years the facilities and type of houses were similar to those in other parts of Fort Collins, small frame homes with shingled decoration in the gables. A few exist today which compare favorably with other older sections. Indoor plumbing had not advanced through many parts of the city proper, though the network of sewers was spreading, so there was not really great differentiation between Buckingham Place and other sections and it was annexed to the city in 1906 without discussion.

Everyone had been excited about the sugar beet factory and the coming of the Russians. On May 19, 1904, some of their homes already had gardens and lace curtains. Then on May 21, the flood came. The engineers predict that a flood of such volume may occur once in a hundred years, but there is no assurance that the interval between two big floods will be one hundred years. It had been just forty since the soldiers had been flooded out at Laporte. By May 28, the flood waters stretched so far north the sugar factory itself was surrounded by water. Three officials and a number of Russians spent the night at the factory. During the flood the Cache la Poudre was a mile wide near the point where George Robert Strauss still lived in his cabin of the '60's. Strauss was one of the casualties of the flood for he refused to take shelter on higher ground insisting he had known floods since he lost his garden in '64.(71)

The immigrants recovered with local help. The paper noted that the Russians would now be wearing American clothes. One family of Russians lived for a while in the Strauss cabin. One member of the Strang family whose home was nearby remembered going to visit them, and finding them with oil cloth on their table, and serving the food directly on it, for they lacked dishes and had scanty silverware.

In spite of the losses in the flood and the fact that many had come from Russia with very few family treasures, there are some items in the Pioneer Museum today from the settlers of this period, among them forks and knives brought from Russia. A lovely painted model decorated with flowers in the museum illustrates a type of wheat grinder which the maker had produced on a large scale many times in the old country. One German used an abacus when he sold wheat in Russia, and brought that along to Larimer County. Some individuals felt prejudice and insecurity, but the general attitude of the older community was one of curiosity and helpfulness. In April, 1905, a reporter at the courthouse observed: "A visitor could have seen lobbies, halls, and vacant rooms, full of Russians. Can it be possible that a portion of Kuropatkin's scampering army has got so far from home so quick?"(72)

The first two decades after arrival were tough ones for the new families but the speed with which the thrifty farmers became prosperous landowners amazed the pioneers of the earlier period. They soon enjoyed the little niceties available in the town. The grandmothers loved to tell stories of the hard life in Russia. Gradually a deep interest in old country genealogy and geography taught children and grandchildren much about the Volga area. One youngster chided her elders for saying they had washed the family clothes in the Volga when she learned they had lived sixty miles from that river! The surprising element was the speed of assimilation.

One custom which impressed the community was the jolly old-country style celebrations of weddings. That of Leah Rommel and John Fabricius in November, 1930, was typical of many given by successful immigrants in the area. The service was performed by C.H. Becker of Bethlehem Lutheran Church. The groom's father arranged a chicken dinner at his farm for two hundred guests. The hayloft was heated for the dance, and those who danced with the bride pinned dollar bills on her dress.

The music supplied by George, Homer, Sigmond, and Harry Deines included violin, banjo, dulcimer, and guitar. Attendants included seven couples, Reinhold Rommel, Alexander Fabricius, David and John Deines, Emanuel Schaffer, Henry Grauberger, Jacob Weidman, Martha Hoffman, Amalie Daubert, Esther Deines, Eva Gross, Marie Janaus, Marie Jordan, and Martha Hoffman. The young couple then planned to live on the farm with the groom's parents. Such neighborly affairs were the pride of the twentieth century pioneers, and even the older set of pioneers enjoyed invitations to these "Dutch Hops."(73)

In the flurry of excitement over the new sugar beet factory, the leaders considered the labor problem a minor one. They promised anyone who raised twenty acres or more of sugar beets "all the Russian help needed and only furnish water and shelter." Charles Evans was hired by the company as foreman to raise 1200 acres of beets for three years. Sections of various farms were leased under Evans' supervision.

The farmers had a lot to learn about beet culture. They were used to grain and hay crops. There was much to learn about handling people too, for bringing in help was not all that simple.

Transient labor, usually men without families, was one traditional source of workers often used to get big programs under way. Swedish immigrants were employed to develop the quarries west of Fort Collins in the 1880's and the men were all housed in the basement of one big hotel. There was occasional use of Japanese help on irrigation ditches and beet fields. In June, 1904, seventy-five Japanese workers were on their way from Greeley to the Grand River ditch west of Fort Collins in the mountains. There must have been some problems for in June, 1906, H. Hokosona appeared before the board of the Water Supply and Storage Company to "talk over the Japanese trouble at the Grand River Camp." Eighty-five Japanese laid some track in September, 1905, between Windsor and Eaton. Then they were sent back to Longmont to resume work in the beet fields. They were under contract, so they had to leave before finishing the railroad work.

Most of the German-Russian and the Spanish-speaking people attracted to the beet fields, however, brought families. Though company officials anticipated the German-Russians would fill the need, there were Spanish-Americans in the beet fields around Fort Collins along with the German-Russians in the early 1900's. Newspapers reported occasional accidents like the drowning in Long Pond of a child, Mariano Herrero, in August, 1904. His parents worked in Mr. Bushnell's beet fields.

"Mexican Frank" was in county court in October, 1907, on a charge of gambling and defrauding workers. He had an office in the City Hotel. He was acting as an employment agent, securing help for growers from the southern part of Colorado, and in New and Old Mexico. He had brought in hundreds of laborers. Mrs. Pablo Gallegos catered to the new food preferences with her chile parlor and chile stand at 347 Jefferson in 1908.(74)

Fort Collins residents had watched the Russians settle in and because of them felt more interest in the politics of the Russian-Japanese war. Around 1910 they followed the news of the Mexican revolution and the civil war against Juarez with concern because of the Spanish-Americans in their midst. James Michener in **Centennial** traced the route of a fictional refugee from the war to the sugar beet fields and described his support of his Mexican family by labor in Colorado. No

Adobe house, Spanish Colony, 1975.

actual record in Fort Collins for such a character has appeared, but the awareness of the war in Mexico and the local community of Spanish-speaking people showed up in the headlines.

Continued immigration was more and more under the recruiting system of Great Western and the people were frequently better off than when encouraged to move here by unscrupulous fellow Mexicans. In 1913 when the company received reports from growers: "We will get our own labor," the reply was: "We are only too glad to have you secure your own labor but be sure you get it." There was insufficient help during World War I and the period of expansion thereafter, and the company's immigration activities grew in importance.

Homes were clustered about the land east and south of the factory. Spanish names were scattered among the German ones in Buckingham Place, which was annexed to the city in 1906.

Andersonville on Peter Anderson's farm was platted outside the city in 1903. Lee Martinez saved a photograph of an adobe house built at East Vine Drive and 9th about 1915. In 1923 Great Western announced plans for a "colony" of Spanish American workers. Space was reserved for an assembly hall

Frame house at 200 Lincoln, Buckingham Place, photo 1975.

which would be built later. An adobe house painted white in the Fort Collins colony was photographed for the official company magazine. Material for a two-room house cost $75.00. Many were of adobe construction in the traditional building method of the southwest.

The company furnished straw, lime, and gravel to encourage the workers to build and own their own homes. The first year no payment was required, the next three $40.00 a year, and the fifth, $25.00 to $50.00 for the lot, 50x85 feet. By this system the company hoped to hold steadier and more dependable workers. A survey of Colorado noted that only in Fort Collins were the Spanish-speaking beet workers becoming farm tenants or owners. The screening process attempted to select the best workers. Character references were required and the company could eject occupants if the home was used for any illegal activities. "Alta Vista" or "Spanish Colony" was officially platted and registered by the company with the county in February, 1927.

The company criticized housing standards provided for migrant workers in general by farmers and praised a few for their improvements. In 1924 Victor Akin had a three-room plastered house built, a type which other growers were urged to copy. E. Chester Giddings was commended for supplying a four-room plastered house.(75)

When the first homes were built in Buckingham Place in the early 1900's and used by German-Russian and Spanish-speaking families, the living conditions were similar to those in homes across the river. As sewage facilities became available throughout the town proper, however, it was practically forgotten that Buckingham Place was part of the city, and the other two areas, Andersonville and Spanish Colony were a kind of No-Man's land for which the county did nothing.

In February, 1924, Buckingham residents asked the city council for protection in spring from the Poudre floods. D.J. Roach, manager of the Fort Collins plant of Great Western acted as spokesman for the delegation. Seventy houses sheltering 500 people were involved. The council studied maps of the existing channel and that of the river in the previous year, but did not know what to do. Among the delegation were Jacob Rommel, Frederick Schmidt and Henry Hahn.

In 1951 Spanish Colony leaders asked the county commissioners for help on road improvement and were told they were not part of the county road system. Some residents had raised funds for road grading, but they needed some public aid. Many people were painting homes, spraying weeds and working on gutter drains.

A summary of the work done by the incoming laborers in 1924 described their arrival in April in time for blocking and thinning the beets. The hoeing was the next big chore, and the second hoeing ended in late July. Then there was no handwork needed till the October harvest. The beets were in that period loosened by horsedrawn machines called "lifters" then pulled by hand and thrown in piles to be topped. The worker with a knife in his right hand hooked up the beet and chopped off the crown of leaves with a sharp downward stroke. He used a knife eighteen inches long with a hook on the end. Fort Worth, El Paso, and San Antonio were the leading recruiting centers for beet field workers.

The basic problem was the fact that many families depended on seasonal labor and had no regular income for large parts of the year. No one was more familiar with the needs of the Spanish-speaking sugar beet workers in Colorado than Father Joseph Pierre Trudel, the first priest to minister to the needs of these people in Fort Collins. He was ordained in Quebec in 1901, studied in Paris, and came to Colorado for his health in 1911. He rapidly learned Spanish and concentrated on the needs of this part of the population. In 1924 he came to Fort Collins and remained till 1936, establishing seven mission chapels for Spanish-speaking people in northern Colorado. The construction of the Church of the Holy Family in 1929 in Fort Collins unified the Spanish-speaking Catholics here.

Church of the Holy Family,
N. Whitcomb and Cherry.

Father Trudel began services in 1924 with a building bought from the Presbyterians. C.V. Maddux in charge of Mexican labor for Great Western attended the dedication. The company had contributed to the purchase price on his recommendation for he "assumed the catholic position that all religions make for social good." There were 500 in the audience.(76)

Father Trudel began holding mass in Spanish in 1924 at St. Joseph's too and many Spanish-speaking residents received the sacraments there. In 1928 his sister, Ernestine Trudel, advertised special Mexican foods available at 610 Cherry, later helping the women make linen mops far superior to the commercial variety.

Interesting sources for Spanish-American relations are two newspapers published for Spanish readers in Fort Collins. Four issues of **La Estrella**, numbered 5, 6, 10, and 13 bear dates from November 20, 1927, through June 10, 1928. These were published by the Spanish Catholic Young Men's Association and contained articles and advertisements, some in English, some in Spanish. A few personal items were mentioned. Nestor Martinez (Lee's father) and family enjoyed a Thanksgiving homecoming dinner. Jovita Vallecillo of 402 Pine Street graduated with distinction from Fort Collins High School. A series of articles covered "civic catechism." It had questions like "What is a democracy?" and "In what ways may a citizen aid?" with appropriate answers. This section had parallel columns with the material in English and Spanish.

The one issue of **El Faro, The Beacon** Vol. 1, No. 1, dated March 12, 1932, is entirely in Spanish and was printed by Robinson Printing Company. A local committee for a united front announced a meeting for beet workers and other agricultural laborers at Redman's Hall, 236 Linden on Sunday, March 13. Among the advertisers were A.W. Scott Drug Store,

Julian's Dress Shop, and the State Dry Goods. These newspapers are extremely valuable for a period with few printed sources.(77)

In 1930 a weaving school for between-season work was in its third season. Jose Ortega was teaching again. There were seven looms in the Franklin school building for beginners. Expert weavers worked in the basement of the Holy Family Church. Fifty to sixty applicants were received. In 1932 the rugs and mops from the Fort Collins Spanish Industrial Center, displayed in Denver, attracted favorable comment.

After the French-Canadian, Father Trudel, left Holy Family in 1936, the church continued to bring in Spanish-speaking priests. They spoke quite a different Spanish from the Colorado or Mexican dialects for they were all drawn from the Theatine order and raised on the island of Majorca in the Mediterranean. Father John Fullana was with the church from 1936 to 1950 and saw his flock through the last of the depression and early recovery. His murder by thieves in his churchyard in Mexico City on December 9, 1956, shocked the Fort Collins congregation who remembered him with affection. The church under the succeeding priests, all from Majorca, has continued to be a vital part of the community.

When a large part of the building burned in March, 1969, some proposed that the time had arrived for integrating all Catholics at St. Joseph's. There was by then, however, a special tradition and heritage for Spanish-speaking Catholics that some valued. A few oldtimers said bitterly: "They didn't want us long ago. Why should we combine now?" Records suggest that St. Joseph as well as other churches welcomed the Spanish-speaking people. But the advantages in personal relationships in a small church outweighed consolidation. The Majorcan priests prepare paella for the fiestas of Colorado parishioners and contribute to the international flavor that has always been a part of the town. They preach a sermon in Spanish at eight o'clock Sunday mass.

Not all the Spanish-speaking people coming to Fort Collins were Catholic, just as the German-Russians were not all Lutherans. In the old days of Sheldon Jackson and the Presbyterians of the 1870's, the Protestant records reflected suspicion of Spanish Catholicism. But in the 1920's the Protestant church began to reach out to the newcomers. The First Presbyterian Church had both Sunday school and church services in Spanish conducted by Lino Sanchez in 1932. In 1948 Spanish Presbyterians met at 514 Wood. La Asamblea Di Dios met at 406 Pine. The Unitarian Church took an active part in the program to eliminate "white trade only" signs which appeared in some of the stores in the '30's and '40's.

Some of the arrangements which seemed unfair were part of the pattern of America, not just Fort Collins. The children in Buckingham and Andersonville walked several miles to the Catholic school near Holy Family since bussing was prohibited for parochial schools though the bus passed them with playmates who were attending public schools. Many examples of public concern are scattered through the records. Waldo Riffenburg, district attorney, turned the action in the court room into a dialogue in Spanish, questioning an accused shop-lifter in 1931 in that language and accepting responses entirely in Spanish. Those deeply concerned about the social inequalities organized community projects to encourage integration.

Librado Martinez, popularly known as Lee, took an active part in the city's Human Relations Commission. His parents moved to Fort Collins in 1906 when Lee was seventeen. His father, Nestor, was a field boss for Great Western, supervising Spanish-Americans raising sugar beets and acting as interpreter. Lee had had only three years of school but he finished the eighth grade in Fort Collins, served in France during World War I and in 1924 married Eva, whose maiden name was also Martinez. Their son, Alonzo, was killed in the Battle of the Bulge in January, 1945, and his name has been honored by

Eva and Librado Martinez, 1964, dressed for Centennial celebration.

the American Legion post. Lee took an active role in the Democratic party in Fort Collins beginning as precinct committee man. Like all political leaders Martinez was criticized. In the activism of the '60's some Spanish-speaking youths felt he was too mild in his requests. For many families however he and his children have given a pattern for successful adjustment to living in this community. A park named for him is under development along the Cache la Poudre very near to the area where so many Spanish-speaking people worked on the beet fields in the early part of the century.

Lee's widow is happy with their home at 728 Sycamore, a quiet street near the river and the park. The house overflows so with grandchildren she hardly has time to discuss the pictures and mementoes of the years when her husband lived. She had admired this particular house with its porch even as a young girl before marriage thinking it would be a nice place to dry diapers and so it had been.

Working in quite a different way from Lee Martinez was another man, Solome Vigil, called "Sam," who determined to improve conditions for Spanish-speaking people and also to make a financial success of his own career. Sam was born in 1916, and had lived in Fort Collins since he was four. He died at forty-four in 1960. His widow, Mary Torres Vigil, frankly expressed the goals and achievements in their marriage— "We wanted a Cadillac and a nice home in a good part of town and we got them both."

Both Sam and Mary knew beet field work as children. Mary's father, John Torres, came to the Bellvue area from Barcelona, Spain, and raised his family in a home developed out of the historic saw mill of Jacob Flowers at Watson Lake on the Poudre. Mary and Sam were married at the courthouse by a judge in 1935. She was eighteen, he nineteen. Sam worked at the street car barn for a while, and evenings occasionally they went to the Lyric Theater where she was allowed to sit downstairs and Sam with darker skin was directed to the balcony. They saw the "white trade only" signs and decided to fight the problem in their own way. Sam took a welding course, then they went to San Francisco and worked together in the shipyards leaving their small son with Sam's mother.

There were disappointments and loneliness. The child died. They returned with a capital of $1100, enough to start a little filling station on Linden near the river where they sold tires as well as gas. They developed a small store with novelties and appliances and made their customers, "Nationals," as immigrant Mexican workers were called in Fort Collins, welcome. Elio Medina, a barber, set up a shop there. Short orders and Mexican food were available. They lived in a house next to the restaurant.

Sam was a corporal in 1944, served sixteen months in Europe, was wounded in the Battle of the Bulge, and discharged in December, 1945. The Alonzo Martinez unit of the Legion met in the restaurant basement. From such humble beginnings they made the restaurant an outstanding success in Fort Collins winning the Anglo community as well as the Spanish-speaking. Though Sam died young, he and Mary had done what they wanted. He was not Catholic. Mary and one daughter, Maxine are. Two other daughters, Betty and Cynthia, belong to the Church of God. In widowhood Mary sold the restaurant officially called "El Burrito" but still popularly known as "Sam's."

"Standing up" for Sam and Mary at their wedding in 1935 were Napoleon Martinez, always called "Nap," and his wife, Ruth. Nap, a well-known figure in the Spanish-speaking population represents a curious American mixture for he had a German father and name. As an orphan he was adopted by a Martinez family. He was born in New Mexico in 1893 and moved to Fort Collins in 1910 at seventeen to work on beets and live with an uncle, Manuel Gonzales. Two years later he began working at the Ingleside quarries near Owl Canyon and that area was his home till 1958. He supervised workers from Spain, Old Mexico, Italy and Germany as well as southwestern United States and he could speak with them all a little in their native languages. In the 1940's he supervised German prisoners.

In 1920 Nap moved the short distance from Ingleside to Owl Canyon and later bought the old school house which he converted into a store. In 1973 he walked over the hogbacks and he recalled his adjustment to legal liquor traffic when prohibition ended in 1933:

Everybody said to me 'Nap, why don't you get a license now?' and so I did, the first one in the county.

Ingleside had a reputation as a tough spot when it was just a loading area for ranchers' cattle to a branch railroad connection. In the first part of the twentieth century it was an important source for limestone needed at the sugar factory.

The barren life there is suggested by the occasional report of trouble in the newspapers. "Mexico and United States in Bloodless War near Ingleside" was the headline for one story in 1909. The Ingleside quarries with surrounding shacks housing families had a special store which was delinquent in payments. Merlin Aylesworth, attorney, with Ernest Fisher, R.M. Ferguson and G.T. Avery, all Fort Collins merchants with interests at stake, went by auto, put the store's supplies in a wagon, pushed them up the hogback, and chained them, putting the store out of business.

In April, 1910, an interpreter for Mexicans notified the sheriff of the appearance of Jesus Vegas, a fugitive from the Greeley jail. He had been isolated with small pox in the Greeley pesthouse and escaped to return to Ingleside where he had previously worked. Judge Bouton sentenced a bootlegger from Ingleside in January, 1917 and the workers complained, "nothing to do at night since his arrest."

The sheriff was in that neighborhood in March, 1924 hunting for stills. He had located three and a quantity of liquor and revolvers when called to investigate a murder. Nap, then foreman, reported the death of Diego Hornelas, a lad, twenty-four, who resided with his father, brothers, and sister at Ingleside. They were an industrious family and the victim was one of the steadiest workers and best men at the quarries. Alberto Aldans, recently arrived from Mexico, had committed the crime. Heavy snows and bad weather keeping the men from work had increased the drinking. Celestino Silva acted as interpreter for the case in court and the killing was termed not felonious.

A few people in Fort Collins realized how wretched the living conditions were, but it was part of frontier life repeated over and over. Max Parshall remembers with affection the patience of his uncle, Dr. Stuver, who accepted many house calls on the sick there though he was rarely paid.

Mrs. Edgar Hilton, the teacher in the school at Ingleside, had twenty-five children in December, 1923, half of them foreign-born. She prepared Madalona Herrera and Hernado Comtrenos to appear in a holiday program at the Livermore Hall with ranch children from schools scattered throughout that area. Walter Swan came from the Adams school, and Sylvia and Juliana Sloan (now Mrs. Lafi Miller) from the Sloan school.(78)

Luisa Garcia Padilla was another of Mrs. Hilton's pupils. She was born at Ingleside in 1919. Her father was seriously crippled in a dynamite accident at the quarry. Her children are among the many Spanish-speaking students making good academic records at Colorado State University today and she is thankful for the contrast of opportunities with those of her own youth, just as the pioneers of the '70's and '80's were proud of the records their children made at the tiny college.

The general area is still used for quarrying in the grove of rare pinon pine and the railroad runs on a limited schedule, though Ingleside itself is a ghost town with little evidence today of the once-busy camp.

Though many ranches in the Rockies had Basque shepherds, no one remembers any in Larimer County. These men came to America with a knowledge of sheep. The Mexican herders in this area did not. They were trained by local ranchers. One with many years in this work is Marguerito Lopez, called "Maggie," born in Chihuahua in 1910. He managed to get over the border and find work on the railroad in Amarillo, Texas in 1927. He tried thinning beets at Sterling, picking green beans at Fort Lupton, and working on the railroad at Wellington. About 1930 he turned up on the Ed Munroe ranch north of Fort Collins where the Calloways long ago dug the first ditches. He had never worked with sheep but Ed Munroe trained him.

Munroe had one of the earliest grazing permits for sheep on the Roosevelt National Forest, getting it in 1924. The spectacle of the sheep drive in July up the Livermore road, down Pingree Hill, and on to Crown Point and the return in September with Maggie in charge was one of the seasonal scenes of the old west that the well-informed in Fort Collins always tried to witness, like seeing pasque flowers in the mountains in April and aspen in October. The drive took four and one-half days going up, and four coming down. There was no other rancher in the area who worked with sheep so successfully and was so highly respected as Munroe. He had worked with Elwood Mead in the early plans for getting western slope water in the Big Thompson project in the 1930's and was an old man when it came through in the 1950's.

When Munroe gave up on sheep in 1969, Maggie had his last drive. He watched dismally from the sidelines as the sheep went on auction and saw Jack Stevens, a farmer south of Greeley, buy most of the Munroe bands. Suddenly he snapped to attention. Stevens was asking: "Where is the shepherd that goes with 'em?"

Maggie stepped out. "That's me."

"Let's go," said Stevens, and off went shepherd, dog, sheep, and van to a new area. Maggie had bought a tiny house at 402 Pine, in Fort Collins in 1958 which he rents out till the time he needs a retirement home. Munroe, too, left the ranch and joined many of his old friends in Fort Collins, enjoying his last years in a modern development home over-looking Terry Lake.

Munroe, Maggie, and the sheep seeking the high mountain pasture looked like the old west but in fact they represented the new era. Forest Service experts watched the mountain pastures, avoiding the over-grazing and destruction of range which made sheep so hated by oldtime cattlemen. They arranged allotments at higher altitudes than cattle and in appriate numbers for compatibility with wildlife. Gradually the long drive had become unprofitable. Stevens intended to move the sheep around on rented fields eating beet tops, fatten them on his own alfalfa, and finish them in feed lots, avoiding the mountain trip entirely.

When Watrous wrote the county history in 1910-11, he felt that the town had come of age. The view from the top of the Opera House looking northeast revealed in the panorama many recent triumphs. In the immediate foreground were the Northern Hotel and the Trimble Block. The next tier back showed the Poudre Valley Bank and the City Hall with its tower. The Tedmon House on Jefferson loomed up back of those, and in the far distance the sugar factory. With the overall view of the modern city in perspective, individual facets and special historical problems may be considered.

View of city northeast from Opera House Roof, 1906.

Part II: Sketches

THE WILDERNESS BEFORE PIONEER SETTLEMENT: REPORT OF JOHN CHARLES FREMONT

The account of John Charles Fremont's trip along the foothills and the Cache la Poudre in late July, 1843, is an excellent source with which to study Fort Collins history in depth. His wife, Jessie Benton Fremont, daughter of the Missouri senator, wrote of her husband's travels: "From his campfires have grown cities," and Fort Collins might be counted one of them. He gave us our first good map of the area. He marked Arapaho country. One member of the expedition, Theodore Talbot, mentioned the reunion of mountain man, Thomas Fitzpatrick, and Friday, his Arapaho friend, at Fort St. Vrain.

Fremont described the wilderness before the Mormon trek west and before the gold rush. His explorations favored converting the fur-trading post of Fort Laramie into a military post. His findings actually discouraged railroad building through the Rockies in northern Colorado and promoted a southern Wyoming route for the Union Pacific. That was exactly what Senator Benton hoped would not happen. Benton wanted St. Louis in his home state, and not Chicago, to prosper by westward expansion.

Fremont recommended Colorado as cow country. Where there were buffalo there could be cattle. He stressed the superiority of Colorado's short grass over the long grass farther east when he reached Kansas on the return trip in 1844:

The beautiful sward of the buffalo grass appeared now only in patches being replaced by a longer coarser grass....The difference in the character of the grasses became suddenly evident in the weakened condition of our animals, which began to fail as soon as we quitted the buffalo grass.(1)

Besides all that, he appreciated the scenery. He thoroughly enjoyed this trip through Colorado, seeing buffalo hunts and grizzly bears, collecting plants and marveling at the beauty of the mountains. A new geranium he had found in southern Wyoming in 1842 was named for him, **Geranium fremontii.** He

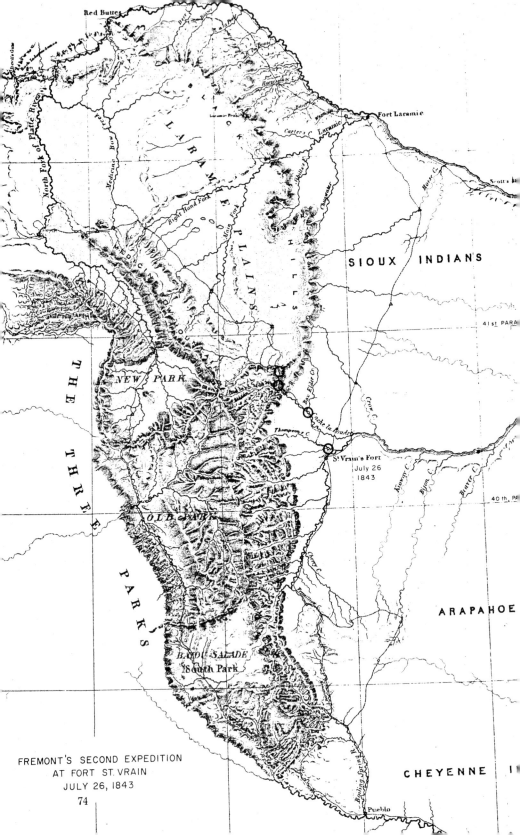

FREMONT'S SECOND EXPEDITION
AT FORT ST. VRAIN
JULY 26, 1843
74

compared the Rockies with the Alps and was excited over the loveliness of the summer flowers shut up in their stern recesses. Talbot, too, was humbled by the view of Pike's Peak and Long's Peak. He wrote: "We have a magnificent spectacle every morning when the sun first shines on the Rocky Mountains. I cannot dare describe its beauty in my plain prose."(2)

Who was young Fremont who became such an enthusiastic booster for northern Colorado? His family background was romantic but tragic. His mother was the wife of a Virginia plantation owner who ran away with her French tutor. He died and left her with three small children. John Charles, the oldest, was only five. Divorce at that time required an act of the Virginia Assembly and the abandoned husband failed in his efforts to get one. Consequently Fremont's mother had many social and financial problems. The family moved about the south, living for a while in Charleston. Fremont, a very bright boy, attracted the attention of Joel Poinsett, South Carolina senator. Poinsett arranged for him to cruise South American waters on a sloop of war in 1833. He learned surveying. He worked in the Carolina mountains and in Cherokee country in Georgia. He traveled with Nicollet in southern Minnesota when that was fur-trading country.

Through all this wilderness experience, Fremont became a good traveler and a skillful observer. He answered questions both for the scientific and political communities in Washington and for the general public. The government printing office

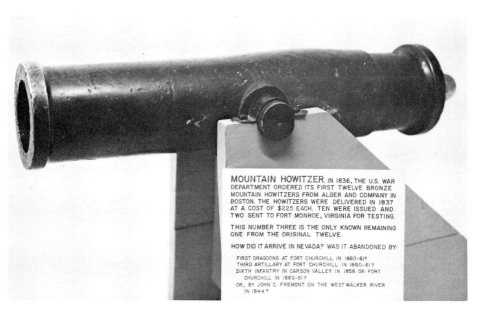

MOUNTAIN HOWITZER. IN 1836, THE U.S. WAR DEPARTMENT ORDERED ITS FIRST TWELVE BRONZE MOUNTAIN HOWITZERS FROM ALGER AND COMPANY IN BOSTON. THE HOWITZERS WERE DELIVERED IN 1837 AT A COST OF $225 EACH. TEN WERE ISSUED AND TWO SENT TO FORT MONROE, VIRGINIA FOR TESTING.

THIS NUMBER THREE IS THE ONLY KNOWN REMAINING ONE FROM THE ORIGINAL TWELVE.

HOW DID IT ARRIVE IN NEVADA? WAS IT ABANDONED BY:

FIRST DRAGOONS AT FORT CHURCHILL IN 1860-61?
THIRD ARTILLARY AT FORT CHURCHILL IN 1860-61?
SIXTH INFANTRY IN CARSON VALLEY IN 1858 OR FORT CHURCHILL IN 1860-61?
OR, BY JOHN C. FREMONT ON THE WEST WALKER RIVER IN 1844?

ordered ten thousand copies of the 1843 report and reprinted the report of 1842 with it. The thousand copies of the latter for public distribution had been quickly exhausted.

Fremont's western travels made him a hero. In retrospect he seems an absurd choice for the new Republican party's candidate for president of the United States in 1856. He had no knowledge of government or politics except casual exposure as the son-in-law of a senator. But he was an excellent leader for the western jaunt in 1843. His political involvement should not detract from this brilliant feat in his career.

Fremont's westward trip in 1842 had been of only four month's duration. It took him along the South Platte to Fort St. Vrain, then northeast to Fort Laramie, not close enough to the mountains to appraise railroad building potentialities. In 1843 he began a tour which lasted over a year. He visited the Poudre only on the outward route between July 26 when he camped on the Big Thompson and July 31, when he was north of the forty-first parallel, the Wyoming-Colorado boundary.

There are many interesting historical points that have been debated ever since by readers of his journals. Jessie claimed that he needed the month of July at Fort St. Vrain because she hurried him off prematurely to avoid recall to Washington. There was suspicion about the cannon he was taking along. Was this an embellishment of later years to enhance the drama of the episode? The Fremonts had financial worries in old age and Jessie explained her reaction to them simply: "I took up my pen."

Fremont divided his group and sent one party with Fitzpatrick northeast to Fort Laramie. He took the rest, including Kit Carson and Preuss, the German map-maker, as well as the cannon along the Poudre. Did Fitzpatrick actually follow the exact route and use the same camping sites as Fremont had in 1842? The map for this part of the 1842 trip and the 1843 trip are identical. Or did they just not have anyone along who could draw a map the second time?

There was nothing very noteworthy in the Cache la Poudre section. The report mentioned the mosquito nuisance on the St. Vrain and the necessity of fording the Poudre eight or nine times. Ansel Watrous believed they must have gone up the Red Feather Lakes road to the Laramie River and then through Sand Creek Pass to Wyoming. One hundred years after the trip, Gertrude Barnes of Wellington challenged that interpretation believing he went along the present highway route 287 to Laramie. In favor of the theory is the fact that

Fremont's map shows the Laramie River rising north of the forty-first parallel in Wyoming instead of having its true source in Colorado. If they had followed the route Watrous outlined, would they have made this mistake?(3)

They did drag the cannon all the way to the mountains bordering Nevada and California. In January, 1844, it became an intolerable burden. The men's moccasins got wet from melting snows, then froze. The Indian guide abandoned them. Their energy was low from a sparse diet of pine nuts and antelope. After they hauled the howitzer into a canyon with no outlet, they left it! That may have been the end of the cannon or it may be the one now reposing in a Nevada museum. There are several theories about this too.

Perhaps it is best just to visit the marked site of Fort St. Vrain on the Platte or the adobe remnants of Fort Lupton under a barn north of the town with that name and say: "Fremont was here." His narrative captured the atmosphere of the west before its settlement by pioneers. It was not written as a guide for later generations to follow in his exact footprints.

Original adobe wall of Fort Lupton protected by barn on ranch north of Fort Lupton, photo 1967.

INDIANS IN THE POUDRE VALLEY

When the Indians were gone from northern Colorado, the pioneers sensed that they had lived through an epoch in history and many contributed stories of their encounters. All during the first stage of settlement during the late '50's and early '60's as well as the brief period when the soldiers were stationed at the fort, the Cache la Poudre was the favorite haunt of friendly Arapahoes. There never was any attack on the post. There was one bill of ten dollars charged to the county in November, 1868, for a casket to bury a man killed by Indians.(4) Most of the pioneers described them as a curiosity to be observed.

Some of the Arapahoes even worked for the ranchers. Black Crow, one of Chief Friday's band, hunted game and his wife cooked for a crew putting up hay for the Cheyenne market. When a sheepherder on E.W. Whitcomb's ranch on the Boxelder was killed by Sioux, Black Crow became too nervous to stay on the job. This illustrates the tension that existed for the decade that whites and Indians shared the Poudre valley. The friendly Arapahoes never knew when Utes from the west or Sioux or Pawnee from the north and east might swoop down. The housewife in a cabin on the river alone while her husband was up in the foothills getting timber was never sure if the strange Indians begging for food were friendly neighbors or hostile invaders.

According to the white man's interpretation, the land bordering the South Platte and its tributaries was all part of the hunting ground for the Arapahoes and Cheyennes after the Fort Laramie treaty of 1851. That settlement had been negotiated by the mountain man and Indian agent, Thomas Fitzpatrick. He was one of the few government officials who really understood the Indian problem and was concerned for their welfare. That treaty, however, did not lessen the warfare between the rival Indian tribes which depended upon finding the enemy wherever he was regardless of white men's treaty lines.

The reason the Arapahoes and pioneers were friends was that their chief spoke English and liked white people. On the Santa Fe trail near the Cimarron River, Fitzpatrick had found him as a child lost from his tribe in 1831. He took him to St. Louis for a period in a Catholic school. During the summers the boy joined him at the fur traders' rendezvous in southern Wyoming, and he eventually rejoined the Arapaho tribe. He was known to the whites as Friday Fitzpatrick and he maintained his fluency in speaking English throughout his life. In 1851 he went to Washington, D.C. to meet President Fillmore with Fitzpatrick's delegation of eleven Indians.

The prestige of this experience made Friday a leader among the Arapahoes. Though he was a minor chief, he had several hundred in his band in the late '50's when the Cache la Poudre was attracting its first white settlers. Gradually Friday came to be associated specifically with this area as Niwot or Left Hand was with Boulder.

A fierce three-day battle between Pawnee and Arapaho near Laporte reputedly occurred in the fall of 1858. Friday described it later to Henry Clay Peterson, the gunsmith at the fort, who related it in turn to Ansel Watrous, the author of the county history. Another account of a battle between these two tribes in the same area in August, 1858, may be a version of the same event Friday recounted.(5)

James B. Arthur located a claim on the Poudre River near Timnath in July, 1860, and his ranch home was an improvised fort where Arapahoes and pioneers assembled in case of alarm. In July, 1862 the Utes stole horses from the ranch of Jesse and F.W. Sherwood near present day Drake road. The events which followed involved a series of mistaken identities. First the Indian wives of the Laporte French-Canadians who were picking berries near Spring Canyon were thought to be Utes. Then Friday and his Arapahoes who rushed out there caused a similar report. By the time all were recognized, the Utes and Sherwood's horses were long gone.

Ebenezer Davis, a Welch miner and trader with the Indians, settled near Arthur and Sherwood. He was counted as Friday's best friend. Friday told Davis the white women should defend their larders from begging Indians with guns. The amount of food the Indians consumed can be guessed by the local belief that Indians ate enough at one meal to last three or four days. Thomas Cline, another early settler in the Timnath area, was such a sharp marksman his wife had only to pretend she heard her husband approaching to frighten off the Indians. Frank Chaffee complained that the Indians stole onions from his garden and he drove them from the premises with a whip. He still cherished in 1933 a hair bridle and knife scabbard made and given to him by Friday.

The farm of William B. Osborn on the Big Thompson near Loveland was another place where Friday and his Indians were well known. The squaws sometimes helped harvest corn and secreted an occasional ear under their blankets. Sarah

Milner Smith, a Loveland teacher, boarded with the Osborns in 1866 and saw the Arapahoes camp on the island near the farm. They liked to make fires there because of the abundance of wood but they rarely stayed overnight because of the frequent flooding.(6)

The Arapahoes as well as Utes took horses when they could. Joshua Yeager near Laporte told of many sleepless nights guarding his stock from the Indians. Long after the tribes were gone, some white men received compensation for reported thefts, Rock Bush in 1886, Abner Loomis and James Arthur in 1899. The Indians were an inconvenience to these early settlers but apparently not a serious worry.

When the soldiers were stationed at Laporte in 1863 and at Fort Collins in 1864 more problems developed. The fort attracted more civilians and both settlers and soldiers hunted game. Friday had to get permission from the commanding officer at Laporte in the fall of 1864 to hunt on the south fork of the Poudre, an area where he had roamed freely before. In 1861 a grandson of Daniel Boone, Albert G. Boone, negotiated the treaty of Fort Wise drastically reducing the Arapaho range, restricting these Indians to a reservation in the southeastern part of Colorado Territory. Friday rejected this for several years but in 1863 when the government threatened to withhold rations and his Indians were hungry, he unwillingly placed an "X" as his signature. He showed his continued opposition to the terms however by asking for a reservation on the north bank of the Poudre. He wanted the land from the mouth of the Boxelder, just across the river from the Sherwood ranch, to the junction with the Platte. The agent pointed out that this choice land already had sixteen white families on it and involved eighteen miles of the stage route.(7)

The cabin that George Robert Strauss built in the 1860's was near one of the favorite camping grounds of the Arapaho on the Poudre north of present Horsetooth Road. This landmark still stands, but the large cottonwood nearby, once called the Arapaho Council Tree, is gone. Friday's late signing of the Fort Wise treaty occurred near Fort Lyon, the new name for Fort Wise, in the southeastern part of Colorado Territory, not near the Poudre. He and his band camped by the Council Tree even if no treaty was made in the neighborhood.

In 1864 Indian raids in Wyoming and in other parts of Colorado caused fear among the settlers and tended to strain normal friendly relations. The agent reported:

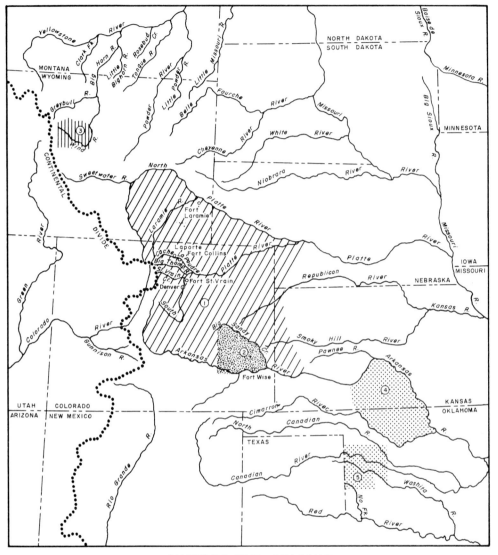

SHIFTING THE ARAPAHO

▨	1	1851 Hunting Area – Between The Rivers
▨	2	1861 Restricted Area – Sand Creek Reservation
▤	3	Wind River Shoshone Reservation–Shared by Arapaho Chief Friday's Last Home
▨	4,5	Other Reservations – Used by Arapaho and Cheyenne

One hundred armed men started out for the express purpose of cleaning out Friday and his friends, but fortunately, hearing of some hostile Indians at Fort Lupton, they went in that direction.

This was a prelude to Chivington's Sand Creek attack in southeastern Colorado on other Indians in November. Friday's band was not involved. Friday still clung to a precarious existence along the Poudre. One of the Sherwood brothers acted as a sub-agent and distributed rations to the band. When his supervisor visited Sherwood in 1864 to see how he was getting on with the Indians he found him in bed, having been badly mangled by a grizzly. In this land of the friendly Arapahoes other hazards were far more serious than the Indians.

Friday camped on the John Coy ranch in April, 1865, and at the Sherwoods in August. Elizabeth Keays Stratton, Auntie Stone's niece, described the fun the ladies had visiting Friday's camp in 1866:

His youngest squaw had a papoose that she was very proud to show. Its entire wardrobe was an antelope wrap, beaded beautifully with just blue and white beads.(8)

Even then the ladies were interested in collecting Indian art objects they reported: "We could not get many of their Indian-made things, as they did not do much such work."

Friday's niece, Success-ca, who was quite a powerful figure in the band, had a lovely robe of fine antelope for state occasions, and the ladies took turns trying it on.

When the fort closed in 1867 the Indians became even more hardpressed for food. Friday appealed to Governor Cum-

Engraving of Chief Friday from original photograph c.1867 on carte de visite type mount, credited to D.S. Mitchell, Cheyenne.

One of Friday's wives called "The One Who Sleeps"

mings in Golden in January, 1867 reporting "game is very scarce and wild this winter." He was given flour, meat, and a few other supplies.

Just exactly when Friday left the Poudre is uncertain. In August, 1868 the agent reported the hungry band near Fort Collins as having only eighty-five members. Henry Clay Peterson said the Indians climbed the framework of his new flour mill during construction and had to be helped down they were so dizzy. Alfred A. Edwards recalled riding Friday's horse, Old Swift Bird, up Rist canyon when he was a boy of nineteen in 1870. The chief sold that horse to a Laporte resident when he left the area.

These Arapahoes really had no place to go that they liked. When the Shoshone chief, Washakie, and the government worked out plans for the Wind River Reservation in 1868, this spot appealed to Friday. He wrote Washakie, asking for permission to share the new reservation. Washakie was not

Friday, seated on right: photo c.1877 by Mathew Brady.

Friday seated with Crazy
Bull photo c.1877 by
William Henry Jackson.

eager to acquire Arapaho neighbors. Nevertheless Friday appeared in the vicinity of present day Lander in 1869. That fall he was rescued from freezing by Captain Nickerson who found him drunk by the roadside. Nickerson recognized his riderless horse at Miners' Delight, a mining boom town, and went to look for him.(9)

In the spring of 1870 a mob of miners and other westerners among whom was A.H. Patterson of Fort Collins gathered in the Lander, Wyoming, area to attack these homeless Arapahoes in retaliation for alleged depredations on whites. Patterson wrote:

We expected to surprise the Arapaho camp, but they were on the lookout for us and we could not get them all. We did get 25 Indians and 14 ponies. We came near getting Old Friday and did kill four of his Indians. We also killed Black Bear. I expect you may know Friday as he used to live on the Cache la Poudre. I got one scalp and it is a fine one you bet. They fought some, but only one of our men was hurt and three horses wounded.(10)

This ended the chief's relationship with the Poudre valley. He was a scout for General Crook during the Indian campaigns of 1876 and finally in 1879 was temporarily permitted space at Wind River where he died at the age of sixty in 1881. During his last two years he served as Arapaho interpreter on the reservation receiving a salary of $300.00 a year. He was the only Arapaho there who spoke English.

The two most famous photographers of that era took pictures of Friday about 1877. William Henry Jackson posed him seated with Crazy Bull standing by his side. Mathew Brady placed him at the front right next to Black Coal in a group of Indians and white men.

There were a few soldiers at Fort Collins who settled permanently in the vicinity and who had had experience with Indians of other tribes. John Mandeville and George Buss assisted Governor Evans at a council with the Utes at Fort Garland in September, 1865. C.C. Hawley, stationed in Denver in 1863 and later a resident of Fort Collins, confirmed the story of the Laporte soldiers' rescue of "Ute Susan." Susan, Chief Ouray's sister, was said to be a captive of Left Hand's Arapahoes in 1863 near present day Greeley. The soldiers freed her and sent her back to the Utes through Denver. In November, 1864, Hawley was the ordnance officer who arranged supplies for Chivington's attack at Sand Creek.

Living in Laporte and Fort Collins were many veterans of that battle. These included Louis Orleans, Martin Farrar, William Lindenmeier, Edward C. Smith, clerk of Larimer county in 1867, and George Pingree, who received an arrow wound in his face at that encounter. What impact did the battle and the racial clash have on their lives? Smith had a nervous breakdown which his wife attributed to the experience. Lindenmeier went into ranching and the saloon business and made no comment. Pingree boasted about it in his old age.

The committee arranging the county fair in 1884 persuaded Chivington to speak in Fort Collins. Interviewers hired by H.H. Bancroft to collect information for his histories came to the Tedmon House in August, 1886. They asked for comments on Sand Creek. George Buss told them "Chivington took the only right course." C.W. Harrington, who lived in Denver and Laramie during the '60's and '70's and then settled near Laporte, regarded the battle as "absolute necessity." J.N. Hollowell of Loveland too supported Chivington and resented the official investigations.(11)

While Indians in general received little sympathy, Chief Friday's reputation remained untarnished. After the turn of the century pioneers gathered in Auntie Stone's old cabin which they restored for a meeting place and swapped Indian stories. Mrs. F.W. Sherwood reminisced at the annual dinners at the Masonic Temple about her husband's work with Friday. She had been a Timnath school teacher and did not marry Sherwood till 1874 when Friday was gone, but her ranch home was already historic as an Arapaho camping ground. She confirmed the fact that the settlers in this area were fortunate in having friendly Indian neighbors.

ANTOINE JANIS: SUCCESSFUL TRADER WITH
THE INDIANS

Antoine Janis represents the era of the French-Canadian fur trader and is an important historical character for early Fort Collins. His reputed presence when powder may have been cached near Bellvue in 1836, his claim to land near Laporte in 1844, and his cabin used on that land from 1859 to 1878, now part of the museum complex in Lincoln Park, are all elements which add to his prestige.

Joseph Antoine Janis, called Antoine, was born in St. Charles, Missouri, on March 26, 1824, third of five children of Antoine St. Charles Janis and Marguerite Thibaut who were married in 1818. The father was a mountain man familiar with the fur trade in the west during the 1820's and 1830's. He was killed by Blackfeet on the Yellowstone River around 1840.

Joseph Antoine at twelve may have been with his father and other fur traders near Bellvue on a snowy November day in 1836 when they cached some powder which they could not carry on to Brown's Fort on the Green River in northwestern Colorado. Ansel Watrous heard this story from Abner Loomis who heard it from Janis. If the river was called "Cache la Poudre" before that date, the incident may have occurred without Antoine.

He knew the Mexican area around Taos and Santa Fe well in the 1840's and the trails from those towns along the Colorado foothills to the Wyoming migration routes. He married a relative of Red Cloud, an Oglala Sioux, and their "home" was near Fort Laramie. Antoine was called "Yellow Hair All-Mussed-Up" and her name was Mary or "First-Elk-Woman." They raised twelve children to maturity: Maggie, Mollie, Pete, Willie, James, Zuzella, Antoine, Nick, Henry, Lucy, Lizzie, and Josephine. Pete and Willie were dry-gulched by Crazy Horse's wild half-breed followers in 1872 and were buried in the Fort Laramie cemetery.

Janis said that he was impressed with the beauty of the Poudre valley in 1844 when he was traveling through it and "staked a claim" near present day Laporte. When the gold rush brought miners and settlers to Colorado in 1858-59 he left Fort Laramie and built his cabin near the Poudre. He intended to live in the area he had admired earlier and to be handy as a guide and interpreter when he could get work.

In 1863 he and Abner Loomis helped train the soldiers at Laporte to western ways and took some hunting parties up the north fork of the Poudre. He continued to live in Laporte when Fort Collins was established down river. His title to the land became official in Larimer County records, May 1, 1867, for eighty acres in Sections 28 and 30, Township 8, Range 69.

Antoine, with his knowledge of the Sioux language and customs, was a successful trader. His personal wealth in the 1860 census was listed as $20,000. He played the fiddle, another skill valued on the frontier. He still lived in Laporte when Ansel Watrous came to the Poudre Valley in 1877.

In 1878 the men in Laporte with Indian wives had to part with them or accompany them to the reservation. Antoine and Mary moved to the Pine Ridge Agency in Dakota Territory. He did not sell his property immediately for he wrote back to a friend in Laporte in August, 1879, with instructions for its care: "You can sell the hay for what you think right....I am glad you fixed the fence."

In October he wrote:

Keep out of the hay money what you have spent for taxes....if $30.00 is not a nuf for my taxes you can rite to me and I will send you the ballance....I want $15.00 per acer and if you can git a offer for less than that rite to me and let me no.

He wanted his area fenced: "If the two wires you put up will not keepe out stock you had better buy and post up another."

Antoine was a resident of the "Pooder" valley, as he spelled it, from 1859 to 1878, a crucial time in its development. For a brief period in 1861 and 1862 he was sub-agent and Sioux interpreter at the Red Cloud Agency in Nebraska. Three years before his death the government paid Antoine Janis $1,625 for damages due to Indian depredation that had occurred long ago on the Cache la Poudre. He died on April 10, 1890, and was buried in the Episcopal cemetery at Pine Ridge.(12)

Antoine Janis with Indian friends on the reservation after he left Fort Collins.

RIDING THE STAGE THROUGH LARIMER COUNTY

Ben Holladay needed a new set of stage coach stops in 1862. He moved the route of the Overland Stage from southern Wyoming to northern Colorado because of Indian unrest. The route generally followed the old trappers' trails, and the trappers had used the buffalo trail, so the easiest way was already known. Holladay used existing ranches or settlements wherever possible. The average distance between stations was twelve and one-half miles. The Sherwood ranch twelve miles below Laporte was a practical choice and Fred Sherwood was good with horses as well as with people. Ten miles above Laporte was Bonner Springs with a fairly good supply of water. Twelve miles north of Bonner Springs was Cherokee Station and north of this, the most famous stop of all in this county, Virginia Dale.

Today there are still a few items to mark these sites: the old ranch home of the Sherwoods, considerably remodeled and used as a residence for the Lewis Morrison family; a marker near the site of Laporte's station; a child's grave near Bonner Springs; an eroded trail near Cherokee Station, and the actual stage coach inn at Virginia Dale. The company owned only about half of the stations in use along its line. In 1866 Holladay ranked second in paying taxes in the county. His bill was 254.88, exceeded only by Joe Mason and his partner who ran the store in Old Grout. Holladay paid the Sherwoods $500.00 to use their ranch.

Grave of Eddie Hale, 19 months, April 17, 1864 near Bonner Springs north of Laporte photo 1947.

Modern photo of home of Jesse and Frederick Sherwood near Drake Road and the river; area used for Arapaho camps and Overland Stage stop.

The route should not be thought of as a modern highway that was surveyed and maintained forever after, on practically the same location. It altered according to season and every new development from year to year. The stage that ran north through Laporte from Denver preferred different stops from the one coming from Latham southeast. When Camp Collins moved from Laporte to its new site, that became a stop instead of the Sherwood ranch. North of Laporte some travelers wanted to go northeast toward Fort Laramie instead of northwest. Some effort to accommodate all these desires was made.

Everyone from Horace Greeley and Mark Twain to the hundreds of less famous travelers felt that crossing the country by stage coach was to experience the Wild West in action. One man's summary of his adventures with baggage trouble in 1863 was included in an official government report of 1864. He found on arriving at Latham traveling east that his valise was lost, having broken through the rotten boot of the coach. Fortunately it was picked up by an honest teamster. To retrieve it, he went back thirty miles to Camp Collins, then ninety miles more—five days on the road. He wrote:

The stages were sometimes in a miserable condition. We were put into a coach one night with only two boards left in the bottom. On remonstrating with the driver we were told to hold on by the sides.(13)

The ramshackle condition of the equipment was matched by the indifferent attitude of the employees. Another account

THE OLD FERRY HOUSE, LAPORTE

described the calibre of staff employed at Virginia Dale by Slade. "They were a drunken carousing set in the main, and absolutely careless of the rights or feelings of the settlers." This unfortunate passenger wrote of his take-off from Laporte:

Six wild mustangs were brought out and hitched to the stage, requiring a hostler to each until the driver gathered up his line. When they were thrown loose the coach dashed off like a limited whirlwind, the wild, drunken jehu, in mad delight, keeping up a constant crack, crack with his snake-whip. The stage traveled for a time on the two offwheels, then lurched over and traveled on the other two by way of variety.. ..Slade and his gang whooped and yelled like demons. Fortunately the passenger had taken the precaution before starting to secure an outside seat. The only way in which he was enabled to prevent the complete wreck of stage, necks and everything valuable was finally by an earnest threat that he would report the whole affair to the company.

Holladay did travel over his line once or twice a year to inspect the situation, but the treatment he received was quite a contrast to that of the ordinary passenger. He went in a special coach with such comforts as coil springs, a bed, a writing table, and an oil lamp with reflector so he could read papers and make notes in the coach at night.

Not all the managers of stops were as tough as Slade who was hanged in Montana in 1867. Some, like William Taylor of Laporte, became respected local citizens. Charlie Clay, a Fort

90

Collins Negro, was famous for the good food he provided at several stops. Travelers welcomed the soldiers' protection on the Larimer County stretch where the danger from white outlaws exceeded that from Indians.

Locating the exact sites of the old stations is a hobby that has intrigued many western history enthusiasts. Not all agree in their interpretation of the old records. The stop on the Sherwood ranch illustrates the vague descriptions which provide some of the clues. Jesse Sherwood prepared an indenture for Ben Holladay to sign on October 18, 1863 which ran:

> **my claim commencing at a point on the North bank of the Cache Le Poudre river about seventy rods below the mouth of the Box Elder and running in a Northerly direction one half mile thence Westerly one half mile thence Southerly one half mile thence down the said Cache Le Poudre to the place of beginning**

and on the south side:

> **commencing at a stake in the Prairie about one mile below dry creek...running thence in an Easterly direction one half mile thence northerly one half mile to the bank of the Cache Le Poudre thence up the stream one half mile in a direct line thence Southerly one half mile to the place of beginning.**

The survey map of 1865 shows both Dry Creek and Boxelder Creek entering the Cache la Poudre at different points from modern maps. Irrigation users may have changed the entry points or the old map may have been wrong. Fortunately the survival of the Sherwood house which oldtimers recall as being near the stop gives some help.(14)

Richard S. Baker, a dedicated local historian and grandson of a pioneer, examined county sites along the whole network and found that the Spring Canyon Station was on the George

91

THE OLD STAGE STATION, LAPORTE

Ross ranch one-half mile north of the Nellie Nichol Fraser cabin which still stands today near Horsetooth Road. George Ross' description matches Sherwood's deed in its loose direction:

I know where the old stage house set. It's out in that corn field of mine. You know where that cattle shed was. The corn field's right east of it. If you come right east about halfway across the corn field, you ought to hit it. You could find glass and broken bits of stoves and such.(15)

Baker with Harold Dunning of Loveland covered the corn field, found artifacts, and took a picture of the hogback including the cattle shed. But now the shed is gone and legend prevails that the Nellie Nichol Fraser cabin **is** the Spring Canyon stop because it does still exist and is easier to point out. Baker has wearied of destroying the myth.

Luckily the grave near Bonner Springs and the Virginia Dale inn are still to be found on their original sites.

Virginia Dale Stage Coach stop - Richard S. Baker on right, J. Evan Roberts. second from left, guides for western history buffs, April 26, 1969.

Trees may mark the ruts of old trail used by stage coaches and covered wagons near the Wyoming border photo April, 1969.

The terrain in Larimer County did not wear into ruts like that of the Oregon Trail in Wyoming, but there are two ecological developments which offer some evidence of the old route. Rancher Billy Logan, fourth generation on the family ranch near Virginia Dale, has observed to the east of modern highway 287 eroding gullies believed to be part of the route from the Devil's Washboard. The nearest stop there called "Ten Mile" or "Cherokee Station" close to Steamboat Rock, was a well-known landmark. On the west of the highway farther north toward Wyoming, Logan believes that the two ruts afforded water and encouragement for trees to grow. The paired lines of trees winding off over the hill today may serve as an outline for the old route. At least it is an interesting theory.

THE ARMY POST ON THE POUDRE

When Lieutenant-colonel W.O. Collins and his Eleventh Ohio regiment got orders in 1861 to go west and fight Indians instead of south against the rebels, their patriotic fervor for war issues was temporarily dampened. "Where is Fort Laramie?" was the question and one western traveler briefed them on the location and character of the Wyoming post.

Colonel Collins seasoned rapidly. He adopted a fatherly concern toward the men, one of whom was his young son, Caspar. He expected them to learn the elements of wilderness survival and felt each should be intentionally "lost" on the desert prairie with nothing but a little salt to see how he would get along. A report of an official inspection of sanitary conditions at Fort Laramie in 1858 noted that the rations were worse than the usual fare of mountain men. The post cattle were tough and stringy. Supplies included hard bread, molasses, apples, rice, beans, coffee, tea, and whiskey. In the '60's there was very little concern for the forts far from the main theatre of war.

Though Colonel Collins was in his early fifties, in the eyes of one young soldier writing down his observations, he was "a very fine old gentleman, rather old for military service but finely preserved, energetic and soldierly." Mrs. Collins sized up the war in the west in April, 1864, and wrote to their daughter, Josephine, in Ohio from her husband's post:

There is trouble apprehended...with the Indians...but if your father is clothed with proper authority, it will not exist long as his wisdom, justice and promptness will enable him soon, to quell disorder and protect the peaceable and industrious, or well meaning either white or Indian.

She noted that he required a soldier to pay for a mare and colt he had taken from an Indian.(16)

Collins' correspondence at Fort Laramie gives many examples of the variety of problems of garrison life in the Wyoming posts. Horse Shoe had plenty of wood but no hay and needed buglers in November, 1862. Upper Crossing was short on books and reading matter. Even old papers would be a treat in December. One man wanted a Bible, "large print as you can get." The men at South Pass in January, 1863, were hungry for publications. "Our books...were taken out of the wagon at Sweet Water Bridge...Our papers are always taken before they reach this post."

Photo of Sutler's store, "Old Grout," when it had become part of the new town of Fort Collins.

Collins himself asked for a new grammar and dictionary of the Sioux language he had heard about in February, 1863. In March he needed instruments and books for nine young men at Fort Laramie to form a band. He reproved Lieutenant Love at South Pass in March:

Am informed that sergeant of your company has seduced squaw and harbors her. Examine into the matter and if proper arrest him. The circumstances as stated here are very disrespectable and injurious to the service.

This was all part of a soldier's life in the west when the stage coach line moved south through northern Colorado instead of going through southern Wyoming, and new arrangements were needed for its protection. At first Colorado soldiers from Denver camped near the river and the Laporte stage coach stop. Their proximity to Provost's saloon and the homes of the mountain men and their Indian wives brought many vexations. Replacement by Collins' Ohio cavalry brought no improvement, and the June flood of 1864 which washed out the Laporte camp gave an opportunity for a new start.

What were the essential buildings for the new camp downstream on the site Lieutenant Hanna and Joe Mason had selected in July? They needed a hospital and Dr. T.L. Smith and Dr. Underhill located that on the northwest side. There had been something called a hospital at Laporte for Philip Smith died there in January, 1864. On the east side they built a guard house. There were often prisoners under restraint, for desertion was common. Many Confederate deserters or prisoners entered the Union army but found western service as "galvanized Yankees" no more palatable.

Officers' quarters, a sutler's store, work space for a few civilian craftsmen like a blacksmith, gunsmith, and good cook to keep up morale—all these were needed to get the camp in order. John Brown, Henry Clay Peterson, and Elizabeth Stone filled the important civilian jobs. Dr. Smith alerted Auntie Stone and her husband to the opening and they were building their cabin even before the soldiers transferred their camp.

Stables, horses, and hay were all important to the cavalry. The haystacks were not enclosed. They attracted local stock which caused hard feelings between soldiers and settlers. Early in 1865 when Indian outbreaks upset the stage line, horses were in short supply and the soldiers went to all the ranchers in the county. They went to Joseph Mason's herd on the Boxelder and to Park Station of the Overland Stage where they were to round up all not belonging to Ben Holladay. They paid Whedbee, Mason, and Loomis $50.00 per horse and $150.00 for one from William Osborn down on the Big Thompson. Abner Loomis and Antoine Janis guided the soldiers on trips up the canyons and taught them the difference between Indian signals and coyote calls. They built a road up Rist Canyon and brought lumber down for the camp.

Of planned recreation, there wasn't much. Sarah Milner Smith, teacher in Loveland, came up to repeat a program she had organized in Loveland at the request of a pastor who was "batching" in a couple rooms at the Army post: "We rehearsed while the older ladies prepared supper on the preacher's cook stove. The large hall at the Fort was well filled." With the admission fees from the appreciative audience she purchased a chair and an unabridged dictionary for her school house.(17)

The bugler set the routine of the soldiers' day. The sutler's store opened with the call for guard-mounting in the morning and closed when retreat sounded at night. The soldiers liked the exercises, parade ground drills, and music. The general rule in Indian country was for all movements to be executed from the signals of the bugler. Many maneuvers on foot as well as when mounted, were coded to the bugle calls. Surprise night practice kept the men's ears sharp.

The notes of the bugle at Fort Collins in November, 1867, floated over the river to the north side where Lieutenant James Hanna's wife was "entertaining" unwelcome Indians in her sod-roofed cabin. The sound caused the Indians to leave, much to her joy. For some reason this bugler was practicing even though the fort had officially closed the previous March 7.(18)

The process of decline for the fort was evident even in 1866 and in the following year civilians acquired buildings as rapidly as the army abandoned them.

Dastarac's 1884 map is one of the few dated drawings of the early army post.

The pioneers considered all log buildings a temporary stage till they could afford something better, so little sentiment was wasted on the structures which the army had erected. They were used as temporary homes and for many other purposes. The neat arrangement of buildings on three sides of a rectangle enclosing the parade grounds and with the open side toward the river was soon lost.

Auntie Stone's cabin on the south side of Jefferson and east of Linden was moved in 1873. The sutler's store of grout on the southwest corner of Jefferson and Linden lasted till 1881. A cabin on the southeast corner of Willow and Linden was William Stover's home. Several of his children were born there. He sold it to his brother, Frank, who later moved it to a new site. The cabin finally caught fire and burned in its new location. A Chinese laundry back of the Tedmon house used one old fort building for a while. John Brown's blacksmith shop on Pine and Jefferson replaced the hospital. Henry Clay Peterson laid out the race to his mill along the southern boundary of the old parade grounds.

Just as the crude buildings were shuffled around and the formation of the camp completely lost in the prosperous new building of the '80's a wave of nostalgia for the good old days spurred the collection of reminiscenses. Sketches of the camp of the '60's fascinated the artists now that the drab reality was blotted out. Pierre Frank Dastarac included in his bird's eye view of the prospering town of 1884 a contrasting scene representing 1865. A crooked tree appeared in the right foreground and a horse and rider near the flag pole. The **Courier** noted in 1884 that Mrs. Judge MacGregor had made a drawing of the camp in 1865 from a pen sketch of a soldier but did not reproduce it. Merritt Dana Houghton, an artist who loved painting ranches and scenes of the old west, worked out his birdseye view of Fort Collins in 1899 and under the advice of George Buss, made a drawing of the fort in 1865 which became a popular post card in the area. He used exactly the same outline of the mountains for the background of the two scenes.

Continued regret for the vanishing fort was expressed in the **Denver Times** in 1901 quoting the **Fort Collins Argus:**

The jail once stood just to the rear of the Tedmon House. Only a few buildings remain and a few more years will remove all unless some measure is taken to preserve them. In after years one of these old landmarks would appropriately fill a space in the city park and something should be done to save them.(19)

This sentiment sparked the movement that rallied to save the Auntie Stone cabin though it was not until 1959 that the simple but historic building got its place in the park. In 1973 it was once more opened to the public. For many years though, it had been a happy meeting place for the Pioneer Society. John Mandeville presented that group with another map of the scene in 1865 and this later was hung in the Pioneer Museum. Mandeville's gift added more complications to the visual representation of the fort for it had a signature and an address—"D. VanLennep, 54 Cedar Street, New York," but no more information. A curator at the museum guessed that it was done by an officer and labelled it thus, then changed it to "a soldier," and finally it was left unlabelled for the viewer to make his own guesses.

The National Archives has no military record for Van Lennep. The New York City directories list the family at various addresses and David Van Lennep, as a clerk in his father's office at that address in 1869. His connection with a Fort Collins scene is clouded with mystery. Mandeville was from Brooktondale near Ithaca, New York, and after his military service here he returned to New York to get his family in 1866. Did he stop in New York City and have the drawing made? There are some points in the drawing on which Buss helped that fit the traditions about the fort better—Auntie

John Mandeville's home 430 Peterson had a box bay window, bracket decoration and interesting design in gable Photo 1974.

Stone's cabin seems in line with Old Grout on the old Denver road. De Lennep has no cabin that resembles hers in line with Old Grout. Buss lived till 1908, Mandeville till 1923. Did they discuss these discrepancies? Mandeville's home was at 430 Peterson, and Buss lived at 209 W. Olive. Both houses are still standing. If they compared ideas as senior citizens, no record was kept.

When Mrs. Collins died some of her papers came to the library of the Agricultural College. Agnes Wright Spring, Colorado state historian, working on a biography of Caspar Collins turned up more family records. Before Caspar's death in Wyoming in 1865 he too sketched and diagrammed Camp Collins leaving his material undated and unsigned. Was this young man a reliable observer? A contemporary soldier described him as "a good poker player, over-indulging in liquor, ambitious for military success who was killed in an engagement with Indians which he ought to have avoided."

As the years went by, one trend was to bury every evidence of the fort while another movement sought to restore it. The city used the area for landfill. Military history buffs searching out the sites of old forts in the west were shocked to find Fort Collins had used its spot for the city dump. William Lindenmeier unearthed a rusty sword which went to the museum. Nicholas Booth, dean of the veterinary college and his wife, Jean, both antique collectors, dug in the dump and unearthed, piece by piece, a lovely old table with porcelain castors and a serial number suggesting government issue.

In 1964 at the time of the centennial, Nolie Mumey prepared a book on Auntie Stone's cabin and included a sketch of the fort apparently based on Mandeville's DeLennep sketch though redrawn slightly. In the 1970's Joe Mason's grandson and namesake retired from a military career, took up residence in Fort Collins, and urged actual reconstruction of the old camp in a gesture of native pride. The National Park Service was already maintaining museums of garrison life at Fort Laramie and Fort Robinson but this seemed insufficient to the enthusiastic boosters. So another movement began to re-create the camp which was used less than three years and had been obliterated casually by the pioneers of the 1870's. The role of the soldiers, guarding the stage coach, attained new prestige and significance.

GEORGE W. PINGREE: INDIAN FIGHTER AND TIE HACK

George W. Pingree, after fighting at Sand Creek, settled for a while on the Poudre canyon and his name was given to a hill and a mountain park in Larimer County. He was born in Orono, Maine in 1832. He enlisted in the army as a private in Central City in 1861, and was discharged in January, 1864. He re-enlisted and was at Sand Creek in November. After he was mustered out at Fort Leavenworth a year later he cut the trail down into the Poudre canyon from the Elkhorn valley and made his camp near the present Rustic Lodge. He located lodgepole pines for railroad ties on the headwaters of the Little South fork of the Poudre and floated them down to Provost's landing at Laporte.

One account credited him with the ability to cut one hundred ties a day when the usual number for a tie hack was thirty to forty. He outlived two wives and was living alone in a tent trapping beaver near Fort Lupton in 1911 when he gave a vivid interview to a **Denver Post** reporter. He combed his whiskers aside and displayed his scar. He was **still** furious that he had been put into the guard house for ten days at Fort Lyon for scalping thirteen Indians after the 1864 battle.

Then Chivington got me out in a blessed hurry. A little while after that I came to Denver. I didn't see what use I had for those thirteen scalps, so I traded them to a barber, who promised to cut my hair and shave me whenever I was in town in the next two years.

Later he went with an investigating committee to the battlefield and was ordered to bury the Indian bones.

'Bury your ancestors!' we says getting mad. And all we did was to take up some stout sticks and play shinny with the Indians' skulls as long as the committee hung around.

The committee wanted him punished for disobedience but Pingree recalled:

Sketch of George W. Pingree veteran of the battle of Sand Creek and tie hack on the Poudre River, made in Denver 1911.

The commander of the fort only laughed. He said that scouts were dinged scarce and that we were good scouts and he couldn't spare us to decorate the guardhouse just then. That was the last we ever saw of the investigating committee.

For Pingree as well as some other participants there were few regrets about the course of Sand Creek. He died at Platteville, August 30, 1921.

As colorful a character as this could hardly go through the legend-spinning web of local history without a few alterations. In Pingree's case it seems possible that the telling of his feats by oldtimers may have even created a second Pingree to make everything fit. The basic facts about Pingree's life, place and date of birth, marriages, and presence at Sand Creek he himself noted in his military record.

Was Watrous influenced by the Kit Carson legend to believe that Pingree came west as early as 1846 when he was only fourteen? It seems more likely he would have drifted to the Poudre canyon area for his camp **after** the Civil War. That was when the railroad needed his tie-cutting skills. Norman Fry, who settled on the canyon in 1889, described him as the man for whom both Pingree Hill and Pingree Park were named. Watrous and Fry apparently knew of one Pingree only.

Charles Pennock in an interview in 1930 when he was eighty years old recalled that the Pingree who discovered Pingree Park was called John W. and believed him of Scotch background. Pennock had known Pingree in his youth for he had a tie camp near Pingree's in the mountains. But this is the kind of inaccuracy that creeps into oral interviews especially when there is no one around to challenge it. One elderly gentleman once observed: "I've told that story so much, it must be true!"(20)

AUNTIE STONE: THE BELLE OF THE BALL

Elizabeth Hickok Robbins Stone lived on many American frontiers and her life spanned the nineteenth century. She was only four when her father moved from Connecticut to upstate New York near present day Watertown in 1805. In 1829 her husband took her to St. Louis, the flourishing center of western fur trade. They eventually settled in Illinois. At fifty-one, she became a widow with eight children to support. She lived in frontier Minnesota in the '50's, remarried, and left that area after the Indian Outbreak of 1862 to move west to Denver.

101

In 1864 through Dr. Timothy Smith, she and her husband heard that the soldiers were moving to a new site downstream from Laporte and they received permission to build a cabin and run a boarding house for the officers. Elizabeth was already sixty-three when she started this enterprise.

The next thirty years which encompassed her life in Fort Collins brought adventures and fulfillment in family and community associations. Widowed again in 1866, she went into partnership with the gunsmith, Henry Clay Peterson, in building a mill and a brick kiln.

Though she lost two husbands, she was always surrounded with relatives. She put a widowed niece and great nephew upstairs in her little cabin in 1866 and they held school there for children in the neighborhood. When the niece married Harris Stratton, the young couple moved into another cabin which had been officers' headquarters. It was a one-room structure with rustic porch and small attic. Mrs. Stratton's sister came west to help when Lerah was born in 1868 so Auntie fixed up temporary housekeeping rooms for herself in the mill. She boarded the men putting in the new machinery, and allowed the two nieces and family to have her cabin for a while.

Boarding kin and paying guests did not rule out parties. Auntie had a dance in the cabin soon after the officers left; evenings with charades for entertainment were common too. When the cabin was moved in 1873 from Jefferson to the Agricultural Hotel, it no longer housed Auntie's family.

She and Peterson really only started the mill, for it required more specialized skills than they possessed. They sold it in the early '70's and Auntie continued in her real career, cooking for people. After a three weeks' vacation in Estes Park in August, 1878, she changed the name of the Blake House to the Metropolitan and ran it until March, 1879 when B.S. Tedmon took it over. She loved outings in the mountains. After all the years of taking care of eight children and running hotels, she considered it a vacation to go camping and fishing for twelve days at Chambers Lake in July, 1880. She was then seventy-five.

Old age brought its ups and downs but Auntie faced its trials and enjoyed its honors. In 1885 the **Courier** reporter noted her involvement in a law suit and described her:

She walks erect, reads a great deal, and talks sensibly. She curls her hair, wears her watch and chain, and dresses up for afternoons as if she were yet a belle. In fact she is a

belle.

The Masonic dance in 1885 with three generations of Auntie's family among the dancers was long noted in Fort Collins annals. Auntie was over eighty-three. Her son, Washington Irving Robbins, was almost fifty-nine. His daughter, Gertie, then a clerk at the Fort Collins Post Office, was almost twenty-two.

Auntie's daughter, Theodosia Van Brunt and family left Illinois for Fort Collins in 1882. She joined her mother's profession by running the Cottage House on Jefferson in 1888. She was hostess for Auntie's eighty-seventh birthday party. Since the guest of honor had given up dancing the year before, she was ready to enjoy the elegant rattan rocking chair cushioned with silk plush, a handsome center table, and a beautiful lamp all presented on that occasion.

Festivities for her birthday in 1890 included a tea given by Mrs. J.A.C. Kissock. The parlors and dining room of the Kissock home were:

Decorated with great masses of pink asters and pink sweet peas intermingled with delicate green adding fragrance to the rooms. The ladies sat around a beautiful tea table with floral tributes. On each napkin was a boutonniere of pansies except Auntie's which contained a beautiful Jacquemenot rose. Mr. Kissock, arriving home too late for tea, wished he was a photographer.

Unfortunately the only photograph of Auntie is a very grim likeness not reflecting the gaiety and friendliness which characterized her life.

Auntie and the Van Brunts were saddened by the death of her nineteen-year-old granddaughter, Mary Theodosia Van Brunt Havener, in September, 1891. The service was held at the new Presbyterian church on Remington. The Knights of Pythias band from Greeley played a requiem and led a procession through the streets to Grandview cemetery.

In 1891 the Masons selected a basket of choice delicacies at their St. John's Festival to send her. When women in Colorado received the vote, Auntie exercised this right in 1894. The bell on City Hall tolled ninety-four times in December, 1895, to mark the passing of this favorite pioneer who, in the days of the fort, had been known from Julesburg to the Green River as "Auntie." This bell in the City Hall tower tolled for significant events, as well as fire alarms and curfews, until 1914 when the tower was condemned and the bell moved to Grandview cemetery where it now rests near the statue of a fireman.(21)

AUNTIE STONE'S CABIN

When the log structures of the soldiers' day were shifted to make room for the growing town, Auntie's cabin was one of the first to go because property on Jefferson Street had gained commercial importance. Through a fortunate chain of circumstances it survived moves and neglect and now remains the only authentic building from Camp Collins still in existence. Marcus Coon operated the Agricultural Hotel on Mountain and Mason and he moved the cabin to his hotel area to use as a laundry. David Harris, an Englishman with a strong Cockney accent, bought that hotel, re-named it the Commercial, and moved the main building to the present site of the Northern Hotel. The cabin was abandoned temporarily on the Mason Street lot. When Grace Harris, his daughter, married James Vandewark in 1893, the young couple renovated the cabin for their home.

The Vandewarks had two children who were born in the cabin. They slept downstairs in the room now restored as the kitchen-dining room of the Auntie Stone period. The parents used the large north bedroom, renting the other upstairs rooms. They also added a shed kitchen and a coal room to the south. There never was a bathroom in the period the Vandewarks occupied it and the outhouse was reached by going through the chickencoop. When the Vandewarks separated, Mrs. Vandewark stayed in the cabin for a while and took in roomers. Eventually she moved elsewhere and the cabin became a paint shop in 1908.

Since the total value of the building was only $150.00, it might soon have been demolished but for the efforts of the recently organized Pioneer Women of the Cache la Poudre Valley. Winona Washburn Taylor, a spirited member, pledged the first ten dollars. The total amount looked enormous to the little club. Montezuma Fuller, the architect, Peter Anderson, merchant and farmer, and John Coy, another pioneer farmer, all helped. Coy's daughter, Mrs. James Lawrence, Mrs. L.R. Rhodes, Joe Mason's widow, and Mrs. McHugh, Auntie's great niece, worked on the project too. Buying the cabin was hard, but so was finding a site for it. The City Council rejected the cabin for Lincoln Park as a possible obstacle to future landscaping! Finally the county authorized placement on Mason near the county garage where the First National Bank now stands.

By December, 1909, the cabin was ready for the pioneers to enjoy as a small museum and meeting house. An addition was arranged for dances. The congregation of St. Luke's Church met there in the summer of 1912 while their church was remodeled. Finally in 1959 the Daughters of the Colorado Pioneers (formerly Pioneer Women of the Cache la Poudre Valley) gave it to the city.

By this time it was considered a precious heirloom and was moved to Lincoln Park without objection. Richard S. Baker, who was in charge of parks and recreation, arranged for matching logs from an old cabin on the Clarence Currie ranch to be brought down to replace missing walls. Lack of budget from the city limited the work to maintenance of the shell and repair of the wall and roof. The cabin remained shut up tight awaiting further interest.

In September, 1971, Delano Scott of Los Angeles died and left a legacy to the museum as a tribute to his childhood and family. His father, Fulton N.B. Scott, had come to Fort Collins in 1873. He worked as a blacksmith and ran a hardware store. He served both as county commissioner and city council member.

Encouraged by these private funds, the Museum Board planned restoration of the interior to Auntie Stone's period. Jane Bass, a Board member, enlisted the support of local Questers' clubs, all antique collectors, as volunteers in refinishing the cabin and locating appropriate furniture. Their work was complete by April, 1973, but more months passed before the Council authorized funds to build a fence around it and make it open to the public. An old stove remodeled to provide heat was contributed by the Public Service Company.

Many of the items displayed belonged to Auntie's relatives or friends. The lace jabot on the wall in the upper small bedroom had been given to her niece at her wedding. Elizabeth Coy, John's daughter from across the river, embroidered the motto: "Eat, Drink, and Be Merry" which is on the kitchen wall. Auntie wanted her friends to drink milk or water, however, and she urged young men to take the temperance pledge. The sewing machine was used by Caroline Taft, another friend. Auntie, with her love for music, must have shared with the Hardins their pleasure in the three octave table zither now on the west wall. She may have seen the picture of Washington's family hanging in the officers' quarters at Fort Laramie. Each piece has been lovingly selected by a committee which appreciated both antiques and Auntie's spirit.

THE OLD MILLS ON THE RIVER

The influx of miners into Colorado in the 1860's created a demand for American flour. The Mexican type was coarse, quite different in character and not popular with the new westerners. American flour went through a bolting process using fine silk bolting cloth which separated fine flour from bran. Around Denver it sold for $16.00 to $18.00 a hundred pounds in 1860, and $10.00 in 1861.

Building a gristmill operated by water power to supply the local market with flour was a priority for settlement. Henry Clay Peterson, the gunsmith at the fort, and Auntie Stone pooled their resources and started one on a wellchosen site close by the little settlement.

In 1867 Peterson surveyed for the millrace. This was a canal that conducted water from a point upstream to the water wheel in a more direct course than that of the real river which meandered so that it lost energy for power. He described it—"One and one-half miles long, thirteen and one-half feet wide at water level, and eighteen inches deep. The grade was four feet to one mile."

Peterson went to Buffalo, New York, to purchase machinery. That was the center of the flourmilling industry till Minneapolis gained leadership as the wheat fields of the middle west were developed. The Fort Collins mill was three stories high which made it tower over, the little cluster of houses along the river. By 1869 the mill was grinding wheat.

Since Peterson was a charter member of the Masonic lodge, he allowed the order to use the mill as a meeting place. It was the practice room for the band too in 1876. Andrew J. Hottel from Virginia, employed at the mill, played the cornet, and Q. Schang, the butcher, the tuba.

In 1873 Joseph Mason became the sole owner of the mill. In 1875 the mill and race were valued at $14,000. Flour was selling at $3.75 a hundred. Mason started modernizing the mill in 1878, spending $1200 for repairs and he took Benjamin Franklin Hottel as a partner. The millrace was improved.

Mason was an ambitious businessman. He had a lumbermill in Leadville in 1879 as well as many enterprises in Fort Collons. In February, 1880, the partners closed the flourmill temporarily to add two more stories to the original three. The newspaper considered the remodeled structure just above

Drawing of Mason and Hottel's mill 1881 from Dastarac map.

Mill in 1894

" Howes Lane' bridge," (now Lincoln), a great advance over Stone and Peterson's "picturesque old affair with broad sides, low roof, and water wheel." After Mason's death in 1881, Hottel ran the mill first as owner, and from 1885, as manager for Colorado Milling and Elevator Company.

One of the terrible hazards of milling is fire; dust prevention to avoid explosions is a constant problem. The first big mill fire was in July, 1886. The structure was rebuilt and in operation by December. It burned again in October, 1895 and was rebuilt. An interesting article on the rebuilt mill in June, 1896, described part of the structure, the crib, for storage of grain and feed ingredients as it still stands today:

The Lindell mill is all ready for expected machinery. The new warehouse being built with ten bins will hold 7,500 bushels. It is built block house fashion. The exterior walls have 2 x 8 planks spiked together one above the other and the division walls are 2 x 6 spiked together.

People who lived near the millrace scooped water from it for cleaning and laundry work; children skated there in winter. In July, 1880, Bush's railroad ties floating down the river went into the race, clogged the headgate, and some ran down as far as the mill, causing a morning's loss of operation. In August, the mill wasn't working again because of a washout in the millrace near S.D. Luke's residence. When the Greeley, Salt Lake and Pacific Railroad was laid out with its route very close to the millrace, radical changes were necessary. In July, 1882, the course of the race was changed to give more space for side tracks because shipping from the quarries at Stout was increasing. In August ten teams and a dozen men were working for Hottel. New sheetiron tubes for the water were installed in September. The new course of the race placed it farther north of Willow Avenue closer to the river.

The water right was challenged in court several times. In October, 1911, the Larimer and Weld Reservoir Company, whose headgate was above the millrace, claimed Hottel water was for power, not irrigation, but water officials let the Hottel ditch take sixty feet, recognizing Hottel's priority over the reservoir company. In 1919 the water wheel was abandoned and that era in milling ended.

The production of flour continued until 1948. Lower grades were packed in wooden barrels or sometimes shipped in bulk, using bran by-products as a base in box cars. Fabric sacking was clean and also appealing to frugal housewives who used it for dish towels and aprons. "Defiance," "Snowdrift," "Pride of the Rockies," and "Jap Rose" were among the brand names.

Hoffman mill, above, early 1890's
right, river side after addition of flour
milling machinery in 1898.

Ranchway Feeds 1975 modern mill on
same site as original mill still using
part of building from 1896.

When flour milling ceased, the operation produced only animal feed. In 1966-67 Colorado Milling and Elevator Company merged with Great Western Sugar Company. Then it was a part of Great Western United. Since 1968 it has been an independent corporation, Ranch-Way Feeds.(22)

John Hoffman's mill reversed the order for he began with stock feed and turned to flour. He came to Fort Collins in 1887 and worked for Hottel. Then he opened his own mill just southeast of the early one and in 1894 was grinding feed. In May, 1898, he enlarged the operation to produce "Golden West" flour. He dammed the river to have sufficient water for his wheel.

The question arose: Could the owners of water rights cause the river bed to be dry? The needs of the new sugar beet factory added to the demands. The factory managed the first "campaign" with an eight inch main to the city's supply. Before the next harvest, the factory bought water from Hottel, ran it through a ditch to a reservoir, and pumped it as needed. This sometimes left Hoffman with nothing behind his dam.

The court decided in Hoffman's favor. It required the sugar factory to pump water below Hottel's mill and return used water above Hoffman's. The factory used city water for boilers and evaporators and kept the old reservoir as reserve.

The reservoir received notoriety in 1919. During World War I, Great Western had revived the Steffens process for making molasses. It abandoned the work when the war ended. The waste from the Steffens process filled the reservoir. It had four inches of worms feeding on the surface. The aroma floated over the town where the object producing it was called the "olfactory elephant." The company used hundreds of gallons of kerosene to burn the surface with no improvement. Finally during a flood stage of the Poudre, the contents were leached into the river!(23)

THE WELCH BLOCK AND THE OPERA HOUSE

Even in 1879 the developers of College Avenue, the Welches, Avery, and Bouton, talked about the need for an opera house. They owned lots fronting on College Avenue, extending north from the northwest corner of the Mountain Avenue intersection. Jacob Welch had operated a store on that corner in the '70's. When a fire destroyed it in February, 1880, they proceeded with a joint plan, included other partners, and built a new store, a hotel, a bank, and an opera house. This last was farthest north, on the second floor, with shops below at street level. Work progressed well in the summer of 1880, and various parts were occupied early in 1881. John Colpitts was the architect and builder.

The whole facade was treated as a unit, three stories high in front, with matching sections. Jacob Welch made his part of the Opera House four stories high. Another fire in 1885 destroyed the store and the Windsor Hotel sections, and these were rebuilt with only two stories, so the facade thereafter was quite different from the original one. While Welch continued his interest for a while in the Opera House, his sons, A. Wilbur, and then Corwin R. took over the store. The initials of the latter and the date "1885" marked the top of the corner structure after the second fire.

The Welch store is an interesting example of prosperity through large scale merchandising. A business rating in 1878 estimated Jacob Welch's business as involving $100,000 a year. Mason and Hottel's mill was listed at $65,000, and then the

Dastarac drawing 1881.

OPERA HOUSE BLOCK

scale dropped to Whedbee at $8,000 and others below that. Even though the figures may be rough, they may give some indication of financial leadership. When Corwin R. Welch reopened the store in September, 1885, he received praise for being the first to introduce gas. "In the evening when two or three scores of jets are all burning, the store...presents the appearance of a veritable palace for fairies." He and his wife traveled east and to Europe several times on buying trips. He made rooms on the second floor available for club meetings just as Wilson, the saloon keeper on Jefferson had in the '70's. The bankers on Linden did the same in the '80's. Welch talked of retiring in 1891, and finally did so in 1900. There were two new owners. Lay came from Grand Junction and made his home in rooms recently vacated by the public library and reading room. Garst had been a salesman of Marshall Field and Company of Chicago and had been coming to Fort Collins for nearly twenty years so he was familiar with the town's needs.(24)

The shops underneath the Opera House had various occupants. In 1882 one was Madame M. Roucolle, the great Parisian dressmaker. In 1885 the Fair was a thriving store carrying "baby carriages, dolls' heads and bodies, express wagons, and toys in endless styles. Prohibition drinks of all kinds which will regulate the solar system and steady the nerves" were sold.

The Opera House entrance was marked by handsome stone pillars and arches. Two-thirds of the seats in the auditorium were arranged on the level floor, the rest on an inclined one. There were four boxes on the east side. Signore E.D. Hurle of Denver, formerly of Milan, did the decorating and frescoing. Harry Learned painted eleven special backdrops with scenes depicting a palace, forest, prison, garden, kitchen, plain chamber, fancy chamber, street and rock gorge. The drop curtain featured a Colorado mountain landscape from the San Juans in Rio Grande County.

Bouton was the local impressario arranging for traveling performers who appeared on the stage. In September, 1881, he introduced Muscular Muldoon and two other wrestlers who gave an exhibition of the Graeco-Roman style of wrestling. In October he had the Georgia minstrels, twenty accomplished performers. In June, 1882, Martel gave a sleight of hand performance and Will Visscher a humorous lecture with impersonations of the American, Irish, French, German and Negro. In November, there was "The Phoenix" and "The Wizard of the World" with new and original illusions and "extraordinary sleep of the angels." In July, 1884, Callenders Colored Minstrels, a troop of forty, entertained an audience of six hundred; they were considered "superior to anything of the kind that travels the road."

More serious productions included performances of Thomas Keene in Shakespeare's "Richard III" in 1881. Mademoiselle Rhea played Beatrice in "Much Ado About Nothing" in 1888. Among the most popular plays produced by traveling casts was "Uncle Tom's Cabin." The many Civil War veterans in the audience never tired of this. It was given twice in 1882, once in 1899, and again in 1904. The 1882 production had trained bloodhounds and camp meeting shouters.

Bouton was extremely angry in 1885 about the city theater license and threatened to close the house to both traveling and home entertainment until it was abolished. "The Opera House Management considers it has donated enough in the amusement line in the past." He refused space to the actress, Grace Hawthorne, and her company so fifty Fort Collins couples went by special train to see her perform in Loveland.

Greeley had similar problems with the circus in 1885. The town raised the license fee from seventy-five to one hundred and fifty dollars and the circus refused to pay it. The town turned a ditch of water on the grounds, but the circus rented land between Greeley and Evans, ran a shuttle to both towns, and profited by the performance.

In the late '90's Bouton had been succeeded by F.C. Parker of Boston, who leased the hall and stage for five years. He fitted it with new opera chairs and scenes, reconstructed the family circle and parquette, and added a gallery. The entrances and stairways were widened. The great Iroquois Theater fire in Chicago in 1904 led to more remodeling.(25)

The programs had tremendous variety. In 1899 a comedy titled "A Boy Wanted" included "an acrobat and a coal-black lady." In 1904 there were billings for "Way Down East" and "Zaza." "The Smart Set" in January, 1904, had a cast of fifty. It was one of the best colored theatrical companies in the world with "ragtime as it should be played." Since ragtime as a musical form was new in 1899, this was an exposure to a cultural development in its early stage.

While one program featured the very latest trend, another might present ideas practically discarded. An unusual billing in April, 1897, was a talk by the widow of O.S. Fowler, who had achieved fame for his theories on the relationship of physical contour to human character. Besides his lectures and writing on phrenology, he wrote a book in the 1850's on the virtues of octagonal-shaped houses and popularized a building craze that swept midcentury America. What ideas his widow offered a Fort Collins audience after his death were not recorded.

Besides providing a stage for imported productions, the opera house was a social center, a court room, and even a gymnasium. The use of the Opera House as a court room was not entirely satisfactory for a hall above the **Fort Collins Express** was selected instead in 1887:

Who has endeavored to listen to the arguments of counsel in the Opera House but what has been thoroughly disgusted with the acoustic arrangements of the drum-like room?

The members of the club, "Entre Nous," held a masked ball there in March, 1881. The dances included quadrilles, waltzes, schottische, and polkas. Costumes included a nun, flower girls, and Minnehaha. Particularly up-to-date were Lelia Loomis as Little Buttercup and Turner Seamans as Captain of the Pinafore, only three years after the Gilbert & Sullivan operetta had been produced in England. There was also a Goddess of Liberty three years before the Bartholdi statue arrived in New York harbor. There were balls on July 4 and in September, 1882. Andrew J. Hottel was dressed as Kalakaua, the reigning king of Hawaii in February, 1885. Costumes were rented from a Denver distributing point, and were available for parties throughout the Rockies, not just for the Fort Collins events.

The political gatherings held in the Opera House were often as entertaining as any stage production. A Republican party leader from Boulder attacked the Democratic candidate from this district in October, 1882, then paid his respects to Mr. Tedmon. "A thrill of delight passed through the house when he declared his enmity to bosses and boss methods." There were:

Ku Klux Klan, red shirt riders, terrified colored people, and down-trodden dough-faced northern democrats chasing each other in ghastly confusion across the opera house stage and in the distance wrapped in the folds of the U.S. flag appeared the thinned ranks of the boys in blue.

The Democrats ordered one hundred and fifty torches from Denver to make their rebuttal equally spectacular.

The Masons had their festival of St. John there in December, 1882. Seven tables "groaned with the weight of roast turkey, chicken, game, boiled ham, corned beef, bread, biscuits, cheese cake, pies, jellies, sauces, honey, condiments, tea, and coffee." Colored servants in dining room uniforms added to the formality.

An evening of stereopticon views featuring scenes from Yellowstone to Mexico and the Great Plains to the Pacific was scheduled in January, 1884, admission 35¢. Governor St. John of Kansas came to lecture on prohibition and temperance later that month. This probably bolstered anti-liquor sentiment for that was the one year in the 1880's when Fort Collins banned saloons.(26)

The Women's Christian Temperance Union sponsored a spelling contest in the Opera House in April, 1884. Ansel Watrous was umpire. The first commencement for a graduating class from the new Aggie College was an exciting landmark for June, 1884. The college lacked a chapel until 1889, so the first few years of its existence it used the Opera House. Home talent provided the cast for the comedy, "A Soldier of Fortune," in 1887, a benefit for the free reading room. After a Memorial Day ceremony held there in 1887 there was a mass march to the cemetery to decorate both Union and Confederate soldiers' graves.

Rain fell in torrents and the streets were transformed into running streams in June, 1898, but that did not discourage the fifteen graduates of the high school and their families. The national flag and that of Cuba were draped over the stage arch, and the audience heard papers on the influence of the Saracens, the Holy Grail, and Norse mythology. In the early 1900's local talent, Fatty Orth and the Cooksie boys, put on entertainment for the children. The nickel admission included a sack of candy.

As movie theaters came in, tastes in entertainment changed and the building itself seemed too old-fashioned. Architect Ansel Pierce of Fort Collins, formerly of Denver, was engaged in May, 1917, to supervise remodeling. The entire front except the old bank portion was torn down. The opera house was converted into a dance hall. A new maple floor was put in, the old false floor removed, the heavy wall of the opera house proper removed too. Balconies built off the third floor overlooking the dance hall were provided. A banquet hall, kitchen, cloak room, and toilets were placed on the third floor. The appearance of the area today is practically the same as that after the 1917 remodeling, when the quaint Opera House auditorium was destroyed.(27)

JEFFERSON BLOCK

JEFFERSON STREET AND OLD TOWN

Jefferson and Walnut Streets, crossed by Linden, formed important segments of the business section. The name, Old Town, suggested that the area was developed prior to College Avenue. In reality the two sections raced one another in construction. Each had old and new shops frequently remodeled or moved. Linden was not built up entirely from Walnut to Mountain until December, 1882.

In 1890 a Denver reporter compared the one-story frame building on the northwest corner of Mountain and Linden with the rake's progress in reviewing its history. It was built in 1873 for a bank that failed. It became in succession Bradstreet's Billiard Hall, the Post Office, and at the top level, Reverend Byrne's shelter for Episcopal services. Then it deteriorated, became a carpenter's workshop, and was finally destroyed. This site got a new start in 1897 with the construction of the Avery Block and now it is going through another cycle.

VANDEWARK BUILDING JEFFERSON ST

J. F. COLPITTS BLOCK — WALNUT STREET

J. F. COLPITTS CONTRACTOR & BUILDER.

Charles Boettcher had a store on Jefferson in March, 1874, where he sold hardware, tinware, agricultural implements, and metallic caskets. He moved to Boulder in September and made his fortune elsewhere in Colorado.

The log cabin once built by soldiers back of the Tedmon house served many uses. Reed had a jewelry shop there before he joined with Louis Dauth, the baker, to build the Reed & Dauth Block at 223 Linden. A Chinese laundry operated in the old cabin for a while. With every new building there was a shakeup of tenants. The **Courier** office was above the jeweler's in the Reed & Dauth Block before it moved to Jefferson. Lauterbach had his cigar store in the Jefferson Block in 1882 before he moved to 208 Linden.

William Quayle, Denver architect, received many commissions from Fort Collins leaders. He designed the Jefferson Block in 1881, the Reed & Dauth Block in 1881, the Loomis and Andrews Building in 1882, and the Franklin School in 1887. He is ranked today as a conservative architect and less esteemed than his more creative contemporaries, but he satisfied the Fort Collins taste of the period.

People were grateful for wooden sidewalks at first. A.B. Tomlin bought Stover and Mathews' store on the northeast corner of Jefferson and Linden in 1879. It had a roof over the sidewalk supported by pillars. Green and white striped awnings were the preferred shelter for the '80's. As the good stone from the quarries at Stout became available by train, wooden

Linden Avenue view toward south 1888 and from Mountain toward north in 1907.

sidewalks disappeared. Rogers of the Collins House laid stone for his Jefferson Street frontage, and Yount and Tomlin were urged to follow suit. Loomis and Andrews got a cheap price for large pieces, twelve by eight feet, for the sidewalk on the Poudre Valley Bank corner to demonstrate the quality of the quarry. Inside too the shops were improving. Seckner's grocery built long bins for sugar, dried fruits, and other provisions, replacing barrels and boxes, in December, 1882.

Completion of every building was a cause for celebration. The city hired J.W. Jordan of Cheyenne to build the two-story brick school building with its imposing tower on Remington and Oak. In January, 1879, the adults met there, fifty couples who were "the elite of Fort Collins, to chase the fleeting hours with nimble feet to the inspiring strains of the Collins string band till past twelve when all repaired to their homes and virtuous couches." Water closets were built on the school grounds in 1891 when sewer connections were available. The tower was dismantled in August, 1895 when it became unsafe.(28)

The drawing of Linden Street in 1888 from the Jefferson Street intersection viewed to the southwest caught the prosperity of the decade. A photograph from 1907 taken at Mountain and Linden looking northeast still showed the horse-and-buggy stage.

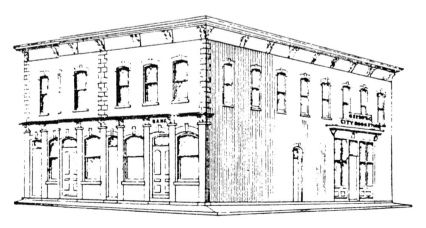

YOUNT BLOCK.

119

THE BATTLE OF THE BANKS

The first successful bank in Fort Collins was opened by Mr. and Mrs. A.K. Yount in 1873. They had a store in a log building on the Big Thompson in the '60's. They moved to Fort Collins, survived the panic of 1873, and started a bank in the fine brick building trimmed with stone from local quarries. It was on the southeast corner of Linden and Jefferson, across the street from Old Grout. Yount was a member of the constitutional convention in Denver and he employed Charles Sheldon to manage the bank in his absence. In 1876 he was accidentally killed and his wife operated the bank for a while. In 1878 she had the old tar, pitch, and gravel roof taken off and replaced with a substantial iron one. She lived above the bank. There was a bookstore on the Linden Street side in 1884.

Sheldon, having gained some experience working for the Younts, joined with William Stover in 1878 to form the Stover and Sheldon Bank. This was in the Wilson Block on Jefferson. They had the simplest appointments, one or two common chairs, a pine table, and a borrowed safe along with a good stock of courage, credit and confidence. There were nervous moments however. On one occasion Sheldon notified Stover that their funds were so low he could not cash a check for one hundred dollars until the afternoon stage from Denver came. Stover, a practical joker, confided in Billy Patterson, who then presented a check for five hundred dollars. Sheldon

grew tense, then relaxed when he detected a twinkle in the customer's eye!

Sheldon and Stover moved in January, 1879, from Jefferson to a one-story brick building at Linden which they shared with

Above Third location of Poudre Valley Bank, corner Walnut and Linden occupied 1883.
Below Interior Poudre Valley Bank 1880's.

Dr. Lee's and Dr. Elston's Parlor Drugstore. This was to be the bank's location only until February, 1883, for they were faced with stiff competition.

Franklin Avery was one of the first depositors in the Sheldon and Stover Bank in 1878 but he soon organized his own bank. It was called the Larimer County Bank, then the First National Bank of Fort Collins. It opened in January, 1881, in the Welch Block on College. The exterior conformed to the rest of that building, but the interior permitted originality. The scene depicted by the fresco painter sounds almost incredibly frivolous for a small town bank, but there is no evidence that Watrous was jesting when he printed a description. It contained a big ox, an African gorilla and smiling Fiji islanders!(29)

Stover and Sheldon determined to meet the competition. They joined with Abner Loomis and Charles Andrews, expanded their capital to form the Poudre Valley Bank, and built the Loomis and Andrews Building on the northwest corner of Walnut and Linden not far from City Hall. William Quayle of Denver was the architect. The three-story structure cost $32,000. In November, 1882, the vault was installed and iron fencing for the cornice arrived from Denver. The bank opened in February, 1883. The floor plan showed a long corridor for the public separated from the cashier's office, the business office, a parlor, and vault. The divider was of cherry with six lights of plate glass set in the railing and brass wickets at

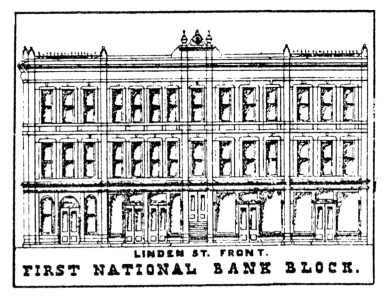

LINDEN ST. FRONT.

FIRST NATIONAL BANK BLOCK.

First National Bank Linden and Mountain: triumph for president Franklin Avery and architect Montezuma Fuller 1897.

the two tellers' windows. The columns with carved capitals and moulded bases separating the glass were highly admired.

Meanwhile Avery was barely installed in the Welch Block when he began planning his next move. He bought the lot on the northwest corner of Mountain and Linden in 1881 from the Episcopalians. In 1884 a design for a new First National on that site appeared. In 1887 there was talk about building. Actual construction did not start however until 1896 and Montezuma Fuller greatly changed the earlier design. A comparison of the drawing with the actual bank affords an excellent contrast of the styles for business blocks of the two decades. The finials capping the pillars on the facade were in the 1884 drawing but became more pronounced in the actual building in 1897. The windows were arched, not rectangular.

The First National Bank was satisfied with this structure only eleven years. The next building was of more classic style just across the street on the southeast corner of College and Mountain. The marble doors and lobby with marble decoration awed the customers. The clock suspended on the corner outside was a welcome innovation. This opened in 1908 with a

First National Bank 1908 Mountain and College.

Interior First National Bank Mountain and College.

gala reception. Members of the Avery family all helped Franklin celebrate the event. The First National Bank had thus made two big moves since its humble beginning in the Welch Block.

Management of the Poudre Valley Bank considered moving from old-fashioned Linden to modish College Avenue but Sheldon resisted any such action. The argument even divided social organizations. A Masonic Temple (now a beauty operator school) had been built on W. Mountain in 1902. Some of

Above Poudre Valley Bank 1917 Mountain and College.
Below Expanded Poudre Valley Bank c.1925.

the members in the lodge wanted to shift their meeting place from the floor above the Poudre Valley Bank over to the new building. Others felt this would favor further deterioration of Linden Avenue property. The Masons did move but the bank stayed on though there were preparations for the inevitable. In 1914 the management purchased the building on the southwest corner of Mountain and College from N.C. Alford and T.H. Robertson. The first floor was leased to A.W. Scott's Drugstore. Tile brick veneer over the outer walls gave a modern appearance. In 1917 the Poudre Valley National Bank moved into this structure. It continued to need more space. In 1925 it purchased Clark's bookstore next door and two years later expanded into the whole building.(30)

Besides the physical changes reflected in architecture and interior decorating, the banks made many changes in policy to adapt to the needs of an agricultural community. In 1893 the Poudre Valley began making loans to sheep and cattle feeders, taking chattel mortgages on livestock. Abner Loomis approved all such loans issued. As a depression measure the Poudre Valley Bank arranged in 1931 with the Casper National Bank for Fort Collins feeders to feed sheep on a contract basis without any ownership interest in the lambs fed. Fred Stover and Claud Stout went to Casper to negotiate these matters. The bank had received trust powers in 1919. It created a separate department for this phase in 1926, but there was not much business until the 1930's. Hottel's death on January 2, 1937, leaving an estate of a half million dollars gave it the first large sum to administer.

Importing Claud Stout, a former national bank examiner, to join the bank staff in the early 1930's was a fortunate decision. He was a critical firm administrator and instituted reforms which proved exceedingly helpful in the dark days ahead.

In 1933 every bank in the United States closed for the moratorium established by President Franklin Delano Roosevelt. The Poudre Valley Bank was the only one in Fort Collins which re-opened immediately.

In 1934 the First National Bank of Fort Collins became the First National Bank in Fort Collins under a new charter. In 1961 it moved into a large modern building on Mason and Oak. The Poudre Valley Bank moved to an equally elegant modern structure in April, 1967, on College and Magnolia and became the United Bank of Fort Collins. Thus neither of the two modern banks is the same as created long ago though the rivalry is just as keen.

SOME OF THE OLD CHURCHES

METHODIST

Traveling Methodist ministers visited Fort Collins in the 1860's and held services in Old Grout, in the Buss or Riverside school house west of Timnath, and in the Pleasant Valley school house. Joseph Mason and Alfred Howes selected the first site for a church building in 1873 on the southwest corner of Laporte and Mason facing Mason. A frame building, 30 x 40 feet, built by Henry Clay Peterson, was dedicated in 1876. When the Colorado and Southern tracks came through in 1877 on Mason, A.L. Emigh gave the church two lots at 252-254 East Mountain and the building was moved there where it served the congregation's needs till 1898.

The windows were painted in 1881 to imitate stained glass. James Milne painted the interior. There was a stencilwork border around the walls above the wainscotting. In 1934 it was in use as a garage.

In 1896, the architect, Harlan Thomas, worked with a building committee composed of Peter Anderson, S.H. Seckner, Elza Silcott, and Franklin Avery. The new church was dedicated on Jan. 9, 1898. It added to the growing number of buildings of distinction on College Avenue since it was located one block south of the Episcopal church, on the southeast corner of College and Olive. Souvenir pitchers from Austria decorated with a picture of the church were sold at the Nimble Nickel store on College.

Above Methodist church College and Olive; designed by Harlan Thomas
       as it appeared 1898-1913.
Below Church after changes in 1913; razed 1964.

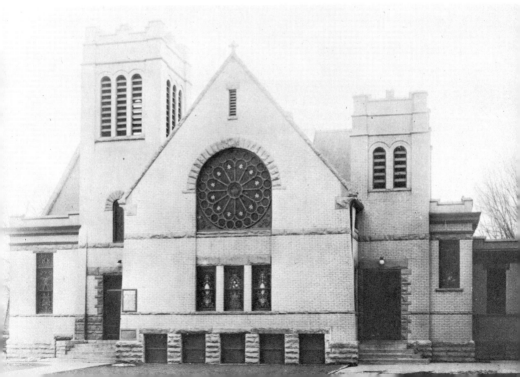

In 1912 the church board planned an enlargement of the auditorium and basement and installation of steam heat. In the changes the Thomas design was completely altered, a second tower added and the original one over the corner entrance rebuilt to match. When this structure was wrecked to move the congregation to a new building on Stover and Elizabeth in the early 1960's, the three stained glass windows were incorporated as a screen in the new church, but the rose window could not be salvaged. The new building was dedicated in October, 1964.(31)

PRESBYTERIAN

The Presbyterians also erected a church in 1876 even before Fort Collins had a railroad. The chapel Sheldon Jackson had built in Fairplay in 1874 was board and batten with scalloped gingerbread around the eaves and belltower. That in Fort Collins two years later was extremely simple with a steeple and pointed windows, probably following a standardized frame design for small rural churches which the Presbyterian church used in the east. It was on the southwest corner of Walnut and Linden.

The families of John Mandeville, George Buss, and Henry Clay Peterson, oldtimers along with Vescelius and Stover, newcomers of the '70's, gave chicken suppers to pay for the organ, red upholstered high Gothic type pulpit chairs and brand new carpet. After the carpet was installed, the sexton who had formerly dressed like other folk, blossomed forth with white vest, cut-away coat, and high hat which he wore as usher and even ringing the bell!

The elaborate gifts which were received at the three church Christmas trees in 1879 suggest that the church rather than the home was the center both for such decoration and exchange. Mrs. Blount received a caster set of rich and massive design, Mrs. By Allen coral jewelry with frosted gold leaves, and furs.

In October, 1881, a twenty-foot brick extension in the rear was added to form a public reading room open during the week. The public was urged to supply the reading matter. In December, 1882 the reading room was the joint project of the church and the Women's Christian Temperance Union. "It

still exists, lives, thrives, and needs more room" was the firm announcement. When Colpitt and Ames & Co. had a force pump installed in 1882 across the street near the new City Hall and fire station, two hundred feet of hose sent a stream of water one hundred feet high over the steeple of the church.

For Christmas in 1883 the walls of the church were handsomely arranged with greens, the branches of the trees groaned with the weight of candies and toys. The church activities were supported by projects like the "social" in March, 1884. "Eighty people enjoyed cake, coffee, and good old-fashioned pop corn balls of mammoth dimensions. The program included poetry, pantomime, music, and the mite basket."

In 1887 the Presbyterians held a series of fund-raising affairs for a new building. On Wednesday night there was a New England supper with roast pig, chicken pie, baked turkey, pork and beans, brown bread, and salads. On Thursday night there was an oyster supper. Friday the speciality was a Japanese tea with a genuine Chinaman passing the tea. Guests were permitted to keep their cups and saucers as souvenirs. The new church on the southwest corner of Remington and Olive was almost ready to use. Montezuma Fuller, the builder, installed stained glass windows from Chicago. The architect was George A. Hall of Denver.

A delightful outing planned for members in September, 1888 was a Tally Ho. There were large four-horse conveyances at the side of this church to take the guests to James Cuthbertson's ranch south of town. There they had a good New England supper and hot coffee.

First Presbyterian Church: second building, Remington and Olive built 1887 photo 1894.

Razing of building 1974.

It served the Presbyterians until 1914, then several other denominations until it was demolished in 1974. The steeple photographed in the rubble contrasts sharply with the new highrise apartment across the street which has taken the site of the old Remington school.

In April, 1914, the Presbyterians laid the cornerstone of their third church on the northwest corner of Myrtle and College. J.C. Fulton, architect in Uniontown, Pennsylvania, promised that it would be Gothic throughout and constructed for $60,000 including heat and pipe organ.(32)

EPISCOPALIAN

Of all the early churches, that built by the Episcopalians in 1882 gave the longest service for it was used until 1965. Father Francis Byrne had been serving as a missionary to miners in Black Hawk in 1875 when he learned of his new assignment to Fort Collins. He traveled by rail to Longmont, then stage on north. He held a service in the Methodist church while it was still located on Mason. Jay Bouton helped the little group purchase a billiard hall and three lots on the corner of Linden and Mountain for $700.00. After the coming of the railroad, the land value appreciated so they sold this ground to Franklin Avery in 1881 for $2,000.00. Benjamin Franklin Hottel was among those selecting the new location on the southeast corner of College and Oak.

Episcopal church 1894 Oak and College wooden vestibule.

Episcopal church with stone entrance, and added rear extension.

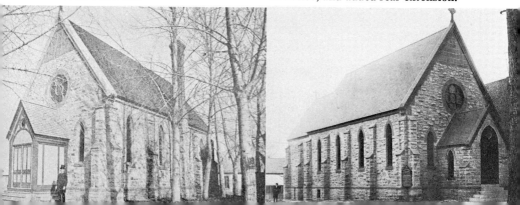

Father Byrne worked hard to draw a congregation together in the tiny town. He traveled by coach to Livermore where he held services in the Livermore Hotel in 1879 and occasionally went on to Elkhorn Lodge. He performed the marriage for his youngest daughter, Emily, to Leonard Allen Smith of Fort Collins in January, 1880. Joseph Mason was one of his vestrymen. Mason's funeral in February, 1881, was held in the Methodist church. A cornet band led the procession to the cemetery which was then southeast of town near east Elizabeth.

Father Byrne made his little rectory on West Oak near Howes cozy but he was abruptly transferred just when the group was ready to build. The cornerstone of "a more churchly edifice" was laid in November 2, 1882. The band of the Masonic Lodge marched from the formalities to the Masonic hall on Jefferson. The ladies gave a New England supper at the Opera House and raised $92.55 for the building. As so often happened in Fort Collins, a terrific windstorm hit it during construction in December. Two-thirds of the east wall fell out, and damage was estimated at $300.00. The building was ready for dedication in 1883.

By 1885 the congregation authorized Professor Lawrence to stop in Chicago on a trip east and select stained glass windows from the George Misch Company. There were many alterations in the years from 1883 to 1965 but the exterior continued to be a credit to the original architect, E.F. Fossett. A drawing in 1884 showed the front facade with simple steps to the door. Among the pictures assembled for the eightieth anniversary in 1955 was an undated one of the church with its wooden vestibule, young trees planted in front, and a very rough road for modern College Avenue. A rear building was identified as the earlier billiard hall-church. Another photograph shows the stone vestibule and a rear extension, alterations made in 1912. The rector, Father C. Herbert Shutt, was the architect for these changes and he did much of the work himself. He designed the rood screen which was a gift to the church from Josephine Collins, daughter of W.O. Collins. While the remodeling was going on in the summer of 1912, the congregation met in the Pioneer cabin. So there were continued connections with the pioneer period as the years went by.

Father Shutt, like Father Byrne, came to this continent from England as a missionary. His life in Fort Collins followed a period in Minnesota where he had enjoyed a lake cottage so in 1918 he bought the Pierce ranch at Log Cabin for a summer home. This is part of the property forming the Ben Delatour Boy Scout camp today.

Another addition on Oak provided Sunday school rooms. This was once attached to the rear of the sanctuary. This section is now part of the store which stands on the site of the old church. Some of the windows were incorporated in the small chapel of the new St. Luke's which was dedicated on October 18, 1965. Other windows are in storage.

The Arthurs and the Hottels, whose homes vied with one another in 1882, were loyal supporters of the church. The lives of the Hottel family spanned the era of the College Avenue church for the father died on January 2, 1937, and the daughter, Mary Hottel Street, on November 12, 1960. The demolition of the sanctuary and the Hottel home across from it after her death removed two of the most distinguished landmarks of old Fort Collins.(33)

CATHOLIC

The first Catholic church at 115 Riverside, as sketched by the artist in 1884, looked like the school house, and that had been its original function. Mass was celebrated in the Old Grout building in 1878. Then the Catholics, led by Frank Michaud, raised the sum of $500.00 to purchase the school, replaced by the new Remington school built in 1879. It was used twenty-two years until the dedication of St. Joseph's in August, 1901. The lots on Peterson near the church on Riverside were added to the Catholic property and a rectory built in 1883-84 under Father J.J. LePage.

The school house-church-home still stands today, though the addition of a porch trimmed with a clover-leaf design in the wood, the changed windows, and a different exterior finish make it quite unlike the simple structure shown in this drawing.

CATHOLIC CHURCH

St. Joseph's Catholic Church Mountain and Howes; dedicated 1901.

Unitarian Church Mulberry and College built 1904; razed 1970.

UNITARIAN

Albert Bryan of Denver designed the Unity Church in 1904 on the southwest corner of Mulberry and College. He had been the architect for the public library and for a while had an office in the Avery Block. The church exterior was gray sandstone. The interior "in old ivory and white with here and there a touch of gold" had transepts lighted by a large rose window. It served as a Congregational-Unitarian church from 1931 to 1970 when it was razed. Traffic noise on modern College Avenue was one of the factors which caused members to build the Foothills Unitarian Church on a quieter site in that year.(34)

AND MANY, MANY OTHERS

At the beginning of the twentieth century the churches claimed the credit for the high moral standard which the little western town had achieved. The appeal in 1902 for a Carnegie library put it simply; this was a town with nine churches and no saloons. Soon there were many more denominations and many divisions within some of those like the Baptists and Lutherans. James Miller has written a charming history of the First Christian Church in Fort Collins.

The selection included here must be regarded as a sampling to show how important **some** church was in the everyday life of most people.

There never was a synagogue but there may have been a few Jewish settlers. The **Courier** ran an apology in June, 1882, to Jewish friends and readers offended by an editorial comment on Russian-Jewish immigration. The paper's objections were to the refugee burden, not the religion. Charles Reingold ran a junk yard at 326 Walnut in the 1920's. He impressed many residents with his quiet dignity and firm observance of his Sabbath, sitting in the sun reading his Bible. One estimate noted seventy-five Jewish residents in Fort Collins in 1927.

Lillie Nicholson Bullard recalled a minor bit of religious conflict in the early 1900's when she lived at Inverness. The Seventh Day Adventist neighbors frequently borrowed the Nicholsons' hay rack on Sunday. When the Nicholsons wanted the neighbors' plow on Saturday and were refused, Mrs. Nicholson took a firm stand: "If your things rest on your Sabbath, ours rest on ours!"

THE ATTRACTIONS OF THE SALOON

In the 1880's no one had to walk far in the business district to find a saloon. College Avenue, Jefferson, and Linden were well supplied. On the exterior, the saloons looked just like the grocery or hardware stores and they were usually located in business blocks with other shops. The owners worked hard to win customers and soften criticism. In the 1870's Wilson's saloon on Jefferson supplied a hall on the second floor for community activities and church benefits. Lindenmeier's "Board of Trade" on College near the Opera House had a bowling alley in 1880.

The sheriff kept a watchful eye on likely spots for trouble. When Sheriff Sweeney saw "four female inmates of the negro dance house arrive at a saloon on Jefferson" in 1881 he was ready. They had come riding in a smart turnout with a white driver. They were decked out in good clothes. When they entered and ordered drinks he forced them to move on.

The contemporary descriptions of the interiors gave a few tidbits about attempts at decoration. In 1882, John Owens installed new bar room fixtures in his saloon, the "Brunswick," next to an ice cream parlor. He made the floor of alternate strips of ash and walnut. It was "splendidly lighted and a gem of its kind."

Johns and Kennedy rented the old "Bon Ton" saloon and added a shooting gallery in 1882. Later that year R.W. Durkee took over as proprietor and hired Thomas Tutton from the Tedmon bar to help. This establishment was located directly under the **Courier** office.

D. Friedlander of Denver came out to decorate both the Bon Ton and the Collins House. He used "fancy-colored paper or netting in plain, grotesque, variegated, and fantastic shapes" to decorate bars, chandeliers, ceilings, and mirrors. The effect was pronounced both pleasing and cheap.

When Frank Miller moved to Fort Collins in 1882 he went into the liquor business with vigor. He started a store on Linden and opened a saloon in F.T. Dunning's business block. He hired Frank Dastarac, the French artist, to paint a fine sign. By the end of the decade he was ready to expand and build his own block.

The two-story Miller Block on the southeast corner of Linden and Walnut was not really completed until 1891 though it was dated "1888" in stone on the exterior facade. The floors, ceilings, and wainscotting were oiled Georgia pine trimmed with cherry. The first fifty feet of frontage from the corner were used by Mosman and Eddy, dry goods. There was a stairway for the second floor offices and apartments. One of these was occupied by C.C. Emigh, insurance.

The next part of the building had Miller's liquor store in front. The rear section was the "sample room". Partitions in this area provided sitting rooms for customers who desired privacy. J.F. Colpitts was the builder. The cost was $30,000.(35)

Miller's license was the last one to expire when prohibition took over in 1896. Part of the building became a department store, the "Fair," managed by Miller's son. In recent years it has become a beer tavern with various names, but little effort has been made to provide the elegance and tone which were characteristic in the 1890's.

"The Fair"—D.C. Armitage and Frank C. Miller, proprietors

CHARLIE CLAY: SYMBOL OF FREEDOM

When the Fisk Jubilee Singers gave a concert of negro spirituals at the Fort Collins Opera House in May, 1889, they inspired memories of the issues of the Civil War to the many veterans in the audience. Fisk University was founded in Nashville, Tennessee in 1866 to educate Blacks. The income from the tours was an important part of the university budget.

A constant reminder in Fort Collins of the period of slavery was the lovable character, Charlie Clay. He started to purchase his freedom in Missouri in the early 1860's. Then as the war progressed he took off for the west. He worked as a cook at Fort Laramie and at several stagecoach stops on the Overland Trail, including Latham and Laporte. He was present at the Battle of Platte Bridge in July, 1865, when Caspar Collins was killed.

Clay entranced the children of Fort Collins with tales of his experiences—how he had cooked dinner for General Grant and had shaved Jack Slade. Frank McClelland thought his humor in face of grim situations stemmed from the way of life in the old slave quarters. McClelland wrote:

When he told of lying behind parked wagons and popping away at red men, it was as though he was relating a game of throwing stones at prairie dogs to see them run for their burrows. If he ever hit anything he never said, but he made a lot of noise shooting.

Clay concluded his stories: "My skin turned white more than once in those days."

In 1874 he was cooking for George Blake, Joe Mason's father-in-law, at the National Hotel. At various times he cooked at the Tedmon House, the Cottage Hotel, the Windsor, and the Toney House. In October, 1882 he moved his home next to the Toney house to make his work there easier.

Even with all the professional cooking, there was time for the Clays to entertain in their own home. In December, 1880 they gave a dance from eight to midnight and then served a supper that was a gourmet's delight. A reporter from the **Courier** observed: "Charlie enjoyed himself...he got up a little dance on his own hook in one corner and the way he 'hoed it down' was a caution."

In March, 1882, his house one mile west of town burned. It was valued at $1500.00. His insurance with Jay Bouton covered a loss of $600.00. Early one January morning in 1885 he was found almost frozen on Mountain Avenue and taken to Dr. Ethan Allen Lee for treatment. He "had been out with the boys looking on the wine when it was red."

His catering and cooking jobs were succeeded by a city appointment. By June, 1888, he was working as scavenger and he received praise for his contribution to the appearance and health of the city. His picture, taken on Linden in front of Robertson & Whitton's store, dates from this period. The painting by Frank C. Miller in the Pioneer Museum depicts both Old Grout, which was razed in 1881, and Clay on his garbage wagon. He had not taken the city job that early but he was such a familiar figure, he belonged in the scene in legend if not in fact.

His wife, Annie, was much younger than Charlie. She died at 37 in 1892 at their Jefferson Street home. They had six children. One daughter, Lillie, was photographed with L.C. Moore and others in front of the late James H. Howe home on Walnut in 1893. That residence was a boarding house for a while as no one wanted to live permanently in the building made famous by Howe's murder of his wife and subsequent lynching.

Charles Clay, former slave, on Linden Avenue; hired by city late 1880's to keep streets clean.

One of Clay's sons was an outstanding runner and he often brought victory to the Fort Collins participants when he helped pull the fire hose in races with Greeley and Loveland. A descendant was reported living in Cheyenne in the 1930's, but there seem to be no relatives about today. Even without loyal family to perpetuate his fame, Clay has his own special place in Fort Collins history. His age was uncertain at the time of his death, August 31, 1910. Hollowell's arranged his funeral. He was honored as a true Christian. He had been a faithful member and deacon of a chapel for Blacks which existed for a time.

Clay's versatile adaptation to whatever employment was available, helper in a brewery in Laporte, butcher, barber, shoemaker, cook, or garbage collector was typical of pioneer America. This art of living along with his friendly personality made him a symbol of freedom, the ideal for which many Fort Collins residents had fought.(36)

SYLVESTER H. BIRDSALL: LARIMER COUNTY'S SINGING MASTER

One of the strange features of local history is the unusual and talented people who turn up on the edge of nowhere instead of in cultural centers where they would be expected. The little Prairie Divide school built in the 1890's for a few children of ranchers and miners working on the "Copper Bug" near Cherokee Park was not a place where a gifted, well-trained teacher of music would be expected. Yet that is where Sylvester H. Birdsall, well-loved singing master of Larimer County, taught. Programs and community gatherings were a regular occurrence at the school house. He bought Will Sloan's homestead in that area in 1893.

Birdsall was born in Pennsylvania in 1839. At sixteen he began studying at Allegheny College, Meadville, Pennsylvania and giving music lessons. At twenty-one he left to serve in the Civil War. At one period he was assigned to guard Lincoln. In 1864 the young lieutenant was commanding Black troops. He must have had a strong interest in Blacks for he worked for the Freedmen's Bureau in North Carolina before returning to study music in the Normal School at Meadville.

The founding of the Greeley Colony brought the Birdsall family west and for a while he lived near Timnath. Like many G.A.R. members Birdsall was proud of having voted consistently for Republican candidates, Fremont, Lincoln, and Grant.

In 1876 he supported Hayes and over-celebrated his victory near Loveland at old St. Louis. He supplied the music and a friend the whiskey. Joseph McClelland firmly criticized his behavior in the **Fort Collins Express** so Birdsall changed to the Prohibition ticket for the next twenty years! He lost his vote for president twice because of his traveling.

There were many singing masters who criss-crossed the country teaching short courses on how to read music and how to play a variety of instruments. J.M. DeMoss taught one in Laporte and Fort Collins in the fall of 1880. These itinerant instructors were like the universal peddlers bringing their talents instead of wares to dazzle the eager public. Birdsall was one who had Larimer County for home base. He trained a choir of one hundred and fifty children to sing at the Grand Encampment in Denver in 1883. For this he wrote special verses using the tune, "Bonnie Blue Flag."

In 1890 Birdsall copyrighted a keyboard pattern mounted on a wooden frame 26 inches by 10 inches, and had it printed in Loveland. The Pioneer Museum has three of these, one of which was found by Josephine Lamb in an old Livermore ranch home. There were two Birdsall daughters, Grace Peterson and Mrs. William Stewart. Birdsall's wife, Amanda, died at the Prairie Divide home of Mrs. Stewart in June, 1898.

Ansel Watrous included Birdsall in his county history in 1911, praising his "happy faculty of versification which he exhibited in the production of many campaign songs." Even then he had not quite settled down, for his address was given as Pine Bluffs, Wyoming and his residence as Kimball County, Nebraska. He wrote verses deriding the Kaiser to be sung to the tune of "Battle Hymn of the Republic" in World War I and lived to be ninety, dying in 1929. His obituary in the **Express-Courier** claimed him as Larimer County's own and his old friends like R.Q. Tenney and other veterans affectionately recalled the gaiety he had contributed to many local gatherings in the "good old days."(37)

FRESH BAKED BREAD DELIVERED TO YOUR HOME

Paint sometimes lasts a long time at high, dry altitudes. Damm's bakery advertisement painted on the north wall of the Colorado Building at 122 South College has weathered for decades since the bakery itself left that locality in 1936. Albert Damm, a German immigrant, first opened a shop in 1889 on Linden Avenue. The family business went through the horse and wagon stage and changed to motorized vehicles before it succumbed to the depression of the 1930's.

Though Damm's bakery was old, it was not the first specialty shop in that field to serve Fort Collins citizens. Louis Dauth from the Rhineland had come to Colorado in the 1870's. He was an honored veteran of the Franco-Prussian War. His medals included the Iron Cross. He opened a bakery in Fort Collins in 1877 because he expected the town to prosper with its new railroad. In 1878 his yearly business was estimated at $4,500.00 tallying higher than a blacksmith, a harness maker, and a saloon keeper, all of whose services might have seemed more essential for that era. He added an icebox and other new improvements to the bakery in 1878.

Dauth got along well with his American friends, many of whom were Civil War veterans. He served as alderman for the fourth ward in 1884 when A.L. Emigh was mayor. With Reed, a jeweler, he built the Reed & Dauth Block at 223 Linden in 1881, a building now occupied by the Salvation Army's Red Shield Room and Senior Citizen Drop-In Center. When new, it was considered a handsome addition to Linden Avenue for it was two-story and brick with "beautiful Norman-arched windows."

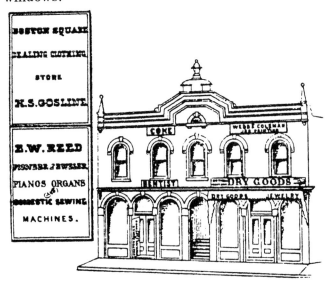

REED & DAUTH BLOCK LINDEN ST.

Damm's Bakery truck in blizzard of 1913 College Avenue.

Bakery truck near Spruce Hall and flagpole, view of Blount home in left background, built 1883, now site of bookstore; Blount home appears in stereopticon view p. 48.

Dauth expanded the bakery to include groceries. He even sold fresh oysters, and he thrived with the growing town. In 1882 he was part owner of a one hundred acre farm near Claymore Lake. His contacts with the old country added a continental flavor to the conversation on Linden. In August, 1882, according to the **Courier**, he expected his brother from Hesse-Darmstadt for a visit. In January, 1883, he was worrying about how the Rhine floods were affecting his relatives in Mainz. In 1885 he made a trip back to Germany.

That same year Dauth bought a new delivery wagon and its arrival in the tiny town was a sensation—"so handsome it couldn't be beaten anywhere. He just about hit the mark." About 1887 he moved to Denver where he became the owner of many apartments and business blocks. Frank McClelland, his friend of many years, described Dauth's happy old age. "He carefully husbanded his resources and in the twilight of life collects his rents and muses in silence over his long active career."

Perhaps it was Dauth's departure which encouraged Damm to try the bakery business. He was born in Magdeburg, Germany, in 1854, and came to America in 1882. He and Ernestine Damsch from Berlin were married in Denver in 1884. The young couple arrived in Fort Collins on April 4, 1888, a date they always remembered for it was not only the beginning of their life in this locality, it was the night of Larimer County's only lynching.

When Damm opened his bakery at 142 Linden in 1889 his family lived on the second floor. Herbert was born there in 1897. In 1903 he sold the shop to F.H. Knemeyer, who continued Damm's name, "The Colorado Bakery & Grocery." Knemeyer's advertisement for "The Best Bread and the Most For Your Money," is painted on the side of this building still though that bakery too is long since gone and the present occupant is T.J.'s Bar.

In 1908 Damm bought Charles Christman's Confectionery Shop at 133 South College and combined this with a bakery business. He was pleased with the new location. It was near to Wolfer's Grocery, a convenience for customers. He used a horse and wagon to deliver ice cream and bakery goods to homes as well as stores. His first car was a two-cylinder Jackson with adjustable tonneau. The family rode in front and rear seats on Sunday, then replaced the back section with a box for weekday deliveries. He next bought an International truck with large wheels, the envy of the town in the 1913 blizzard when even the streetcars were stuck.

This vehicle advertised the confectionery as well as the bakery. Mrs. Herbert Damm still has a 1916 menu, listing plain sodas at five cents, with ice cream, ten. Sundaes like fresh strawberry, Billie Burke, Damm's Special and Tin Roof were ten cents. A Mary Pickford or a banana split cost fifteen.

As times changed delivery service was kept up to date by changing to a fine Dodge Brothers' truck which was photographed on the campus near the flagpole and Old Main.

After the Damms sold the Linden Avenue bakery they lived for a while in a cozy little house at 209 S. Sherwood. This is a neat white structure still standing. Its oldfashioned door with oval glass opens on to a porch shaded by a huge lilac. The hitching post is at the curb. One of the Damms' four children is a Fort Collins resident today. Herbert and his wife, Julia, live at 215 Remington, the house which the elder Damms occupied in their later years. Albert died in 1929 at 75 and Ernestine in 1932 at 72, before the worst of the depression hit which ended the company.

Frequently old residents tell Herbert they miss the marsh-mallowfilled cream puffs from the bakery, a remembered delicacy of their childhood. Besides such concoctions, the Damms made a nourishing loaf of bread sweetened with molasses which everyone knew was nutritious. When a men's apparel store succeeded the bakery in the same building, it was years before the basement was thoroughly explored. Dean Berg of Hughes Men's Wear now uses the building. He recalls finding a forgotten barrel of molasses in the basement corner covered with dust in 1943. "It weighed a ton" he was sure when they lifted it to clean out the area.

It is interesting that professional bakers found a niche even in the early town. Tradition has it that Theodosia Ammons, developing a home economics curriculum for the Agricultural College around 1900, maintained staunchly that every girl should bake a good loaf of bread to graduate. The galvanized iron bread mixer was a common utensil in most kitchens. These antiques are popular again with a few determined cooks. Breadmaking courses have drawn eager students. Most Fort Collins households, however, rely today on the supermarkets and modern bakeries for their bread. The housewife, instead of the baker, supplies the transportation.(38)

THE GOOD OLD DAYS OF THE WOODEN INDIAN AND THE FIVE CENT CIGAR

Carl Lauterbach had a shop at 210 Linden in the 1880's which bore a sign, "Cigar Factory." The building still stands today, with the facade unaltered. He and his wife lived in the rear of the store so it was easy for them to pose for the photograph. The tailor, McDougall, and his wife were neighbors so they joined the Lauterbachs in the picture. The hitching post serving both shops is outlined against the black background of Mrs. McDougall's skirt.

Lauterbach retired in 1900. He and his wife, Catherine, lived at 521 Howes till he died in 1915. J. H. Swan and Lawrence Nightingale managed Lauterbach's store in 1904. They promised the best in cigars and tobacco. They had many other business interests however, and apparently soon gave up on this one.

Fred Watson, who came from Iowa to Fort Collins in 1906, made and sold cigars for many years. For a while he worked on Linden, then on the second floor of the Eastside Grocery on the southwest corner of Whedbee and Magnolia. This building is now used by the carpenters' union.

Watson was delighted when C.R. Welch rented him the little shop at 131 S. College, now Garwood's Jewelry. He had as neighbors on the south side Damm's bakery and on the north a tea speciality shop which had a large teapot sign over the sidewalk. The Watsons lived in the rear of the cigar shop. Six employees helped make the cigars. The large leaves came in three hundred pound crates. The men moistened the leaves to make them pliable and used special knives to prepare the filler.

Watson had cigars with brand names like "Great Divide" and "Town Boast" which sold for a nickel and "Old Master" for a dime. He posted advertisements in Ault, Eaton, and other neighboring towns and the products sold well.

A photograph of the street taken in 1914 at the time of the semi-centennial showed the shops, but the wooden Indian was hidden in the shadow. In 1917 Ray Williams, an employee, carried the statue inside every night to protect it. It was then a valuable antique. The art of carving wooden Indians for cigar stores may have developed when sculptors no longer made figureheads for sailing vessels. They were most popular in the middle of the nineteenth century and somewhat outmoded by the time of Teddy Roosevelt. Apparently people in Fort Collins appreciated this one since it received such special care.

Haulcie H. Roberts learned cigar-making under the Veterans' Vocational Training Act after World War I. He purchased Watson's factory in 1924 along with the trade names. He produced the cigars which Watson sold until 1935 when machine competition made the craft unprofitable. Watson turned to the coal business. The tools and equipment used by both men were given to the Pioneer Museum.

"What this country needs is a good five cent cigar" is a classic quotation. It has survived while the name of the man who voiced it, Thomas Marshall, Wilson's vice-president, has been forgotten. Though that priced cigar has long been extinct in Fort Collins, a sign advertising one remains painted on the wall of the Robert Trimble Block, half-hidden by the sign for a Chinese restaurant, and just a few feet from where the wooden Indian once stood.

Building the Larimer County Courthouse 1887.

FRONTIER JUSTICE AND A BRAND NEW COURTHOUSE

The building of the Larimer County Courthouse in 1887 was a big achievement for the political leaders. Fort Collins had been the county seat since 1868. Officials worked in Old Grout, the Opera House, or rented space above stores in other private buildings. These were makeshift arrangements till the expense of a real courthouse could be met.

LARIMER COUNTY COURT HOUSE.

Residents were justly proud of the edifice. It was located in the center of a pleasant square, well-shaded with trees, south of Mountain and west of Howes. The two-story red brick structure with attic dormers and tower with flagpole loomed up on the skyline like Old Main on the south and Hottel's mill on the northeast. Each formed a center for specialized activities.

Construction began after voters supported a bond issue in November, 1886. In July, 1887, the Fort Collins Foundry was making castings for pillars, columns, and lintels. On August 11, the Masons conducted an impressive cornerstone-laying ceremony. The builders paid honor to the tradition of Roman law by carving a Latin motto in Germanic letters on the stone: **"Justitia non est neganda non deferenca."** Justice is not to be denied or delayed. William Quayle of Denver was the architect. He arranged for electricity since that became available during the period of construction.

This all sounded as though crude practices of administering frontier justice were over and trials would follow normal legal procedure. Yet the one lynching in Larimer County occurred in April, 1888, just after the courthouse was finished. There was another in Greeley in December. The event in Fort Collins was covered by the newspapers. That in Greeley was photographed and the scene displayed on the courthouse wall as a powerful reminder more potent than a Latin motto.

Howe's home on Walnut near Linden was haunted by sad memories after the lynching, avoided as residence, used as boarding house; photo c.1892 showed Della Welch Miller, Daisy Welch Bosworth who ran it, Lilly Clay and Clark Moore.

James H. Howe, the victim of the Fort Collins lynching, had found a job in Hottel's mill and sent for his wife. His father-in-law, Oliver Vandewark, traveled west with her in September, 1880. While in Fort Collins, Vandewark invested in some property north of the river. Howe and his wife acknowledged the neighbors' help when their daughter, Cornelia, died in 1881. His mother-in-law visited them in June, 1882. In August that year his wife had a bouncing girl. He was "smiling and setting them up for the boys."

In December, 1882, the Howe family moved to a brick house on Willow near the mill. In December, 1887, he was engaged by the city to locate each water tap in the city system on a map. In 1888 they were living in a white clapboard house on Walnut near Linden. These everyday incidents gave no hint of impending tragedy.

Passersby on Walnut were shocked on April 4 shortly after noon when Mrs. Howe staggered from their home and collapsed, fatally wounded by her intoxicated husband. Howe offered no resistance to the night watchman and others who arrested him and confined him in the jail near the new courthouse. That night the lights blacked out at eight o'clock. A mob took him from the jail and hanged him on a rope tied to a derrick. The machine was in the yard for it had been used to lower flagstones for the new jail floor. By 9:30 the lights were on again. The following day the jury of inquest reported his death "by hanging at the hands of an infuriated and unknown mob."

Greeley in nearby Weld County had constructed a new courthouse in 1883 ahead of Fort Collins. The yard of that building was the scene of a lynching shortly after Howe's death. The victim, a cattleman in Evans, had killed his former partner in a dispute over some flour. On December 29, 1888, the grim scene was photographed. Some thought one city set an example for the other. The Fort Collins paper supported both actions:

Much as lynch law is to be deplored in the abstract, yet there are times, or at least, seem to be, when the checking of crime can be accomplished in no other way.(39)

Above: Greeley lynching December, 1888 next to Courthouse and church.
Below: Weld County Courthouse 1883-1915.

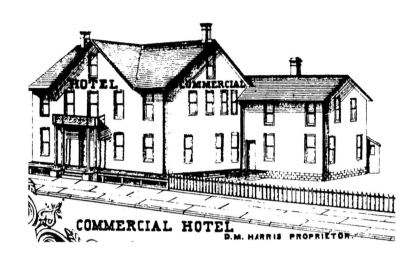

COMMERCIAL HOTEL
D.M. HARRIS PROPRIETOR

HOTELS: ONE BATHROOM FOR EVERY FLOOR

When Isabella Bird stopped over in Fort Collins in 1873 on her way to climb Long's Peak, she found her hotel revolting and she omitted any mention of its name. The first floor was swarming with locusts. She may have been describing the Agricultural Hotel, for Marcus Coon built that in 1873 at the corner of Mountain and Mason. He moved the Auntie Stone cabin over from Jefferson to give additional work space.

In 1874 there were three other hotels besides the Agricultural, the Collins House on Jefferson, the National across from it, and the Blake House nearby. Accommodations were much improved and "the boys no longer slept three deep." Every coach arrived with new customers. The Agricultural Hotel arranged a maple sugar festival in May with that delicacy imported from Cortland, New York.

D.M. Harris bought the Agricultural in 1877, moved it to the southeast corner of College and Walnut, and changed the name to Commercial. In 1881 it was quite spacious, though not as elegant as the new fashionable Tedmon house under construction on Jefferson. It must have been completely re-built by the end of the century if the drawing for an advertisement now in the museum is an accurate representation. Everything was changed again in 1905 for in October the three-story Northern Hotel opened on that site. Construction had run to $100,000. Dr. McHugh, Sam Clammer, and other town leaders were proud of its Tiffany-like dome in the dining room and the balcony over the entrance. William Jennings Bryan considered addressing townsfolk from the balcony in October, 1906 but changed to the Opera House instead.

The modifications through the years in the exterior appearance of this hotel present interesting examples of changing tastes in styles. The pilasters, which resemble columns but do not stand out separate from the wall, ran to the cornice under the roof. In 1924 the management boasted the hotel was getting the first steel furniture in Colorado. A fourth story was added and elevators installed. At first, the original design was retained as much as possible, and the pilasters still ended near the band which had once been the cornice.

Then the Exposition Decoratif in Paris in 1925 popularized a new style now called "Art Deco." With this inspiration the College Avenue facade was altered replacing the three-story classic pilasters with new four-story ones and adding medallions and doorway trim in the same spirit. This face-lifting occurred only on the College Avenue side so the Walnut Street wall still bore the old-style pilasters. When the building was damaged by fire February 18, 1975, some people remarked on the disagreeable jazzy exterior of the College Avenue entrance yet this one facade provides a unique example of the taste of the 1920's. It is as interesting in its way as the dome in the dining room, installed in 1905, later covered over and forgotten, and re-discovered and treasured in a restoration in 1973!

Northern Hotel exterior early 1900's - three floors with balcony over entrance.

Northern Hotel after addition of fourth floor c.1924; City Hall and belfry on Walnut in left background.

TEDMON HOUSE   GEO S BROWN PROPRIETOR.

THE TEDMON HOUSE

Bolivar S. Tedmon and his wife came to Fort Collins in 1878 and the next year he took over the management of the Metropolitan House from Auntie Stone who retired at seventy-eight from the hotel business. Mrs. Tedmon had a millinery shop on Linden where she "trimmed hats and bonnets to order at short notice in the latest styles and at reasonable rates." She also took orders for goods, patterns, and magazines from any of the eastern cities.

From this small beginning grew the ambitious plan for the construction of the Tedmon House in 1880, an elegant hotel which dominated Fort Collins' business area for the next thirty years. It was located on the northwest corner of Jefferson and Linden, three stories high of brick and stone. Its oriel window, a bay cantilevered out from the wall over the drug store doorway was an innovation. It set the pace for the improvement of Jefferson from humble wooden structures and flimsy livery stables and blacksmith shops left over from the days of the fort to good brick buildings.

The new hotel had nineteen rooms on the third floor, seventeen on the second with parlor and ante room, and each floor had a bath room and linen closet. The first floor had baggage room, barber shop, sample room for traveling salesmen, a dining room with two chandeliers, china closet, dishing and serving room, and kitchen with cooking range, steam table, boiler, and pastry room. Brussels carpets covered the stairways and halls. A special carriage picked up clients at the railroad station and conveyed them in style to the hotel.

"Old Grout, your days are numbered," ran the headline the next year and even that venerable structure which had served as sutler's store for the fort and housed the temporary courthouse, post office, and community center had to go when faced by such a modern edifice as the Tedmon House across the street. Tedmon soon sold out, but the succeeding proprietors maintained the style with which it was begun. When the Northern Hotel appeared in 1905 and the Union Pacific wanted to build along Jefferson, progress doomed the Tedmon House and it made way for the railroad after thirty years of service. (40)

Tedmon Hotel 1880's Jefferson and Linden
Stover Drugstore in Tedmon Hotel.

THE EVOLUTION OF THE MODERN DRUGSTORE

The pioneer drugstore relied on patent medicine and whiskey with a few additional frills to attract customers. Uncle Ben Whedbee had the post office in his drugstore in the 1870's. Frank Stover's store on the Tedmon House corner prominently displayed the mortar and pestle symbol of the druggist on a corner post. Stover sold St. Jacob's oil, a German remedy. He had "iced Congress and Seltzer Mineral Water on draught" and presumably the appropriate additives. In September, 1880, he had a telephone exchange in his house on Linden and Willow with two connections, one with the drugstore and one with Mac's Tinnery. It was expected that "soon our city will be traversed by a bewildering maze of these wires." W.S. Taylor had anticipated him in 1879 by getting a right for telephones in Laporte where the new invention was advertised as a convenience for camp meetings and other large assemblies, though "there should be one in every house for it works like a charm."

In the early '80's Dr. Lee and Dr. Elston had the Parlor Drugstore in a small brick building at 237 Linden with the Poudre Valley Bank as their neighbor. They had a local exhibit to entertain customers. A prairie dog and a black-footed ferret, possibly from the colony still on the vacant lots nearby, were placed in cages. The prairie dog was scalped in short order when he got into the wrong cage!

A.W. Scott in his drugstore on Linden anticipated the modern jukebox when he installed automatic drop-a-nickel-in-the-slot phonographs. The reporter noted in December, 1891:

The cylinders are filled with stump speeches, recitations, music, etc. and to listen to the machine is very interesting and amusing. The cylinders are changed to make a new program every day, and the little machines are almost constantly surrounded by curious crowds.

Stover met the competition in 1906 by getting a new gramophone from the east. "All people on Linden will be happy" because of his automatic winding machine which was loaded with twenty-five or fifty rolls and run by batteries.

The basic purpose of the shop, however, was to dispense medicine and Scott exhibited high quality leadership in that area. Scott's father had been a minister in the Dutch Reformed Church, then professor of mathematics and president of Hope College, a church school. Scott came west to find in primitive Fort Collins a business challenge. His first job was as clerk in the Parlor Drugstore. He took a partner and bought the store from the doctors. In 1888, the year of his marriage in the Loomis house, he became sole owner.

In 1887 the state initiated a license program for pharmacists. Scott made himself such an expert in the field he was appointed to the State Board of Pharmacy in 1895 and served for seventeen years. He was on the State Board of Health for twelve years. He prospered financially, was active in the Episcopal Church, and treasurer of the Country Club. When he died in 1927, the quality of drugs sold was standardized, a change which he helped bring about.

The Scott Drugstore occupied several sites on Linden, Mountain, and College. The photograph in the 1920's showed it in the Physicians' Building on College. Walgreens occupies Scott's location today.

Scott's management was not entirely without blemish. In 1907 he pled guilty to selling more liquor than his proper quota. Fancher Sarchet in making himself the champion of the underprivileged, arrested for liquor violations, was quick to criticize the socially elite who evaded prohibition regulations through cronyism. But Sarchet himself apparently saw no ethical conflict in the practice of young lawyers' helping themselves to confiscated liquor stored in the Courthouse attic. In spite of the occasional slip, Scott earned his comfortable home on College, the electric car for his wife, and the other privileges he enjoyed by providing a modern drugstore.(41)

College Avenue view north toward Mountain; Scott Drugstore and Robert Trimble Block on left.

A.W. Scott home 403 S. College, site of United Bank photo c.1912.

DOCTORS IN THE CHOICE CITY

Dr. Timothy Smith, the first doctor, improved Fort Collins at the outset for he advised Elizabeth and Lewis Stone to settle here in October, 1864, and and thus got the first woman at the fort. His own wife was still at Fort Laramie for Christmas that year. Mrs. Collins mentioned her presence at the festivities. He liked hunting and fishing. On an outing to North Park, a rancher who had been a soldier at the fort recognized him as the cavalry's former doctor and recalled with good humor the treatment the doctor had once prescribed to sober him up: "Put him on ice." The other soldiers had done just that and it worked!

The founders of the Agricultural Colony named a street for Dr. Smith. He was county treasurer for a term beginning in 1872. At the end of that decade he built a house near the Mason & Hottel Mill. He had his family temporarily rooming in the Welch Block the night it burned in 1880. He called for medical help from Greeley and elsewhere when Joe Mason was fatally injured by a horse in 1881.

Dr. Smith was a popular figure in the town and apparently expected to continue his practice here. He revised his plans however when his wife gave birth to twin girls in October, 1881 and he was sixty-five. He told the reporter, "Twenty-five

Dr. E. A. Lee.

Dr. Ethan Allen Lee Physician-
mayor photo 1890.

years ago I would have celebrated with jollification. Now I am pleased." He sold his home and moved east.

Besides Dr. Smith the town had two other doctors for a while in the '70's. A Dr. Miller operated on Jacob Flowers' daughter for a tumor in May, 1879. He had help on the anesthetics from pioneer, Captain Post, and from the patient's sister. Dr. Ethan Allen Lee who arrived in 1883 was the familiar physician for the next twenty years. He had his office at 241 Linden near the Parlor Drugstore and posed in front of that in a silk hat. He vaccinated the quarry workers from Stout for smallpox and arranged for the care of one patient with that disease in March, 1889. The man was placed in an unoccupied house on the outskirts of town. Dr. Lee was mayor that year.

The University of Michigan offered good medical training in the late nineteenth century. One graduate in 1883 was Will Mayo who went to a small Minnesota town, Rochester, to practice with his father and brother. Dr. W.A. Kickland graduated in 1895 and he investigated Fort Collins partly because of his weak lungs and because he saw a challenge in the needs of a small town. The population was under two thousand. Dr. Lee accepted him as partner and in the next year as son-in-law. The two doctors had their offices on Linden but when the Kicklands built a brick home on S. College they moved to that. Then as the commercial aspect of College developed, the Kicklands moved to a new home at 430 W. Mountain and built the Colorado Building on the site of their earlier home. Dr. Kickland's fame as a surgeon grew and he studied in Vienna in 1907 and 1919.

Other doctors' offices were scattered about in various business buildings. One sign on the Avery Block still says "doctor." Magnetic healing was advertised on the window of the Trimble Block in 1903.

Dr. Peter J. McHugh was a physician-mayor too, like Dr. Lee. He moved here in 1890, married Auntie Stone's great niece, and after 1899 had his office in his home, the Andrews-Harris house at 303 Remington. He converted the carriage house into a private hospital. He too studied in Vienna.

Hospital care was a new idea at the turn of the century. Christian White built a frame dwelling in the Loomis Addition in 1893 and fitted up part of it as a hospital where he gave nursing care. The county hospital provided limited facilities. An association formed in 1903 succeeded in building a substantial brick structure on the southeast corner of Magnolia and Mathews in 1906. A really modern hospital started in 1924 and additions since have made it a medical center. Many doctors' offices are clustered nearby.

While many remember with nostalgia the home visits of family physicians like Dr. Lee in his horse and buggy and Dr. Kickland in his curved-dash Oldsmobile, the seriously ill are grateful for the modern laboratories and other facilities of the twentieth century hospital.(42)

THE BIRD'S EYE VIEW
TWO ARTISTS' MAPS OF OLD FORT COLLINS

While Pierre or Frank Dastarac, in a company with R.J. Selway, worked painting signs, hanging paper, calcimining, and painting a grain on woodwork, he sketched new buildings appearing in the city. He produced two maps, one in 1881 (published in August, 1882) and a second in 1884, and framed these with drawings of the buildings. The first one had sixteen buildings, the second seventeen. Only seven were repeated: Old Main, the Avery house, City Hall, the Hottel mill, the Tedmon House, the Remington school and the Opera House.

The 1881 map included with these the Commercial Hotel, which was then on the present site of the Northern Hotel, the Reed & Dauth Block and the Haynes Building on Linden, the Yount Block, the Jefferson Block, and the Vandewark Building on Jefferson, the Standard mill, a competitor of Hottel's, and Colpitts Block on Walnut adjoining City Hall. He gave the names and boundaries for the new additions in 1881, thus illustrating the expansion west and south.

In 1884 he completed one of the "birds' eye view" maps which were so popular in nineteenth century America. By

Enlargement of 1884 Dastarac map showing millrace, mill, Tedmon Hotel, Jefferson Block; early churches.

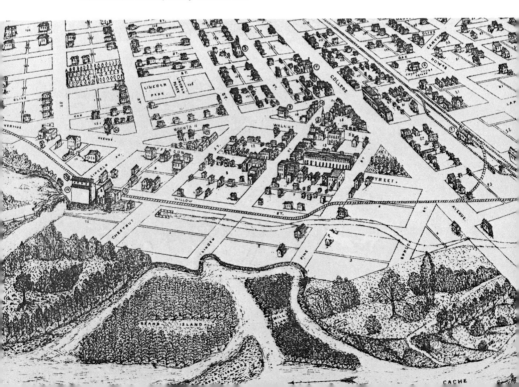

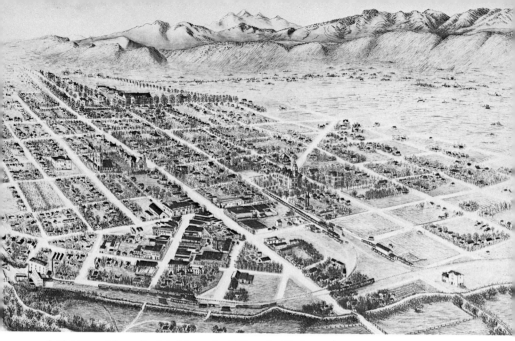

Artist Houghton depicted town in 1899 and added many buildings like the Courthouse and Franklin school which were part of the expanding town; many more trees had been planted.

representing actual buildings on each street, he recorded which lots had been used and what ones were still open space. For his special border drawings he added four churches, a category omitted in 1881. He dropped some of the business buildings and added four other residences along with the Avery house, including his own home on Mountain. Spruce Hall represented the campus as well as Old Main. To add to the historical significance he included Old Grout, already razed, and a scene of the fort in 1865.

Though there is a photograph extant of Jefferson Street in the '80's which shows the steeple of the Presbyterian church on Linden and Walnut, Dastarac's drawing of this building is the only contemporary representation of it now known. The Episcopal church appeared without its vestibule and before it acquired stained glass windows. Since the mill was rebuilt after several fires, its appearance in the early '80's is especially interesting.

Dastarac's overall concept of the city is very important. He showed the entire route of the millrace. The meandering curves and islands of the river with its border of trees in an almost treeless town are revealed. The lake for which Lake Street was named appears in A.L. Emigh's Lake Park addition. Since there is no lake at all there today this is especially illuminating. Dastarac solves some mysteries with his beautiful map, and creates others, but the document is one of the most valuable in tracing the history of the town.

Dastarac's own life in Fort Collins is somewhat mysterious. A Miss Dastarac was a princess at a masked ball in February, 1882. In June that year Dastarac painted and put up a new sign for the Boston Square Dealing Clothing House. He also did some "artistic painting" on the Reed & Dauth Block. In October, 1882, he furnished signs for the Women's Christian Temperance Union oyster sociable. In November his fine job painting Campbell brothers' new residence southeast of town was a good recommendation for further employment. In December, he was working on a sign for Frank Miller's place on Linden. The terrific wind tore one of his cloth signs to shreds that month.

In July, 1893, Dastarac was advertising for work in artistic paper hanging, frescoing, and painting. He gave Reed's as his address. One commission outside Fort Collins was reported in June, 1896. He was engaged to paint scenes for a new San Francisco theater. The **Courier** reported: **"He has few superiors with brush and pencil and his services are in demand in all parts of the country."** He had a boat on Terry Lake. These are the few personal details that are known, but he must have loved the town to delineate each tiny detail with such precision.(43)

Merritt Dana Houghton's map of Fort Collins in 1899, made fifteen years after Dastarac's, provided an interesting picture of the development in that interval. Houghton's showed many of the same landmarks as Dastarac's, the Jefferson Block, the Episcopal church, the Hottel house, along with the new construction, the Courthouse, the Methodist church, and a re-built mill. There are many more buildings on the campus. There is a luxuriant growth of trees. Even in the old parts of town many blocks were not yet occupied.

Houghton's personal interest was more in Wyoming than in Fort Collins and he moved to Laramie where he went around the countryside sketching ranches and recording the west of the end of the century. Many of his drawings are cherished family treasures or in Wyoming libraries. His map of Fort Collins was not highly appreciated at first and Mayor Sam Clammer who owned it sold it to Elwin Hunter for $25.00. Hunter arranged for its display on the wall of the Home Federal Savings and Loan Association where it may be seen today. Postcard size copies were reproduced and one of these is in the Pioneer Museum. Houghton, under the tutelage of George Buss, veteran from the days of the fort, made a view of the fort too which was printed as a postcard.

Left, wedding picture Montezuma Fuller-Anna E. Graham in Fort Collins; ceremony June 27, 1881; below, Fuller's home at 226 W. Magnolia built c.1889.

MONTEZUMA FULLER: PIONEER ARCHITECT

When a son was born in 1858 to the Fuller family in Nova Scotia, he was given the colorful name of Montezuma. Another boy in the family was called Fred. Both came west, Fred to be a blacksmith in Eaton, and Montezuma a carpenter in Fort Collins. The mother followed the boys west too, and died in Greeley in 1897. In the present period of nostalgic viewing of the past, Montezuma has become a romantic figure, the town's first architect and the only one in residence for many years. His home at 226 W. Magnolia with its flavor of the 1890's still stands, though it is unoccupied. The interesting patterns in the red brick, the shingled gables, the tinted windows, and

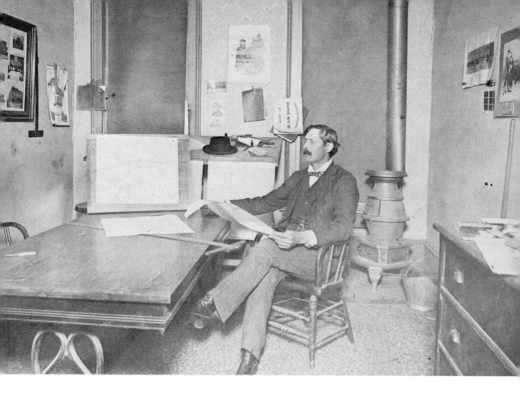

Fuller's office possibly on Mountain, 1880's complete with potbellied stove.

His office in the Avery Block early 1900's.

Robert Trimble Block west side, College Avenue south of Mountain early 1900's.

Trimble Block east side College Avenue, north of Mountain early 1900's.

the elaborate woodwork of the porch all attract the antique-minded today.

Fuller was a young man of twenty-two when he settled in Fort Collins in 1880. The town's population was well under two thousand. Like many new arrivals, he was untrained, but he came on the eve of the town's burst of substantial building and the changeover from rough frame to good stone and brick construction. Fuller watched the building of the Welch Block and Opera House, the Jefferson Block, and the City Hall. His technical skills grew along with the expanding town.

The Agricultural College hired Fuller in 1883 to convert the college barn into a laboratory and scientific classroom. This is still in use in 1975 as the southeast wing of the printing and publications building. Its south side has been re-faced with buff brick to match newer buildings on the Oval but the old red bricks still show on the east and north.

In 1885 Fuller invented a circular swing which was shown at the Old Soldiers' Grand Encampment at Cheyenne and at county fairs. It was sixteen feet in diameter. It had twelve arms eight feet long, and sixteen seats covered by an awning. By 1887 Fuller had progressed to "carpenter and builder" and had an iron shop on Mountain Avenue. The Presbyterians chose him to work with a Denver architect for their new church on Remington and Olive. This building was demolished in 1974. In 1888 he returned to his native Nova Scotia for a visit.

Y.M.C.A. designed by Fuller, 140 E. Oak (now Elks Building) cornerstone dated June 6, 1907.

Charles B. Andrews hired Fuller to work on his stone house at 202 Remington in 1889. By 1890 Fuller was called "architect" and he had a respectable list of clients for stone and brick houses which he designed and built. The homes ranged in cost from $1,000 to $10,000. That of Andrews just completed was the most expensive and included stables. His own brick residence cost $1,700. He completed the Kissock and Murray Block too at 115 E. Mountain. Its cost was listed both at $15,000 and at $22,000. It burned in 1895 and was rebuilt. Now it is used for a furniture and pet store. The front and west side have been re-faced but the rear shows its antiquity.

By 1891 the city's new sewage system was progressing. Fuller received a contract to build water closets connected with it on the playground for the Remington school. In 1893 he built a home for William Metcalf at 322 E. Oak which still stands, north of Lincoln Park. A later owner was Robert James Andrews. This was red brick trimmed with red sandstone. It has three columns decorating each side of the large arched window on the porch and one separating two small arched windows on the second story.

The peak of Fuller's career came when Franklin Avery chose him to make the final plans for the new First National Bank in the Avery Block which was completed in 1897. Fuller had his own office in that building for many years. With its round arched windows and massive entrance decorated with the head of a lion, it was the pride of the town.

In 1904 Fuller worked out the design for the German Congregational church on Whedbee and Oak. He received public contracts for many school buildings in the district. He built the Pleasant View school No. 16 at Shields and Drake in 1896, the Laurel Street school, the LaPorte Avenue school, and the one in Laporte, these after 1900.

Business was really good at the turn of the century. He built a slaughterhouse for Beach & Steward in 1899. He began the design that year for a business block for Robert Trimble at 109-115 S. College. It took time to complete it for the exterior, unaltered, bears the date 1906. The original facade of the other Trimble Block at 132 N. College resembled Fuller's style in the treatment of the windows and may have been his design too. He built a home for A.A. Edwards at 402 W. Mountain in 1904. This dignified frame dwelling with a Palladian window is still occupied by Edwards' children. The hexagonal pergola effect on the corner of the porch added a romantic touch to the formal exterior.

Senator William A. Drake hired Fuller to build an elegant barn in 1898 on his farm on Drake Road, the present site of Ghent Motors. It had the shape of a Greek cross. In 1908 Drake turned the farm over to his son and moved to an imposing town house on Magnolia and Remington which Fuller designed. It was buff brick, cost $18,000, and had dull brass fixtures for combination gas and electric lamps.

Fuller worked with Arthur Garbutt on the Young Men's Christian Association building at 140 E. Oak in September, 1906. This is the Elks' building today. It cost $60,000, even more than the third First National Bank going up at Mountain and College at the same time, which was listed at $50,000.

During the early 1900's Fuller had contracts outside Fort Collins too. He planned school buildings in Loveland, Berthoud, and Longmont. He was architect for ten Larimer County churches ranging from "small village ones costing a few thousand to elegant structures costing $25,000." The United Presbyterian church in Loveland was highly praised.

One client, Alvina Koeper, for whom Fuller built two houses eventually became his wife. Montezuma's first wife had died in 1902. He built a new brick house in the 1890's for the Koeper family in Bellvue. They had been living in the old Bingham homestead across from the place where the powder was cached long before. When Koeper died, his widow retired from lamb-feeding and had Fuller build her a new house at 1101 W. Mountain, in which she was hostess for the wedding of Fuller's son, Robert, on May 12, 1909. The young couple occupied an apartment in "Fuller Flats" on Howes right next to the family home on Magnolia.

On March 28, 1912 Montezuma married Mrs. Koeper. She and her family moved into the Fuller house on Magnolia. The Koeper-Fuller family album is filled with pictures of Montezuma on the porch watching the children, snowdrifts and icicles from the eaves in the blizzard of 1913, and trips up the Poudre canyon to see the convicts building the new road. When some of the children left home, Mrs. Fuller preferred the newer house at 1101 W. Mountain and they moved there, leaving the one which seems much more colorful and charming in detail today for a nondescript home, now converted into apartments, described as "wellbuilt." It still has a hitching post in front. It has a built-in storage area for dishes in the dining room, and an old-fashioned window in the front parlor.

On February 1, 1910 the State of Colorado awarded architectural licenses to both Montezuma and Robert Fuller. The father had been practicing architecture for thirty years and the son was two years out of Cornell, working with his father. He then moved to Denver to begin work with Robert S. Roeschlaub who was licensed architect No. 1 in this state. Later Robert Fuller had his own company with his two sons, also architects. A grandson too chose the same profession so Montezuma influenced a great-grandson through this family chain. Fuller died on January 29, 1925 at sixty-seven having enjoyed a happy life and a successful career in his forty-five years in Fort Collins.(44)

FRANKLIN AVERY AND HIS HOUSE

When Franklin Avery sold his small white house on Mountain and Meldrum and laid the foundation for a new stone house in April, 1879, he was only thirty years old and had been married four years. It was a propitious time to build, for the stone quarries west of town were supplying good material. The construction of Old Main that year on the Agricultural College campus encouraged faith in the town's future. Railroad connections had been completed between Denver and Cheyenne two years before and growth had been the pattern ever since. Avery already had a barn on the property built in 1878 at a cost of $250. Later in the '80's his house was called a "cottage" but when it was built it led the list in quality stone houses. The two-color sandstone gave a sturdy appearance and the many gables and dormers in the roof added variety to the second floor. No name was given to the style by contemporaries. It was considered "elaborate in design" and it cost $3,000.(45)

Avery had come west from the Finger Lakes area of New York in 1870. He surveyed Greeley's streets and then moved upriver to join the new colony starting Fort Collins where he repeated the procedure. He became county surveyor. He followed up the platting by supervising tree planting along the new streets and avenues.

RESIDENCE F. C. AVERY MOUNTAIN AVENUE.

Avery courted Sara Edson by mail and returned to upstate New York to marry her in 1876. She did not say farewell to her family in the east and part with them forever by this big step, for her sisters later came out and found husbands in the little town. Phebe Edson married A.A. Edwards and they eventually built a house across the street. Mary Edson married Alexander Ault, and both sisters had daughters who later joined the teaching staff of the college. Mrs. Avery's parents, Delano and Elizabeth Edson, joined the family too. Mrs. Edson, however, never became reconciled to leaving the familiar surroundings of her youth. She watched the trains arrive at the depot on Mason when she sat in the Averys' back yard and wished she could take one back east. She died in 1884.

The Averys lost two children in infancy, one in December, 1883, and one in August, 1886. When the city acquired the Grandview cemetery in 1887, the Averys arranged for a family plot and the babies were placed there near Grandfather and Grandmother Edson.

Franklin and Sara had three children, Edgar, Ethel, and Louise, who grew to maturity and added many grandchildren to the family circle. Two of Avery's brothers came to live in Fort Collins while a sister chose Greeley.

With such an expanding family the little house was much too small and Avery selected Harlan Thomas, a former Fort

Collins boy who was winning acclaim in Denver, to design an addition. This was completed in late August, 1893, at a cost of $4,000, and was so beautifully integrated with the old part many people today believed the whole building dated from 1879, the year which is marked in stone over the entrance door.

Avery's action to expand and renovate his house helped the town's morale in a period of financial depression. He also got a good bargain for his investment. Thomas turned the cottage into an unusual family home. The stone porch was one of the innovations. It extended from the front entrance around on the east to an outer entrance of the back parlor. One room upstairs was a sewing room. It opened on a broad balcony on the east side. Plumbing and electric lights were installed. No one recorded any of the day-to-day activities. Was the sewing room used for quilting bees? In 1895 Mrs. C.C. Edwards offered a reward for a silk quilt stolen from the porch. She had it ready for lining when it disappeared.

Did Thomas include the stone fountain in the front yard? He liked fountains and built one in Denver near Richthofen Place. Was the gazebo part of his plan? A drawing in 1899 showed the old barn still on the rear of the lot. When was that barn replaced with the stone one matching the house?

Much of the social life for the family revolved around their interest and support for the Methodist church. In July, 1888, the Averys had an ice cream social on the lawn which was brightened with Chinese lanterns. Vocal and instrumental music entertained the guests and a sum of sixty dollars was collected toward the minister's salary. Avery served on the committee for a new church building. Before the dedication in 1898, his brother George had become minister. Thomas designed this building too.

The Averys were thankful for their deep religious faith which helped them face several tragedies. When William, Franklin's brother, died in 1890, his widow and her new husband were tried for murder. They were acquitted but the family never agreed with the verdict. Later they lost a son-in-law through murder. Louise Avery had married Newton Crose, a young lawyer, on October 10, 1906. He practiced with Judge Bailey and had an office in the Avery building. A disgruntled client shot him there in August, 1914.

For all the sadnesses that touched the family, Avery lived to see many projects he had sponsored succeed and he maintained a reserve and quiet dignity in his leadership in the community. His business interest encompassed irrigation, real estate, and ranching as well as banking. He and William had a cousin bring them one hundred head of fine Merino sheep from Vermont in 1884. He was one of the owners of the Northern Hotel completed in 1905. He served three terms as alderman and also invested in the sugar factory.

During the thirty years he was president of the First National Bank which he had founded he saw it occupy three of its four locations and he was proud of its growth. He established it first in the Welch Block near the Opera House, then the Avery Block on Linden and Mountain and in 1908 on the southeast corner of Mountain and College. At a gala reception for the opening of that building his daughter, Ethel, and nieces, Pauline and Beth, helped Mrs. Avery at the party. There was a hidden orchestra and a table decorated with carnations and sweet peas. The marble portals opened into a tiled lobby with marble counters. This was the last big public event in which Avery shared. He retired from the bank in 1910. By 1915 when the city was excited over the possibility of the first paving, Avery was too ill to take any part in the planning. In June, 1917, Mrs. Avery announced they were moving to California, hoping the lower altitude would improve his health. He died in 1923.

Avery's descendants owned the house until 1962 when it was sold and rented. That decade saw the demolition of so many dignified old homes, a movement began to preserve Avery's as an example of its period. The support in a city-wide election permitted the Council to purchase it in 1974. Its restoration will perpetuate memories of one of the city's founders along with those of a talented architect. The remodeling under Thomas gave Avery the house he really needed in maturity, and the era of the 1890's will be featured in the interior.(46)

HARLAN THOMAS: ARTIST AND ARCHITECT

Harlan Thomas' life is a happy example of talent rising above adversity for the conditions in his early education hardly favored the development of artistic ability. The family came west from Iowa to Fort Collins when Thomas was nine years old. He later described the town of his youth:

Every other building on Main Street (College Avenue) was a saloon. Twice a year the cowpunchers from nearby roundups rode in on their broncos, filled up on firewater and took the town over. Each spring a hundred tie-choppers came out of winter quarters in the adjacent mountains, dressed in red flannels, and had their way. During these raids we boys remained snug in our shelters.

In September, 1886, Thomas enrolled in the Agricultural College, but even this opportunity ended, for his father, a Civil War veteran, died. At sixteen the boy became a carpenter's apprentice earning three dollars a week. The next year he moved to Denver to work as a carpenter. In 1889 he became a draughtsman with an architectural firm. In 1891 he designed the prize-winning menu card for the first annual dinner of the Colorado Association of Architects and was praised for "considerable ability as a colorist and draughtsman" in the office of A.M. Stuckert.(47)

Mechanic Shop designed by Harlan Thomas in 1891 still in use on campus.

Harlan Thomas in 1894 when he was graduating from the Agricultural College and beginning career as architect.

THE NEW MECHANIC SHOP AT THE STATE AGRICULTURAL COLLEGE.

This building is to be constructed of brick laid in red mortar, with red stone trimmings. The arched entrance
urel street will be decorated in carved stone and heavy panelled oak trimmings. The main addition is 32x70
The old building is that portion between the two front projections. Harlan Thomas is architect.

The desire to give the former local boy a chance must have favored his selection to design two buildings for the Agricultural College in 1891. He was only twenty-one when he drew plans for the Agricultural Hall and the Mechanic Shop. The latter, now called "Industrial Arts," on Laurel Avenue is still in use, the former demolished. He then re-entered the college in March, 1893, and had classes in the building he had designed! He received a degree in June, 1894, having taken a few miscellaneous courses in shop practice, elocution, mathematics, psychology, the U.S. Constitution, and the philosophy of history. In September 1896, he designed a third structure on the campus, the Chemistry Building.

While he worked on the Avery house addition, he continued his student life. In June, 1894, he debated the negative in the proposition: "Independent action is better than party allegiance." He courted Edith Partridge. Her father had been a minister in the First Presbyterian Church on Remington. The young couple started housekeeping in a cottage in Denver but soon went to Europe for sixteen months. Thomas described his study in Paris:

I was a member of an atelier whose patron was Marcel Peruse de Montclo, a Prix de Rome winner independent of the Ecole National des Beaux Arts.

Fort Collins was bursting with pride when he returned to Colorado in April, 1896. A reporter believed his designs would stand among the first in any part of the country. He was a logical choice for architect of the new Methodist church on College Avenue and Olive begun that summer. He worked out of Denver, getting commissions all over northern Colorado. In 1896 he built a school in Fort Morgan costing $25,000. The Fort Collins paper, announcing this, concluded: **State agricultural boys are always in the front rank of whatever profession they elect.**(48)

Although the building trade was recovering from depression he advanced rapidly and built a mansion in Montclair for his family home. This was ready in 1897. It was twice the size of the one he remodeled for Avery, the bank president! It is still standing today at the northeast corner of Olive and East Seventh, a dignified stone house, surrounded by an iron fence. The district is part of Greater Denver today.

Thomas was mayor of Montclair three times and a member of the school board. He kept up his Fort Collins' connections and served on the Board of Agriculture. During his term the college offered course work in architecture.

In 1903-04 he took his wife and small children around the world, spending six months in Japan. There he collected Japanese prints. In 1906 he moved to Seattle. He designed the Corner Public Market in 1912. This is part of Seattle's historical district under restoration today. He was head of the School of Architecture at the University of Washington from 1926 to 1940. After his retirement, he painted in water colors and held a one-man show at eighty-one. He died in 1953.

RESIDENCE J. R. ARTHUR MULBERRY ST. & PETERSON ST.

Arthur cabin south of Timnath used in early 1860's still standing incorporated in other building photo 1975.

FROM CABIN TO MANSION IN TWO DECADES

Some ex-freighters and Indian fighters becoming prosperous business men in the new city had a series of homes which reflected innovations in style currently popular and suited the different social life they later enjoyed. James Arthur lived south of Timnath in the 1860's. The cabin identified with the Arthur family still stands though moved from the river. His life style was considerably altered when he built his big two-story brick house at 335 E. Mulberry in 1882. The yard was enclosed with a handsome fence. The coach house in the back is now converted into a residence. There were only a few barns between his home and the Remington school which appeared in the background in an early photograph.

Arthur hired Denver architects, Nichols and Canman, and they promised to make his home one of the finest in Fort Collins. The cost was about $7,000. The style was called "Queen Anne." The hall windows were of frosted glass embellished with a smooth sunken flower design. On the right from the entrance hall were the parlor and diningroom, separated by sliding doors. Both of these rooms had "magnificent mantels of Tennessee marble faced with tiling." The staircase in the entrance hall had solid black walnut balusters, and was lighted by a tier of three windows, the upper half of each with variegated glass. These windows today with the afternoon sun pouring through them or interior lights shining out at night give an impressive beauty to the old home.

The rear of the first floor contained a bedroom, back staircase, kitchen, pantry, and store room. Upstairs there were

Arthur house 335 E. Mulberry built 1882 - early photograph still standing in 1975.

three spare chambers, a sewing room and four servant rooms. Gas fixtures were installed and a furnace in the basement heated each room through registers.

The Arthurs had no children, so they used this spacious home for friends and church affairs. In 1890 Arthur gave a euchre party for seventy men. After the games when Mrs. Arthur and her helpers were serving refreshments noises arose outside, bell, whistles and commotion. The guests saw many of their wives with signs: "Home Rule," "Give me back my Hubby!", "Innocences Abroad," "Where is my wandering boy tonight?", "Who'll take care of the baby now?" They all fled, escaping detection!

A more formal event was a reception for the Episcopal rector of St. Luke's and his wife in 1896. Rev. and Mrs. D.H. Clarkson received with Mr. and Mrs. Arthur. Mrs. Clarkson wore a white corded silken train trimmed with pearls, white gloves, white flowers in her hair, and carried a white fan. Mrs. Arthur wore pastels and Mr. Arthur a full dress suit.(49)

Abner Loomis lived in the '60's in Pleasant Valley, developed a ranch in Spring Canyon, and in the '70's was living in a frame house on Linden where he had many business interests. His house had been built by Dr. McClanahan in 1872. In 1879 he added on to it. By 1889 Linden was becoming commercial and the house was moved to Peterson Street. Later it may have been moved to 401 Smith where with its modern siding it hardly appears old.

Loomis bought a lot on the southwest corner of Remington

Abner Loomis' home c.1885 still standing at 405 Remington.

and Magnolia in 1880 but he probably did not build upon it until 1885. In November that year the grounds were fitted up for ornamentation and in December the cost of the house was listed at $12,000, the barn $3,000. It was all set for the marriage of his daughter, Lelia, to Thomas H. Robertson in June, 1888. This was a double wedding for A.W. Scott married Anna B. Maxwell in the same ceremony.

The double parlors were decorated with flowers, bouquets, festoons, and wreaths. A wedding bell of flowers hung in the arch between the two parlors. The brides wore neat and becoming travel costumes and the grooms regulation black.

In December, 1893, Lelia helped her mother give a surprise party for Loomis on the occasion of his sixty-fourth birthday. Fred Sherwood, George Robert Strauss, Stover, Arthur, Andrews, and Alford were among the guests who swapped stories of the early days while enjoying the elegant supper. Strauss still lived in his rustic cabin on the river and Sherwood had given up his simple frame house near Strauss only that year.

Hottel house 1882 on present site of Penney's store.

B. F. HOTTEL'S RESIDENCE.

In 1893, the Loomis daughter and her husband built their home at 420 W. Mountain, somewhat like her father's two-story brick. It had front and back stairways, sliding doors, and large verandas. The balcony over the entrance gave a fine view of the town. The Scotts who had shared the wedding eventually had a big two-story frame house with pleasant veranda and bay windows at 403 S. College where the United Bank is now located.

Benjamin Franklin Hottel, the miller, and his wife, lived on Remington in 1881 when their infant daughter died. In 1882 they completed an imposing home on College Avenue where Penney's store is now. That mansion awed Fort Collins for decades as it survived until the 1960's, staying in the Hottel family, while other big homes sold many times and proved impractical to maintain as one-family homes in a servant-less society.

A contemporary description called the Hottel house "bracketed Italian villa style." Richard Burke, local builder, designed it with double parlors on the left, a central hall, and sitting room and dining room on the right. Above these were four large chambers, trunk room, store rooms, bath room, wardrobe, dressing room, and closets. The back wing had kitchen, pantry, kitchen cellar, coal room, sink room, dish closets, and bedrooms for servants on the second floor.

Mrs. Arthur helped Mrs. Hottel entertain the cast of "The Victims" playing at the Opera House in 1887. She sponsored a "donkey social" for the ladies of the Episcopal church that year. In 1890 the home was the setting for a masked ball when guests appears as Helen of Troy, William Tell, Lafayette,

Linden and Willow: cabin on left used by both William and Frank Stover for early home.

William Stover's home on Willow near the mill; town in 1880's.

Later view of Stover's Willow Avenue house, typical frame home of early period.

The Stover family built three houses on Remington; all exist today. This photo shows the big brick house on the corner with one-story porch. William's son, Fred, used the other two houses.

Uncle Sam, John Bull, Kate Greenaway, Gypsy Queen, Spanish lady, and Polish King. One of the most elaborate affairs there was a reception in 1899 for the Columbian and Women's Clubs in honor of the state president of Women's Clubs. Ground pines and palms were scattered about the parlors. The arches were covered with green pines, with festoons attached to the center of a large Japanese umbrella over the dining room table and extending down to the four corners, softening the lights from wax tapers in the candelabra in the center. In the entrance hall fruit punch was served from a table "under a lovely Chinese umbrella."(50)

For a Women's Club evening with Dickens in April, 1899, the house was decorated with flags and buntings. The table was spread with the star-spangled banner, napkins matched, and the ice cream was in red, white, and blue. The need for meeting space outside homes was already evident for the ladies thanked Mr. C.R. Welch for providing club room space in his building during the year.

W.H. Miner's brick house at 503 Mathews looks neglected today but when he built it in 1884 it had a fine enclosed yard, shade trees, and barn. The "oculus" window resembling a porthole was a popular part of many Fort Collins homes. There were bays to the east on both first and second floor and a graceful protected corner entrance. Miner had made a fortune in sheep-ranching but liked having a town house. He was still living there in 1914 as a widower. Then he married his wife's sister, a friend for years. They went to Portland, Oregon, to the rose festival and promised to be back in Fort Collins "When they were good and ready."

The Stover brothers went through a log cabin stage using an old fort building but in the '70's advanced to comfortable homes on Willow. William's clapboard was very near the Hottel mill and showed in an early view of Fort Collins taken from the mill roof. The train for the mill ran right in front. It had bay windows on both the east and west. A neat fence enclosed the yard. Stover built a handsome two-story brick at 503 Remington in 1887 (now called "The Point") and wired it for electricity in anticipation of the city's installation planned for 1888. It had originally a one-story porch which revealed the fine design of stone at the windows better than the present two-story one.

In 1894 when Emma Stover was hostess for the Epworth League in the big house on Remington she arranged for Madam Topolambampo, the celebrated Mexican clairvoyant to entertain her guests.

Brick house built by Frank Stover August 1878 on site of log cabin Linden and Willow.

Frank Stover's home on Canyon built 1894.

Peter Anderson's town house 300 Howes photo 1975.

Montezuma Fuller's entry competition in Farm houses second prize Carpentry & Building, May, 1902.

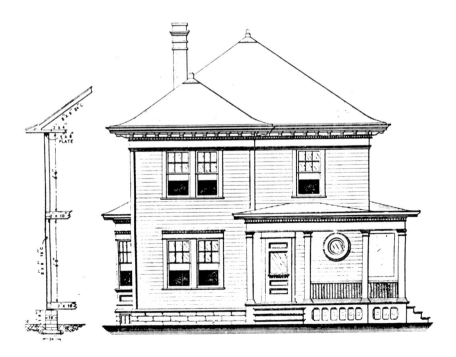

Mayor Frederick Baker's home 304 Mulberry built in 1895 photo 1975.

Andrews-Harris-McHugh home 202 Remington still standing photo 1894.

Frank Stover was close to his drug store on Linden and Jefferson when he lived on Linden and Willow in a cabin and then a neat brick house. But he was ready to enjoy more space in the new house on Canyon and Howes built for $2,000.00 in 1894. This had a large veranda and curved bay windows on both first and second floor.(51)

In 1866 Peter Anderson found a log cabin on his claim. He developed a farm near 9th and Vine and used the cabin for a decade before replacing it with the simple frame house still standing. In the 1900's he enjoyed a large two-story white clapboard house at 300 Howes. This resembles in so many details a prize-winning design of Montezuma Fuller, it seems likely Fuller was his builder.

Fred Baker had several houses, one in the country which he sold to Charles Andrews in 1891, a neat two-story frame at 103 Sherwood which he sold to Jesse Harris, and one he built at 304 Mulberry in 1895 when he was mayor. It cost $4500 and resembled the other imposing brick homes of that decade.

Charles Andrews hired Montezuma Fuller in 1889 to complete the house at 202 Remington. It cost $10,000 to finish the unique large stone house and barn. Andrews came to Fort Collins in 1872 and like Miner and Loomis, who was his partner for a while, made a fortune in ranching. He bought Henry Clay Peterson's home on the Poudre Canyon and had Shetland ponies there. He lived in the house on Remington only five years. In 1892 he hired a nineteen-year old English boy, Norman Fry, to tend the furnaces, milk the cow, and take care of the driving horses. Fry had "a nice private room with a stove in the barn and ate in the kitchen with the Swedish hired girl." He drove Mrs. Andrews about town in a small wagon with ponies. Jesse Harris bought the house in 1894 and

Charles B. Andrews home built 1902 on Canyon, present site of Rocky Mountain Bank; occupied by his widow and son, James, for a while, later moved to East Elizabeth. The Andrews fitted up a gymnasium in carriage house for James. photo on new site, 1975.

Fancher Sarchet - David Atkinson home 903 W. Mountain.

Dr. McHugh in 1899. He developed the barn into a private hospital for his patients. Mrs. McHugh, Auntie Stone's great niece, worked hard to improve the new Carnegie library. She had Christine Schlitt, a young German-Russian girl to help when her children were small. Christine, now Mrs. John Amen, sighed in 1974 recalling how many times the McHugh boys left crumbs in the pantry after raiding the cookie jar.(52)

The Bouton house, built in 1895, was clapboard, not brick or stone like the Loomis and Andrews house. Fortunately it was situated off the busier streets at 113 N. Sherwood, and the grounds around it and large shade trees make it a handsome place today. John C. Davis was the builder, and the cost $6,000. The stable was added in 1904. There was a separate walk-in cellar, probably for vegetable storage, not wine, because Judge Bouton was a strong supporter of the city ordinances for prohibition throughout the eighth district and was noted for his vigorous help to the anti-liquor cause. Fort Collins itself was dry the whole time the Boutons lived in the house.

Aureli Bouton gave a party in the family home in January, 1897, which featured a bean hunt. Beans had been hidden from garret to cellar. The young ladies were given little silk bags to collect the ones they found, and at ten o'clock the young men were auctioned off for partners, some bringing as high as eighty beans! The house was too large and expensive for the Boutons in their old age and they moved from it though they stayed in the neighborhood.

In the late 1890's and early 1900's the trend in big houses was for square massive structures planned without the romantic touches, verandas, turrets, and gables. The Welch house built in 1899 (later owned by the Evans family), the T.A. Gage house next door (later owned by Fred Stover) also built the same year, the Senator Drake house at 415 Remington in 1908 and the Sam Webster house at 301 E. Olive in 1913 represented the new style. The Drake house designed by Montezuma Fuller cost $18,000. When it was wrecked in 1963 the walls were found to be much thicker nearer the ground and at the foundation eight feet thick.

Of this group, only the Webster house still stands. Jack Goodrich, adapting it for his funeral parlor, encountered similar broad bases in the walls. The change to buff brick from red in the big houses was typical of the 1900's. The pattern showed in the college building as well where Old Main and its neighbors had been red, and Guggenheim buff.(53)

The home of Fancher Sarchet at 903 Mountain, now owned by David and Doris Atkinson, illustrates the square substantial look that the twentieth century preferred.

Welch, the merchant, was considering retirement at the time he built his palatial mansion and did not occupy it long. Evans, the next owner, entertained in state for a while, and Emil Lambotte, the young director of the boys's program at the Y.M.C.A., attended a dinner where a servant behind each guest assisted in serving. This house became a rooming house and a fraternity house before it was wrecked to make way for Safeway.

Mrs. L.R. Rhodes, once married to Joe Mason, advertised in January, 1903, for help in her spacious two-story brick home at 604 Remington: **Wanted—good girl to do general housework. Must be a good cook. Good wages and no washing.** Gracious living in the big homes depended on household servants who used the back stairways.

Artist's sketch of Walter DeWitt Taft home built 1876, drawn 1880's on Taft Hill Road.

STYLE AND COMFORT IN THE SMALL COTTAGE

Some of the pioneers did not succumb to the grand house syndrome as the years went by. Walter Taft built his farm home on Taft Hill Road in 1876 in two sections. A quaint drawing by an itinerant artist the family befriended in the 1880's show the early shape. By 1916 when the pioneers gathered there for a party it had a third wing. Jocelyn Bellairs bought it in 1922 and the half moon window, put in the middle section to give light in the attic, was called "Sylvia Bellairs' eyebrow."

A carpenter, Grant Ferguson, built a plain clapboard cottage at 401 Mathews in 1876. John E. Coy got this home in 1895 and in 1897 married Nina Ingersoll, daughter of the college president. She was interested in music and china painting and her piano and examples of her dishes are in the museum. He walked back and forth across the river to the old Coy farm where he worked with his father. He retired in 1928 and sold his interest in the farm but lived on for many years in his neat cottage.

Salty Joe McClelland with his red beard and fiery temper, turned from newspaper editing to fruit farming. His first Fort Collins home was a little house near Lincoln Park, then he built a simple clapboard farmhouse near Fossil Creek and got the orchard going in the 1870's. When he retired to live in town at 143 Remington he had a small well-built brick house with interesting stringcourse decoration and an arched splayed window in the front. Ansel Watrous lived in a small frame house at 400 Meldrum while he wrote his history and in 1917 at 218 Remington in an attractive one-story brick house still standing, much like Joe McClelland's last home.

Taft home photo 1975.

House at 401 Mathews built 1876 owned for many years by John E. Coy photo 1975.

THE FOSSIL CREEK FRUIT FARM, OWNED BY J. S. McCLELLAND.

Captain Josiah and Lucy McIntyre engaged Richard Burke to build their cozy home at 137 Mathews in 1879.(54) McIntyre became totally blind in 1885 because of unskillful care as a Confederate prisoner. He went to the University of Michigan in 1889 and received the first law degree in the United States given to a blind person. Both he and his wife were highly admired in Fort Collins and after his death in 1892 she lived on in the house till her death in 1940. Her epitaph at Grandview Cemetery reads: "The Last of the Crusaders: Faith, Hope, Love." One daughter, Loa, became a missionary to the Utes on the western slope and her Indian costume given by the tribe is one of the Pioneer Museum's treasures. One son, Clyde, wrote a history of the First Presbyterian church covering the days on Linden and Walnut, now a rare document for early Fort Collins.

George Bailey's house at 517 Howes had nine rooms. It was a local gray sandstone trimmed with red and cost a bit over $2,000 in 1888. Bailey was a cowboy and freighter, then studied law and began legal practice in 1885. He attained recognition in politics, lost an election to Mack Mills during the

McClelland's home 143 Remington in his retirement to town photo c.1908.

Ansel Watrous never had a famous home; he lived at 400 Meldrum when he worked on his famous book. All early local history research begins with that work. photo 1975.

House built by Andrew Jackson Hottel at 426 E. Oak; later owned by John Hoffman and his family; it has a bay window on one part balanced by porch on the other half of the facade, a popular arrangement in Fort Collins photo 1975.

John and Rose Lee Havener built the stone house at 147 N. Washington in 1897 when the area was all country and laid out a fruit farm around it photo 1975.

Populist wave in the '90's and was appointed to the state supreme court in 1905. This small but distinguished house remained his home throughout his career.

Andrew Jackson Hottel who worked in his brother's mill for a while built a house at 426 E. Oak. John Hoffman who first worked in Hottel's mill and then started a competing one, bought the house and his daughter, Lydia, was born there in 1893. After many years in other parts of the country she has returned with her husband to occupy this "period house" in her old age.

John Havener, a junior member in Peter Anderson's company selling agricultural machinery built a neat one-story five room stone cottage at 147 N. Washington in 1897. The interior had pantry, closets, and bathroom. The simple handsome "country" look of the exterior was popular throughout nineteenth-century America. The sunburst design over the door and the small window panes in the gable are interesting details. The Haveners bought ten acres from Loomis and Maxwell, and started an orchard of 1700 apple, plum, and cherry trees even before the house was finished.

Havener's first wife was Theodosia Van Brunt who died of typhoid in 1891. He married Rose Lee in December, 1894, at the home of her father, Dr. Ethan Allen Lee, on Oak Street. They sold the home in 1902 and since then tasteful additions to the rear have not disturbed the cottage appearance, and it has been maintained as an attractive home.

These are only a sample of the interesting "vernacular" architecture that developed in late nineteenth century Fort Collins. The carpenters consistently captured solar energy through the long-tested bay window, and many houses like William Stover's near the mill had two. Rarely were two identical houses built next to each other. Some little flourish made each distinctive. Especially in the treatment of the roof, there was room for originality. The simple gable of the '60's and early '70's gave way to hip, mansard, and gambrel with variations and combinations giving light and ventilation to attic space in one-story or one and a half-story homes. Porches provided the owners with protected areas in which to sit and do quiet chores while enjoying passersby. These disappeared in the construction of the 1920's when paved streets and whizzing automobiles made them less attractive.

Often a kind of balance was achieved by having a bay on one side of the front facade and a porch on the other. Varied arrangements and patterns in shingles in the gables combined with clapboard or brick walls added individuality.

The lots were long and narrow, reducing the upkeep and expense for watering lawns in an arid region and giving the advantage of placing barns and outbuildings for animals as far as possible from the house and on the alleys. "Every man's house is his castle" ran the old adage and both carpenters and owners felt pride in these homes. The W. Robert Nickerson family restoring a house at 515 Mathews found a newly-minted coin, placed perhaps by the carpenter, dating every addition. Though disinterested landlords and students with their dogs have permitted much deterioration, there are many lovely cottages well maintained today. In June when the syringa, lilacs, and old-fashioned roses are in bloom they present the type of home many retired people prefer.

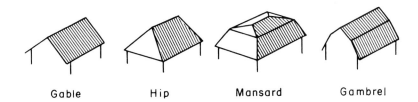

Gable   Hip   Mansard   Gambrel

A CARNEGIE LIBRARY IN LINCOLN PARK

While the men were busy raising sugar beets, building irrigation reservoirs, and feeding lambs, the ladies had leisure to study and improve their minds. The Women's Club, meeting at the Loomis home in November, 1893 had a German evening with reading and tableaux from Schiller and Goethe. In 1899 Mrs. Hottel entertained them for an evening of Dickens. In 1900 their theme was recent scientific discoveries. Captain Post was a guest speaker. He reviewed the history of astronomy from Galileo and demonstrated how to determine latitude and longitude with quadrant and chronometer.

The Columbian Club was equally industrious. In 1897 Lerah Stratton McHugh discussed the Bretons from 360 A.D. In 1899 they had papers on the English kings, George III, George IV, and William IV. In March, 1900 they were studying Marie Antoinette, the Reign of Terror, Charlotte Corday, and eighteenth century French philosophy.

There was no lack of enthusiasm, but there was a terrible shortage of books, and the club ladies sparked the movement for getting a public library. It was a fortunate crisis, for a way to solve the problem was at hand. Andrew Carnegie had decided to make his special philanthropy helping establish public libraries. He began with a gift in 1881 to his birthplace in Scotland and experimented with giving large amounts and few buildings to big cities. Often these structures were community centers with auditoriums, gymnasiums, and swimming pools. Then he changed to a policy of funding libraries in small towns where books were the main emphasis. He brought James Bertram from Scotland to manage the new policy.

Mrs. Donald McLean, president of the Columbian Club, and wife of a Fort Collins doctor, wrote a request for aid in June, 1902. She received a promise of $10,000 in July, so rapidly that the library board with Mayor Frederick R. Baker, Ansel Watrous, and Lerah McHugh instructed the secretary to write for verification. "Is this authentic and is the money available now?" wrote Mary Kilgore.

Carnegie and Bertram had set up simple requirements. They would help towns of over one thousand population who had a good site, an annual maintenance pledge in tax support and city officials who favored the movement. The amount given was estimated on a ratio of $2.00 per resident. Mrs. McLean gave 6,000 for her estimate of the population, the census of 1900 had 3,000. Thus a grant of $10,000 was generous.

Other nearby towns were making the similar appeal. Grand Junction received a grant in 1897, Canon City in 1901, Denver and Pueblo in 1902, and Laramie and Colorado Springs about the same time as Fort Collins. Boulder, Longmont and Loveland got theirs a few years later.(55)

Many towns needed a hundred letters to complete their arrangement with Bertram. The average was thirty. Fort Collins was awarded the initial grant with five. Mrs. McLean's appeal stressed nine churches, no saloons, five hundred students at the Agricultural College, and new families coming to very humble homes because of the sugar beet and brick factories.

Walter Sheppard at the **Fort Collins Express** wrote a sensible letter with a summary of the local situation. He gave New York references, noted his own graduation from Yale, and said:

The chief industries are farming and stock raising. There are no very wealthy people. The few who have a competence acquired it laboriously from the farm or ranch and are not the people to found libraries...The simple truth is that the average town in the West needs and actually appreciates a library more than the average town of the same size in the East.

Later Carnegie and Bertram developed a guide for architects on library-building but in 1902 each little town was on its own for the planning. It took so long that Fort Collins had a new mayor, Dr. P.J. McHugh, and the city council decided to ask for $5,000 more and promised to increase its maintenance allowance. Mrs. McLean wrote again and the gift was raised to $12,500. Again the Board was amazed and insisted on confirmation beyond the evidence of Mrs. McLean's answer from Bertram. Her opinion of the Board was rather scorching:

The fact is that we have a lot of old women on the board, some wearing pantaloons, some petticoats and they seem unable to comprehend anything and as I am anxious to see the building complete, I write even while I consider it a piece of foolishness.

The site in the park facing Mathews was part of the original city plan, for that land was city-owned. Mayor Baker arranged for purchase of the part fronting on Peterson increasing the public square to the whole block. Avery, Gage, C.R. Welch, Hottel, N.C. Warren, Alexander Ault, and others petitioned to have the building placed in the center of the Mathews street land, not on the corner as first considered, so it would have lawn and trees on every side. The OTA Club with Anna Coy, Ada Ault, Mildred Seckner, and Lura Miner

327 E. Oak opposite Lincoln Park 1880's owned at one time by James Andrews, but not his residence photo 1975.

322 E. Oak red brick house designed by Fuller, built 1893; occupied by Robert James Andrews after 1906 for many years, then his nephew, James who had an electric elevator to avoid use of stairs.

helped on the project too. Albert Bryan, a Denver architect who had moved to Fort Collins for a while, designed it. The cornerstone was laid November 14, 1903. None of the pictures of the exterior were taken to show the roof clearly, but there must have been a dome, so characteristic of Carnegie libraries. In 1932 the city hired Orton Davis, contractor, to remove the domed ceiling, and rebuild and replaster that section to conform with the other ceilings.

There were many defects in the design which became apparent as the years went by. In 1917 the Board appealed to Carnegie and Bertram for remodeling help. Bertram replied that their budget estimate if the city had 12,000 people, should cover a whole building, not just an addition, according to his scale. They had less than 9000. Elfreda Stebbins wrote in 1917:

No one knows better than we that some space in the present building has been put where it can not be used. Toilets were not put in the basement because the only sewer connection was too high.

Bertram was unsympathetic and felt the city itself must rectify the problems.

By 1936 the staff groaned under the inefficient arrange-

The basement of the remodeled public library became a city auditorium in March, 1939. Individuals and clubs contributed funds for furniture.

Children enjoyed the space formerly used as auditorium as the library adapted to different needs. April 19, 1967.

The biography of George Buss, soldier at Camp Collins, was part of the treasured history copied by modern machine at the Public Library, December 19, 1972.

ments. They needed more room, office quarters, study group space, and public toilets. There was no separate coal bin. "Coal is everywhere it should not be." They needed a new furnace. By this time there was also widespread desire that the library fill other needs for the community. It could have an auditorium and be more comfortable as a center for club study. Under the financial arrangements with federal aid through the Works Progress Administration this was secured.

The club ladies again worked hard. The Women's Club under the leadership of Cora Gibson gave $1,000. The Elks Club, the Pioneer Club, the Business and Professional Women all contributed. A long list of private individuals gave chairs for the auditorium. The WPA library consultant spoke at the dedication on March 29, 1939.

As the years went by the children's needs gradually crowded out the auditorium. The library continued to give gracious and intensely personal service to the many users while the population grew. When copying machines were made a useful tool, one of these was installed. Everyone expected the library to be richer than any other area in reading matter on the city's own history and the clipping files were worn from their use by school children. The American Association of University Women initiated a study of the history of the Cache la Poudre which was covered in film, and continued its historical work by copying many of the sketches of pioneers. The building, planned for 3,000 people, enlarged for 12,000, was serving 65,000 in 1975.

A NATIONAL FOREST AND A NATIONAL PARK JUST OVER THE HOGBACKS

The advantages of having a national forest within a half hour's drive from the city seem so obvious today that it is difficult to visualize the violence of early opposition to such a recreational wonderland. The formation of the Roosevelt National Forest was bitterly fought both in the town and county. Only the steady support of thoughtful, far-seeing leaders made it a political reality.

One of these leaders was R.Q. Tenney. His Civil War uniform with its eighteen handmade buttonholes is one of the treasures of the Pioneer Museum. Tenney's surveying instruments are at the Museum too. He had worn the uniform when he shared Grant's victory at Appomattox. The surveying tools symbolize a more peaceful victory in Tenney's life, the creation of a national forest along the Cache la Poudre.

In shade near top of photo is bridge on Flowers wagon Road in the Roosevelt National Forest photo c.1915.

Hazards of mountain driving along the Poudre, Roy Portner checked his car after the drive photo 1926.

The system of national forest reserves was devised in 1890 and the first one was officially established by President Benjamin Harrison at that time. Just one year later, R.Q. Tenney and John G. Coy circulated a petition in Fort Collins to have the three tributaries of the South Platte included in a reserve to protect the watershed. Coy and Tenney were charter members of the Larimer County Stockgrowers Association and they realized that their industry depended on water. In 1893 the State Forestry Association forwarded the petition to the president. Tenney used his surveying equipment and often guided inspectors during the next ten years while the project was under investigation. In 1898 a public meeting in Fort Collins favored the proposition. Peter Anderson and N.C. Alford added their endorsements.

The opposition then gathered 208 names on a counter-petition. Even Ansel Watrous questioned the need of such a reserve. He was a Democrat and the forest reserves had become part of Roosevelt's conservation policy in the early 1900's. Regardless of these protests, Roosevelt set aside the reserve in July, 1902. L.G. Carpenter, an irrigation expert at the Agricultural College, supported Coy and Tenney. Their intelligent leadership was of primary importance in the crucial decade while the land was still in public ownership.

Fort Collins, like Denver, is almost a "Mile High City." The foothills which rise immediately west of the city are called "hogbacks" because of their long, crested ridges. The forests begin here and grow in the area of rising altitude until the two mile mark is reached. Thus, as an early dean of forestry at the college put it, Colorado's forests are "in the second mile up." Above that the trees gradually give way to a treeless tundra.

The mountain forests were a great source of pleasure for the early settlers. Some camped, like Auntie Stone; some stayed at Rustic Lodge, built in 1880; others enjoyed Campton's Resort at Cherokee Park which was built in 1890. Another choice was Zimmerman's Keystone Hotel, built in 1896. While campers and fishermen explored the wilderness and found a cool retreat in time of summer heat, the ranchers and irrigation experts realized the harm sawmills could do to the watershed.

The Roosevelt Forest went through many changes in name, in administration headquarters, and in its boundaries during the years after the reserve was set aside. In 1905 it was part of the Medicine Bow Forest. In 1910 Colorado National Forest became the official name. Finally in 1932 it received the name of the president who had bravely established it against much local and state opposition.

The headquarters had been in Wyoming, then in Estes Park, but after 1908 Fort Collins became the permanent site. Space was allotted in the new Federal Building in 1911. As the staff grew, other quarters were found; the construction of a second Federal Building in 1972 brought it to that building. Tenney's pride in the Forest as a treasure for posterity led him to deposit the notes on its history with a forestry professor at the college just before his death in 1932.(56)

H.N. Wheeler was one of the early directors of the Roosevelt. He left Fort Collins occasionally to lecture in various parts of the country to win public support for the movement. One of the slides he liked to show was a photograph of the bridge over the Big South Fork of the Poudre near Peterson Lake in 1915. This bridge was on the trail Jacob Flowers had opened in 1879. The Flowers Road served the forest rangers long into the twentieth century and parts of it are in use today.

Another who knew the Forest as thoroughly as the rangers was Roy Portner. He roamed through the mountains searching for reservoir sites and then building on them. One reservoir south of town was named for him and his name was unofficially given to an area along the Poudre canyon because of an accident there on June 11, 1926. Portner was riding in a car with two others just west of the point where the Little South joins the main river. The car missed a curve, shot into the high waters, and was caught upside down on a rock in the raging torrent. The one occupant who could swim had just received his salary from Portner. He chose to swim downstream after his billfold before rescuing the other passengers. They clung to the wheels as he left them! The three men did get to shore safely, billfold and all, but word of the accident spread to Fort Collins rapidly and with embellishments. The first story Portner's wife heard was that he had drowned. However safe and dry, he returned to the site of the near-catastrophe for the photograph later in the day. Many other mountainous areas have their "Lovers' Leap" but the Roosevelt has "Portner's Leap."

There were many users of the Forest besides those on holiday. Students from the forestry school used the area around Pingree Park as a laboratory after 1915. Ranchers had grazing permits for stock and after 1911 reluctantly paid fees for each animal. The right to charge for stock on public lands was upheld in a court decision involving a national forest elsewhere in Colorado. It was a blow to Larimer County ranchers. Clarence Currie threatened to shoot R.C. McConnell, local ranger, if he came near his ranch but later he mellowed and invited him to dinner.

The necessity for regulation was eventually accepted. Currie and J. Arthur Sloan were among the ranchers who cooperated with the Forest Service and the Agricultural College in grazing studies in the 1950's. The whole program today developed from the battle for the general welfare as phrased by the little petition of Tenney and Coy back in 1891.

Another concept of the value of the mountains required special attention. While the Forest Service coordinated the multiple uses of the forested areas, protecting the tundra involved specialized knowledge of quite another type. Training in the field of recreation was needed to protect the people who chose to explore the high country. Yellowstone National Park was established in 1872 to preserve its wilderness character for the enjoyment, education, and inspiration of all people. This established a pattern appropriate for Long's Peak and the recreational sites around it.

The area became more accessible as the twentieth century opened. Several Fort Collins residents helped in the development. W.H. Schureman, Presbyterian missionary, Myron Akin, and E.J. Gregory began a summer resort for Presbyterians at Glen Haven in 1903. That same year Frank Stover prodded the county to complete a good road between Loveland and Estes Park. Added to the work of local people was the ingenuity of a newcomer, F.O. Stanley. He opened his hotel in 1909 and invented a car, the Stanley Steamer, to transport guests from the railroad in Loveland to the hotel.

Enos Mills, third from left, with Fancher Sarchet fifth, and families, Long's Peak Inn in background, summer, 1918.

The greatest promoter of all was Enos Mills who settled in Estes Park in 1886. He bought Long's Peak Inn in 1902 and quickly rebuilt it after a fire in 1906. He climbed Long's Peak two hundred and fifty times.(57) His guiding, lecturing, and writing won friends for the area. His campaign for the creation of a national park succeeded in 1915. He posed for a photograph with Fancher Sarchet and his family in 1918 when they visited the Inn.

The improved roads and growing throngs of people visiting the Park have added to the awesome responsibility of the federal employees and the local people. The number of visitors in 1974, two and a half million, exceeded the total visiting Yellowstone. Finishing Fall River Road in 1920 was the first big engineering triumph. Trail Ridge Road, opened in 1932, made accessible a height of 11,796 feet by car. Climbers scale Long's Peak which rises to 14,256 feet.

The fact that plants, animals, and climate change as man moves north from the equator is observed so gradually as people travel north, it may lose its impact. Going up a mountain provides the same experience but the transition is so rapid awareness of the contrasts in geography is inescapable. People in Fort Collins are privileged to go to the Arctic and return in one day every summer and most of them do so. There they can see the exquisite dwarf flowers of the tundra. Some are short-stemmed and grow in a carpet form. The fairy primrose, Alpine forgetmenots, dwarf sunflower, and Arctic gentian resemble larger forms found at lower altitudes. They are so tiny, people kneel to see them and the study is dubbed "belly botany." These plants survive the low temperatures, storms, and winds of winter but are threatened by the feet of tourists in summer.

It is part of Fort Collins' responsibility to support a program which preserves the wilderness in this unique area from exploitation by short term commercial gains. Mills got the Park started. Later generations must maintain it.

THE AUTOMOBILE AGE

The purchase of an automobile was the most revolutionary change that an individual could make in his life style in the early 1900's. Larimer County judge, J. Mack Mills, read the literature about horseless carriages and though he had never seen one, he audaciously took the train to Denver, shopped for two hours, got a little instruction from the salesman, spent $700.00 for a 1902 black Oldsmobile, and drove it home. It was seventy-five miles by wagon road from Denver, and it had been raining the previous night. His daughter, Freda Mills Hubbell, recalled the wild excitement of his arrival:

By nightfall there was standing in our driveway a mud statue that looked like a man sitting in a horseless carriage.

The Mills family always carried a bucket in the car to get water for the radiator. When they went to crank the motor, they were taught to avoid entangling their long watch chains on the crank.

Advertisement for Maxwell automobiles, Fort Collins Express, March 11, 1908, p.2 depicted streetcar, horses, and cars. Doctors, veterinarian, butcher, rancher, and photographer were among the proud owners.

B.B. Marshall, the photographer, had his 1902 Cadillac in the group picture and also snapped individually.

In July, 1906, the news was that Dr. McHugh had been seen on Mountain Avenue serving as chauffeur in a big automobile, the property of an agent who was beside him. This looks as though the doctor is thinking of owning a buzz wagon which he could no doubt use to the best of advantage.

In a photograph advertising Maxwell automobiles in the *Express* in March, 1908, car owners had their vehicles lined up across College Avenue south of Mountain. Some of the individuals identified included Dr. McCarroll, the veterinarian, Dr. Quick, and Dr. Killgore, physicians, Allen Greenacre, former instructor in mechanical engineering at the college and rancher, Frederick Schroder, a butcher and livestock feeder, and

Bradley and B.B. Marshall, photographers. Marshall arranged for a special photograph of his car which showed the luxurious upholstery on the bucket seats to advantage. The group photograph included also the street car, new that year, and several teams with wagons hitched to posts along the avenue in the background.

No wonder hats for the ladies had to be modified. Ones with voluminous veils were recommended in the **Courier** in 1906:

The new small sailor is not a bad motor hat if it is trimmed in ribbon and wings...and is fitted comfortable to the head by a cleverly adjusted bandeau. Despite its coquettish tip to the left, it has not brim enough to be unmanageable, and with plenty of hat pins it can be made very secure.

There was a special Mary Pickford auto cap named for the popular movie star available for the ladies for forty-nine cents in 1915.

The automobile line to the Cherokee Park Dude ranch in 1909 helped vacationers. A twelve passenger Rapid car with twenty-four horse power covered the forty miles to Campton's resort in three and one-half hours while the stage had taken all day. "It will climb hills and skim through the glades." Cas Zimmerman ran Stanley Steamers up the Livermore road to another hotel in 1912. He changed to a team for descending Pingree Hill and going farther west. Gardner I. Cushing, clerk of county court, was arrested in April, 1915, for driving to the court house at a speed of more than twelve miles per hour. He modestly admitted that his vehicle was capable of even more speed.

With private individuals reporting so favorably on the new invention, the city council considered updating the fire department in 1912. The White Auto Company of Cleveland brought Cripple Creek's new auto fire truck down for a demonstration. Unfortunately it went too fast, and the councilmen, following in another car, did not witness the whole event because the clouds of dust prevented observation.

Judge Mills believed that anyone who could start and stop a car could drive it, and he initiated his daughter, Jessie, into the problems of traffic by jumping into the back seat and telling her to drive home. They passed by the Post Office then on Linden, and encountered a street carnival. She had to maneuver the car around the merry-go-round, shooting gallery, and guy ropes of tents pitched in the middle of the street. She never found any pleasure in driving a car after her first effort.(58)

Most people preferred a better trained approach. In 1909 the Young Men's Christian Association gave a special course in use of autos, having an instructor come from Denver two evenings and one day. In 1916 the Agricultural College scheduled a summer class on autos and tractors. Old livery stables were converted into garages. In 1917 the council passed an ordinance requiring drivers to be licensed.

Somehow the friendly concern for both neighbors and strangers which typified the little western town was kept alive even when the population grew. Construction of a road up the Poudre Canyon was an example. In 1914 the way into the mountains was still by the route up Rist Canyon which the soldiers at the fort had first used. There was a second route farther north by way of Livermore and the Red Feather Lakes Road, then dropping south to the Poudre. Now with the automobile and the advance in technical knowledge on road-building that accompanied the invention, construction began on a highway following the main branch of the river. By October, 1914, the road had reached Hewlett's Gulch. This was celebrated by a public picnic. Auto owners were asked to register and provide rides. F.C. Avery and others arranged for two hundred pounds of fried chicken. People were asked to bring well-filled baskets with sandwiches, cake, and doughnuts, enough for themselves and a few strangers. A hundred autos with six hundred happy people picnicked at Farrell's grove.

This was only the beginning of even more wonders to unfold. The same year college boy, George T. Avery, wrote home from Harvard describing his impressions of Cambridge:

If these people lived in Fort Collins, Mayor Clammer would have half of them in jail by night for auto speeding.... The splendid paving is a temptation. The surface is smooth but not slippery, and it is as noiseless as rubber.

It was just six months later, June, 1915 when petitions were circulating among downtown merchants to ask for two blocks of paving. C.G. Buckingham signed and was congratulated for his cooperation since he did not even live in the town. Avery was too ill to be concerned. Some business men opposed it, fearing higher taxes. Negotiations by the city on the contract required a lot of haggling and the season was too far advanced to chance the work that year. Finally by October, 1916, the first pavement was a reality and the celebration far outshone the arrival of the railroad in 1877 for there were more people and much more town spirit.

There were floats of Columbus, Plymouth Rock, and Franklin's press. The precious area was roped off for the dance. Cornmeal and soapstone powder were used on the pavement. Sugar beet wagons were not allowed to cross it. The Foltz boys' band played. Mayor Clammer sat on a throne. People jostled against the roped-off area with baby buggies. Women fainted. Everyone had a marvelous time.(59)

The times were indeed changing, but the merchants did not want things to go too fast. A headline, "Hitching Posts must go," ran in the **Courier** in 1916. The shop keepers resented the new ordinance removing the posts from paved streets. They felt the farmers must be allowed to hitch at the curb even at the hazard of a little manure on the precious stretch of pavement. Though some were taken away, old Fort Collins is dotted here and there still with hitching posts. Hitching rings in the curb on College Avenue, south of Laurel, spaced about the same as the parking meters, are relics of the older era.

A FEDERAL BUILDING IN FORT COLLINS

When Joseph Mason applied to the federal government for a post office to be located in his sutler's store in June, 1865, he noted that the nearest post office was on the Big Thompson, twenty miles south. Fort Halleck, one hundred and thirty-five miles to the north, also had postal facilities. Holladay's Overland Mail Stage arrived in Camp Collins daily. In support of his request Mason drew a map showing the highway through the town along the river on the south side to a point east of modern Shields and north of Vine, where it crossed the river and continued northwest. As sutler, Mason was already handling the mail dropped by the stage for the soldiers.

Billy Patterson succeeded Mason in the job. The office moved across Linden to Whedbee and McClanahan's drugstore when McClanahan took over the work. The post office moved with the drugstore to Mountain and College in 1873. For many years the job of postmaster was a part-time one combined with other work and done wherever the man had his office. When Joseph McClelland was postmaster in 1879 he used the office of his newspaper, the **Express**.

Such appointments were part of the spoils system and the incumbent's political views reflected those of the victorious party in the national elections, though few comments on this surfaced in the papers of the day. In December, 1884, the

Federal Building under construction 1912; tower of Hottel home on left.

Interior Federal Building post office workers c.1912.

Architectural designs prepared for Federal Building.

Courier mentioned two would-be postmasters, Ansel Watrous and Charles Evans. If Evans received the job he promised to build a two-story brick building on Linden on the site of the meat market a few doors below the existing post office. However, Watrous was appointed.

The period of wandering ended and the post office became stationary for sixty years with the construction of a Federal Building at Oak and College. It was completed in 1912. The land cost $12,000 and the building almost $88,000 for its 19,825 square feet of floor space. The stonework, Alabama marble, and sculptured designs were worked out with tremendous care and shipped in for placement in the new structure. With a red tile roof and the facade of an Italian Renaissance palace, it did not really match the rest of College Avenue, but it weathered well and gave a sense of prosperity to the business district. The quality of workmanship impressed residents as they watched it being assembled. It was a good period for building in Fort Collins. The big houses which rose then were built to endure too, though many of them have since been razed.

The post office building was outgrown and finally offered

for sale in 1972. Occasionally groups have toured it to consider its potential uses because of its prime location in the core of the city. All are intrigued with one architectural feature, the provision of an observation place from which employees could be watched at work without being aware of the surveillance. Such arrangements are common to all post offices, and are known to regular employees. Outsiders, however, are startled at this cryptic method of enforcing honesty.

The second Federal Building completed in 1972 cost $3,500,000 and provided 65,000 square feet of usable space. Its somber gray appearance, while functional, has been a disappointment to residents. In 1911 federal buildings were not necessarily expected to fit in with the town, but were intended to bring proper style to it. Since then a preference for use of native materials whenever possible has favored local variation. New federal buildings in Wyoming, the state buildings on the university campus here in Fort Collins, and the new courthouse have used native stone. The practice has produced warm, cheerful structures which relate to the Rockies. The present post office does not.(60)

Night Scenes in Fort Collins, Colo.

THE SMALLEST AMERICAN TOWN WITH A
STREETCAR SYSTEM

Fort Collins was essentially still a "walking city" in the early 1900's and had no need for mass transit. Fortunately before the city expanded and could use a streetcar, the experimental stages in developing this facility were over. Denver had horse-drawn cars in 1871. San Francisco's cable car began in 1872. During the next thirty years many improvements were designed, and by the turn of the century, street cars were the mark of a successful city. The Colorado and Southern Railroad regarded the field of local transportation in towns served by its steam lines as an area for expansion. The Denver and Interurban Railroad, a subsidiary of the Colorado and Southern, was developed as part of a unified transportation system. When this company applied to the city council for a franchise in 1906, few people had automobiles and some never bought them, becoming instead devoted customers of the new trolley.

The decision to allow the company to come in was momentous. August Rohling, Peter Anderson, Fred Stover, Thomas Quinn, and F.N.B. Scott favored it and swung the vote. Among the dissenting voters on council were Chris Philippi, harness maker, and A.A. Edwards, irrigation expert.

During the forty-three years that street cars operated, the town grew only from 8,000 to 14,000. It was still even in 1951 a small town, and the street car was a leveling popular factor that bound the town together. It was never simply mass transit like the subway or elevated in New York or Chicago, but a cozy hometown affair, part of the local spirit.

The company built a car barn and power house on Howes and Cherry in July, 1907. In December the paper praised the Denver and Interurban for employing only local men, adding twenty substantial citizens, owning their own homes and rearing families in Fort Collins. By Jan. 1, 1908 the inauguration was reported as having gone without a hitch. One trolley party had been held. Cars could be chartered at low rates and decorated for the purpose.

When the line was extended past the sugar factory to the Lindenmeier farm, it provided transportation to two big recreational areas, Sheldon or City Park and Lindenmeier Lake. At the latter there were boats, picnic areas, and many forms of entertainment. In April, 1915, the company provided twenty minute service on Sunday afternoons to get people to the ball games.

In 1924 Superintendent W.A. Johnson arranged a schedule with one car every ten minutes on Sunday morning to get people to church. Since most of the churches were on or very close to College or Mountain Avenues, part of the street car route, this was a tremendous convenience. In 1923 there was a ten minute street car service on Saturday and Monday just before Christmas to aid holiday shoppers and they could see the municipal Christmas tree at College and Laporte as part of the fun. Downtown merchants arranged free street car days to entice customers to big sales in July, 1932. Pulling the connection from the overhead wire was an easy trick to tantalize the conductor-motorman and many boys considered it a prank to do once as part of growing up - particularly in the area of St. Joseph's church.

The service was provided with relatively few accidents or upsets. Two mules were killed by a street car in 1912. The great blizzard of 1913 left one car stranded on Whedbee. Lydia Schlitt Weber, daughter of German-Russian immigrant, Peter Schlitt, posed for her picture in front of it. On August 21, 1915, the car operated by William E. Vandewark collided with a heavy steel bucket of a crane of the Sugar Company. He was severely injured and a beet worker, Peter Schmeidner, also was a casualty, but no lives were lost.

Beloved though the street car was, running it at a profit was not easy. The entire railroad system in the United States was shaken up by nationalization during World War I under President Wilson. The company was in receivership in 1918 and service ended in July. The city had the opportunity of buying the operation at $75,000. The original cost was $315,000, but the company had been losing money for some years.

Everyone loved the street cars but could the city afford them? "What will you have, a city or an old-fashioned country town?" appealed the supporters. A special election in 1919 ran 940 in favor of purchase, and 32 opposed. So the city took over the task, built a new car barn which is standing today.

The **Saturday Evening Post** featured Fort Collins street cars in an article in 1947. It praised "the smallest town in the United States to boast a trolley system," the cheapest fare—five cents, and "operation at a profit." Careful statistical study might contradict the last point for such figures depend on juggling questions of maintenance and replacement. Receipts in November, 1929 showed $1,261.03 and disbursements, $1,931.29. In November, 1930, the figures ran: Receipts, $829.10, disbursements, $1,365.56. In 1951 the loss was running $1,200.00 a month.(61)

In 1950 there were 1677 voters who still wished the cars to run as a subsidized service, 880 for abandoning them. Fiscal problems, not sentiment, led to the city's action. The last car ran on June 30, 1951. Fort Collins held out longer than any other city in Colorado. Denver had given up in 1950.

The story of Fort Collins street cars would be incomplete without a comment on the loyalty to the system of Nellie Landblom. She was an able mathematician, a Phi Beta Kappa from the University of Minnesota, and her home on Pearl Street near Mountain was so close to the street car route, that it was a part of her daily existence. She never owned a car. The conductor often jangled his bell on the outward run to City Park and she would be waiting to board as he headed east toward the business district. Once when she missed it and he went without her she waited till he made that trip again to catch the same man and reprimand him for such action. She felt that abandoning the street cars was a sinister plot of city officials. In her youth she was advised to wear a green visor to protect her eyes from the bright Colorado sunlight. She never yielded to the innovation of sun glasses. At eighty-six, in bed with a broken hip in January, 1972, and still wearing her green visor, she sat up and fumed angrily at the government which had parted with her treasured trolleys.

The cars on the different loops met at the intersection of College and Mountain, once the site of the horse-watering fountain. Then they took off on different routes on single tracks. It was a Toonerville Trolley system in the eyes of tourists and street car fans who came from elsewhere to view it. But probably no other service the city ever provided aroused such fond emotions.

FORT COLLINS' PART IN THE WILD WEST SHOW

BILLY PATTERSON

Arthur H. Patterson, called Billy by friends, was a freighter and Indian fighter who turned into a town builder and solid citizen of Fort Collins. In the '70's his influence was felt in building the town ditch, encouraging the Agricultural College by giving land for the campus, and planting trees along College Avenue to that site from the tiny town. In the '80's he participated actively in city and county government. He served as alderman in 1885 with James Evans, Bouton, Hottel, Arthur, and Alford. He supported the Democratic party. Though he was a respected leader in the town with other business men, he provided a special touch of glamor because of his early day friendship with Buffalo Bill Cody. His personal contacts with Cody continued throughout his life.

Patterson was born in Pennsylvania to a family that drifted westward. He went to grammar school in Cincinnati, and spent part of his childhood in Leavenworth, Kansas, where he met Cody. They were only sixteen when they moved west to

Billy Patterson's home in the 1870's 211 Myrtle photo 1975.

Denver. Patterson worked with mule trains and government freight and stage lines. He was a wagon master before coming to the Poudre Valley about 1866.

In 1870 he joined a punitive expedition against the Arapahoes around Lander, Wyoming, when Black Bear was killed and Chief Friday barely escaped. This was his last fling for, with his marriage to Alice Watrous in December, 1873, he settled down to the problems of building Fort Collins and making a living for his wife and six children. Their early home at 211 Myrtle, a building still standing, was then in the country and he gave eighty acres of his farm for the college. His early experiences with horses helped him operate the Grout Livery stable on Jefferson. In 1879 he had carriages from Tom Connelly's celebrated manufactory in Dubuque, Iowa. He sold feed and coal there too. The very first train arriving in Fort Collins in 1877 had three carloads of Rock Spring coal for Patterson. He sold the livery stable to Jesse Harris in 1880. On the site of the old fort hospital on the northeast corner of Jefferson and Pine, he built a big stone structure for his business enterprises.

In the early '80's the county had no official court house and Patterson was among those offering temporary solutions to this problem. In July, 1882, he proposed that the county rent the upper rooms for court rooms. They were spending $600.00 a year for space in the Opera House and elsewhere and incurring additional expense transporting prisoners to Golden. Apparently the plan was rejected for in December, 1882, he was

Patterson's warehouse on Jefferson 1880's.

Advertisement for model home in Loomis addition 1887; house purchased by Patterson.

Patterson's home 121 N. Grant now home of Don McMillen family; photo 1974.

using the building as a grain warehouse in partnership with H.B. Emigh. They built a street crossing over Jefferson to the **Courier** office on the other side.

In 1885 he urged the county to buy his building and postpone construction of a courthouse. It was described as two-story stone, 50 x 100 feet, with frontage on Jefferson. It was connected with the city waterworks. The roof was of iron. He even offered to buy it back in three years if the commissioners decided to go ahead with building plans.

The Pattersons must have lived in the area of the warehouse in the early '80's though Bill had built a home on Remington south of the school building in November, 1879. In 1881, when he was recovering from illness, he could watch the train on the new track near Jefferson from his home. In 1885 he added a new front piazza. There must have been great excitement when he purchased the exhibition home in the Abner Loomis Addition, a house still standing at 121 North Grant. The family moved in September, 1888 to this house "fitted with all modern conveniences." The change from the first to the second ward lost him his seat on the city council.(62)

There was short time to enjoy the new home before disaster hit. A fire destroyed the warehouse and contents in 1889. Patterson went to Salt Lake City and tried selling real estate with little success so he returned. His health was poor and he died on December 27, 1892, at forty-eight.

A happy thread in Patterson's life in the '80's was vicariously enjoying the triumphs his friend, Bill Cody, was then having in the show business. Buffalo Bill had finished his tenth season of stage melodrama in 1882 when he went to North Platte to organize a Fourth of July celebration. He expected one hundred cowboys to apply, and one thousand did. He insisted on authenticity in the exhibitions, getting a Deadwood stage coach from the manager of the Cheyenne and Black Hills line. In 1887 Cody was in London for Queen Victoria's Golden Jubilee. Four kings and the Prince of Wales rode in the Deadwood coach. In 1889 he was in Europe again. That decade was the golden era for the show.

News trickled back to Fort Collins of Cody's exploits. Patterson had an elk at the Grout stable in 1883 which he had captured for the show. In September, 1885 he got pictures of Sitting Bull and Cody. In 1887 there was a letter from London. Cody was concerned about Patterson's financial misfortunes and there was talk of hiring him to manage a game preserve somewhere in the Rockies or in northern Mexico. This remained one of Cody's dreams. In March, 1892, Patterson visited Cody in North Platte for two weeks.

Cody's loyalty to his friend led him to visit Fort Collins in July, 1915, and he scolded the oldtimers for their failure to commemorate the deeds of the pioneers like Patterson. On this trip Cody went about reviewing memories and sites important in the early days of the stage coach and the town. Just one year later, again in June, the pioneer societies responded to the challenge. The headline ran: "**Col. Cody's Admonition Made Good on Campus.**" They unveiled a commemorative stone near Old Main and the Jesse Harris fountain with Patterson's name heading the list. President Lory formally accepted it for the college and many grandchildren of early settlers assembled for the occasion. Cody died in 1917 so he had put in his support for this action just in time.

Stone commemorating land gift for college campus near Spruce Hall.

FRANK C. MILLER, JR.

Could Cody's mantle of glory as a showman descend to a native son of Fort Collins? Many of the personal friends of Frank C. Miller, Jr. believed so. Miller was born May 11, 1886, in the family home on Laurel and Mathews. His father was in the liquor business and served as alderman on the city council in the 1890's. The young boy grew up admiring Cody and copying many of his techniques when he began organizing his own shows in the 1900's. Miller's professional life developed around three areas: business, art and showmanship. His major business ventures included a department store, the Fair, in his father's old saloon on Linden, the Northern Garage at 100 Pine, converted from a livery stable and run by Miller intermittently from about 1917 to the late 1930's, and a dude ranch, known as "Trail's End," northwest of Livermore, which was his big interest from 1920 to 1940. He took painting seriously and hoped to make this more than a hobby, choosing as themes landscapes to catch the beauty of the west and episodes to illustrate its history.

His showmanship was evident when he displayed his tremendous skill as a crack shot. His marksmanship was developed by practice with cowboys as a child in a gallery below his father's saloon. By 1914 he was getting many summer engagements in rodeos, county fairs, and pioneer day parades and winter ones in vaudeville. He estimated that he gave 3500 performances.

Miller's business affiliations with the store and garage were interrupted by his travels and exhibitions to the detriment of his financial status. Running a store was much too

Northern Garage Filling Station is Pioneer in Opening New Field of Useful Work for Young Ladies

Site of Miller's ranch Trail's End photo May, 1971.

Frank C. Miller Jr. center of group below one of his paintings at Trail's End.

quiet a pursuit for the young man who loved the crowds and adulation he received for his marksmanship exploits. Even at the garage the gasoline he sold was called "sharpshooter" gas. When he bought Trail's End he hoped he had found a business where his special talents would enhance instead of handicap the venture.

The Union Pacific advertised "Trail's End" in a special pamphlet and noted that Frank and his wife could be coaxed to give performances for guests on weekends. He really loved wild animals and arranged cages and pastures for mule and Siberian deer, buffalo, bears, owls, eagles, hawks, skunks, wolves, coyotes, and porcupines. There were ponds for ducks and geese. The trout in the north fork of the Poudre responded to the feeding. He charged $25.00 a week for adults and took boys for periods of five weeks at $100.00.

Entertaining famous show people like Fred Stone and Will Rogers added glamor but was also expensive. The "mountain paradise in summer" meant plain hard work in winter. Frank was ill in Denver in 1927 and Peggy, his wife, tried to keep things going. She reported that they put up 122 cakes of ice 18 x 18 from the pond. They were feeding hay to the animals. She thought she had hired a good mechanic for the garage, and she was going to pay bills and continue with the old car. He must get well before coming back:

I have got my hands full without having to take care of you unless you are well enough to help me and don't think we don't want you but we do want you well. She was discouraged about some guests more interested in drinking than fishing. In fact, running a dude ranch was a strenuous undertaking.(63)

Frank had always needed a good business manager. Having never had one, Peggy found they needed a good lawyer to extricate them from financial entanglements. She looked for advice in Fort Collins and Denver. She wrote that she had heard one man described as "another Fancher Sarchet and he can see our side of the case." Depression days were bad, local bankers saw Miller as a delightful person but a poor risk. His loans from the Home Owners Loan Corporation helped only for a short time. Peggy sold five elk and three or four deer for meat by going to the Brown Palace, the Albany Hotel and the Denver's Tea room.

Frank had always been especially proud of "Uncle Sam," a bald eagle, saved on Armistice Day, November 11, 1918, from a coyote trap on one of the Folsom point sites north of Fort

Collins. Its head was completely white in 1921. The bird's photograph taken September 16, 1934, appeared in the **Denver Post** and national magazines. It died May 25, 1939, the day the Millers received the eviction notice. All the animals had to be disposed of or released, and residence at the ranch ended in 1940.

Frank's failure in the business world was softened by his local success as an artist. He told people he was at first influenced by a German commercial artist, Eisele, living in Denver around 1900. Eisele painted a western landscape for the walls of the new Northern Hotel and a scene of old Fort Collins, including Old Grout. Miller felt he could do better and he took a few lessons in Chicago though not at the Art Institute as later believed. The paintings he did of his ranch, of the Poudre canyon, and of scenes in Wyoming were admired by all his friends and are still sentimentally cherished locally today.

Frank's performances as a showman were the real joy of his life. One woman wrote "Cheyenne's Frontier Days will never be the same without Frank and his two bears riding in a car in the parade." The Irwin family were show people who developed the spectacle for Cheyenne and they hired Frank to demonstrate shooting. The Fort Collins paper noted

Frank and admirers with his famous coach.

Exhibition oxteam used at shows photographed 1904 College Avenue; Watrous illustrated his county history with the same team, p. 47.

Miller's vaudeville show c.1914.

that Frank was taking the bears to Laramie for a ride on the Ferris wheel. In later years he regaled audiences with tales of his experiences with shows. One role required him to be tied on top of his stage coach struggling and writhing when an Indian was to blow it up. The Indian whispered he didn't have a match!

Frank used a stage coach discarded by Buffalo Bill, and reputedly the same one that once carried Queen Victoria and other crowned heads of Europe. He often had a team of eight horses pulling it, as he shot and waved his hat from the front. Later it was placed on a motorized vehicle and arranged as a float and hauled about. Banners on the coach advertised Marlin Fire Arms and Peters' ammunition. The fun of such shows had been long appreciated in Fort Collins. In 1904 the **Larimer County Democrat** proposed that a park be developed north of the river for bronco busting and kindred sports. In October that year there was a wild west parade with cowboys, a pioneer stage coach, and a double ox team. The latter was one of the big attractions of Carnival Week at Prospect Park.

The rodeo grew out of everyday life on the ranches in pre-barbed wire days. A really good cowboy had to have an excellent horse and a knack with his rope. The most skillful competed with those from neighboring ranches with other ranch hands as audience. After 1900 the open range was modified by fencing and grazing leases, and the old skills were not quite so essential but handy to have and greatly admired. Gradually the idea of performing for city folks grew in popularity. Fort Collins was never a big center for such shows since it had to compete with Cheyenne's Frontier Days and the Denver Stockmen's Show. These two events were growing in importance and attracting talented performers from the whole west. Miller's scrapbook noted that the word was pronounced "rod-ee-o" in northern Colorado where they really rode 'em, and "Ro-day-o" in California with its more authentic Spanish accent.

Miller arranged a pioneer day for Fort Collins in 1921. The souvenir program listed the usual offering and guaranteed authenticity for rough and ready horsemanship, roping, and shooting. There was an Indian war dance with bona fide Indians and a "stage coach holdup with Spittin' Bill Davis, an original driver."

Miller's own part sometimes included throwing a can into the air and hitting it twelve times using a pump action twenty-two rifle. He could stand on a saddled horse, twirl a lariat with his right hand and shoot an aerial target with his left,

Ivy Baldwin, Miller's friend, dazzled crowds with his performance.

having the gun balanced on his left shoulder. He shot chalk from his wife's mouth at twenty-five feet with the sights of the rifle covered and gripping the rifle with just one hand. At the same instant he fired a revolver to break an egg resting twelve feet away on a vase. His friend, Ivy Baldwin, then seventy-two, walked a tight rope three hundred feet long stretched two hundred feet above the north fork of the Poudre at the ranch on July 4, 1934.

These deeds were illustrated by syndicated cartoonists, Ripley in "Believe It Or Not" and Hix in "Strange as It Seems."

Such spectacular offerings made the disappointments of the next decade even more poignant. He lost the ranch, his marriage broke up, and his adopted son, Teddy, was killed in Berlin in 1946. Miller had intended the old stage coach to be a precious heirloom for Teddy. In 1948 he gave it to the city as a memorial to his son. The Council accepted it. Miller's friends contributed money to cover it for display on LaPorte and College Avenues, labelling it "The Passing of the Old West." They clearly considered it more a memorial to Cody, Patterson, and Miller than to the son whose name was listed with the others lost in wars on a tablet nearby.

Miller was pleased and touched with the arrangements for the coach. When the structure was finished he invited some Sioux to stop here to see it. In Nebraska they were misdirected to Fort Morgan instead of Fort Collins and by the time they reached Longmont they were so furious they threatened to return home. Miller placated his old friends and they finally arrived to pose in front of the old coach in its new home.

In his last years, Miller's residence was the Linden Hotel near his father's old building. He died on November 21, 1953.

FANCHER SARCHET: TRIAL LAWYER

When a grade school teacher in Iowa received a paper from a pupil who signed his name "Fancher Sarchet," she thought he was deceiving her. She instructed him to write that name ten times on the blackboard as punishment. The boy responded by writing it once in large script covering the whole board! His name was unique and so was his personality.

Sarchet was born in 1879 and came to Denver in 1900. He became a lawyer through the nineteenth century system of apprenticeship under a practicing lawyer and a little night school study. E.A. Ballard, his mentor, had practiced law in Fort Collins from 1880 to 1896. After moving to Denver Ballard returned two months each year for spring and fall terms of court to "reap a little better than a modest harvest." In 1906 he retired to Fort Collins and persuaded his secretary, Sarchet, who had just passed the bar examinations to move with him.

Sarchet married Nellie Herring of Laporte in 1908. Her uncle recommended the young lawyer for deputy district attorney. Sarchet held this job the next seven years and developed an interest in criminal law and a confidence in his own ability in trials. He was a flamboyant character among the more conservative ranchers, businessmen, and the new crop of lawyers out of formal law schools.

One acquaintance described Sarchet as "a conscientious objector to the eighteenth amendment." He enthusiastically defended clients prosecuted for liquor offences. He considered the amendment ridiculous and the local sheriff corrupt.

The oil boom near Wellington in 1924 brought him much publicity and some ill feeling. J.J. Ver Straten refused a client of Sarchet's the right to redeem a mortgage on some property in the oil field area. Sarchet won the case in the higher courts. In September, 1927, a gunman shot Sarchet from a moving car. The wound cost him the sight in one eye. Sarchet apprehended his would-be assassin who was later convicted. Sarchet's accusation that Ver Straten had hired the man was not sustained by the court.

Sarchet was tremendously interested in the litigation with Wyoming over water rights. He went to Europe in 1929 with William Kelly, the famous Greeley lawyer, who was a specialist in that field. In the 1930's he and Albert Fischer, another water law expert, were office neighbors. Fischer's office was above the First National Bank then located on the southeast corner of Mountain and College. Sarchet's office was above the shop now used by an auto parts company.

There were three generations working together in Sarchet's office. His parents followed him west. His father became a justice of the peace and often sought his son's legal advice. Sarchet's own son, Clark, graduated from the Law School of the University of Colorado but was killed in an accident after only a short period of practice. Sarchet's daughter, Doris, became a legal secretary and worked in his office.

Sarchet analyzed the effect of women jurors on his cases. Though women could use the ballot after 1893 they were not allowed on juries in Colorado until 1945. Sarchet became head of the county bar association in 1940. In 1948 the **Rocky Mountain News** placed him in a Hall of Fame for criminal lawyers in the state.

Sarchet loved the drama of the trials and described his affection for the old-fashioned building: **"I have come to feel as much at home in the old courtroom as a Huckleberry Finn on the Mississippi River."** On April 1, 1957, he participated in the final session for the Eight Judicial District held in that courthouse. He died in 1960.(64)

Last session of court in the old courthouse, April, 1957.

W. CHARLES GRAVES:
DAIRYMAN FROM THE DEPRESSION

As Charlie Graves recalled his childhood on a ranch in Pleasant Valley north of Fort Collins in the early 1900's, he emphasized the family's interest in raising Hereford cattle. His father had managed a grocery store in southern Illinois but was attracted to Colorado in 1898. He hayed one summer in North Park, then bought land near Rist canyon.

Charlie was eight when the flood of 1904 hit the valley. The bridges on the Poudre were all swinging bridges—just planks wired to a couple of cables—so the flood took them all. Charlie and his father wanted to shop in Laporte. They took their team up Bingham Hill into Fort Collins to use the Lincoln Street bridge at Hottel's mill, then went on the north side to Laporte. The return trip took the same route and the errand required an entire day.

The family enjoyed watching the college students on their May Day outings. The students came by train, then walked the last part of the way through the Graves' ranch carrying ice cream freezers to their favorite picnic site at Lew Stone Falls. Charlie himself became a college student in 1913.

Graves thought of himself as a cattleman. He wore a big western hat and had his special saddle. He didn't really like boots however; he tried one pair and never bought another. He didn't plan to become a dairyman. He thought that occupation degrading, but his practical nature accepted a change in viewpoint during the depression.

The Graves had hospital and doctor bills for a new baby and no money even for groceries. Elihu Ellis, running the Westside Grocery, suggested an exchange of cream for groceries. They sold him twelve bottles at fifteen cents a pint; these retailed for twenty. All were gone by noon of the delivery day. They found a second customer, "Chink's little place north of the courthouse." This brought a query from Dr. Glover of the veterinary college who was city inspector. Even in 1971, W.C. Graves remembered the exchange between the two men vividly. He was asked: "Charlie, I understand you are 'bootlegging' milk in town. Do you want in or out?" He answered: "Well, I'm eating better than I've eaten for a long time, I guess I'll just stay in."

Glover promised to come out to check his equipment and Graves hesitated. "All I have is a bucket, stool, strainer, and a funnel." Glover replied that that was about all anybody had, so he "came out and inspected the place and offered to be the first customer. He bought from us as long as he lived and his widow also till her death."

From this small beginning the Graves Dairy, the only dairy in the immediate Fort Collins area, developed. The family purchased more land, installed a sprinkler system to help raise alfalfa, and converted that crop into pellets with a dehumidifier plant. Many stages of the new venture were experimental, storing the pellets, for instance, and farmers came from Russia and Africa to see the Graves' operation. The Graves themselves became world travelers and visited many of their friends in distant countries. Helen Graves always insisted on rural outings when they arrived abroad, firmly stating: **"We must see farms. My husband is a farmer!"**

Their son, Robert, graduated from the veterinary college in 1957. He carries on the dairy since his father's death in 1974. He is proud that people still can whip their regular dairy cream just as they could the first twelve pints back in the depression.(65)

STATUS OF WOMEN

Did women find life more difficult and limited in old Fort Collins than in older cities or were there opportunities which favored them? Modern activists search the accounts and attempt to generalize from the sampling. In actuality a case can be made for either side.

Ansel Watrous' summary of the life of Agnes Mason Giddings may well represent the male viewpoint of the day. She was the first white child born in the area, arriving in 1867. The family farm was near Willox Lane north of the river. She grew to "women's estate" and married E. Chester Giddings in 1888. He provided her with a fine farm on the Boxelder from which he annually accumulated "a snug balance of profit". In 1909 he bought a handsome home on West Mountain for the winter months. Agnes "shared in his burdens and rejoiced in his successes" while joining clubs. She "found her greatest pleasures in the duties of her home surrounded by her husband and children."

This was the type of woman who received space in the biographical section of the county history. Watrous expected all who could afford it to pay for their entries. To some, books were unnecessary luxuries and they rejected that invitation much to the regret of their descendants. There were

Mary Hackerd Calloway ranch wife 1880's.

Ida Patterson Fairfield, nurse 1890's.

about nine pictures of pioneer couples and about thirty individual portraits of women placed along side the husband. The many wives omitted were probably not neglected because of their unimportance but because of deaths, second marriages, and other complications. People may have liked to forget the struggles of youth when economic security had been achieved. In a paragraph on Mrs. Bolivar Tedmon, Watrous wrote details of her ancestry including Ethan Allen, but made no mention of her little millinery shop. He did note that Mrs. George Buss sold good cheese which she made in her home.

The widows with children had to make their own way and some did remarkably well. Kate Trimble, widowed in 1876, raised her family, sustained and encouraged by relatives, and she put her own picture with her husband's in the county history. She died in 1911. Mary Calloway came west as a bride in 1869, was widowed in 1879, married her brother-in-law, and lost him in 1891. She put both men in the publication and tucked the book's proof for the Calloway entries carefully away in a trunk with her own picture and a lock of hair.

Mrs. Edith Simpson's hair dressing parlors.

Auntie Stone, most famous of all widows in the area, set a distinguished example for other women who wanted to work by her skill in running boarding houses.

Throughout the following years many came to support and educate their children and be close to the college while filling this important economic niche in the community. William Watrous' daughter, Ida, became a pretty nurse. Vincenz Demmel, the shoemaker had a school teacher daughter, Maggie. Laura Makepeace, the butcher's daughter, taught country school, became a librarian at the college, and wrote on Aus-

Interior of Mrs. M.C. Coleman's "Nimble Nickel"

Theodosia Ammons, Agricultural College faculty early 1900's.

Lilly Bullard and friends in Riding Club on College Avenue.

tralian libraries as well as enjoying her home town. These were the usual professions along with dressmaker, milliner, and all the others advertised in the papers.

Some of the businessmen found their match in shrewd capable women who managed ranches and lamb feeding projects efficiently. Roy Portner observed them on many occasions around Fort Collins and respected their business judgments.

Mrs. Ledru Rhodes, married first to Joe Mason and then to Rhodes who had worked on irrigation law in the '70's, ran a newspaper for a while. Mrs. Edith Simpson had a hairdressing parlor in the early 1900's. Mrs. M.C. Coleman ran the "Nimble Nickel." She dealt in ladies' furnishings, combs, neckwear, and novelties of glass and china. Over her counter passed three to four thousand different articles. "Everyone knows Mrs. Coleman and her ability to handle such a trade."

Since the land grant colleges were coeducational from the beginning there was always opportunity for the gifted woman in the field of scholarship. Grace Patton, whose family home was on College Avenue, graduated in 1885 and was on the faculty in various capacities till 1895 when she became superintendent of education for the state with her office in Denver.

She got out a newspaper, first in Fort Collins, then one in Denver called "The Colorado Woman." Theodosia Ammons, the governor's sister, joined the faculty in Home Economics. When she entertained in her home on Howes Street in 1896, "intellectual and memory test games were indulged in till half past nine when a dainty lunch was served."

While home economics was the field most open to women, they got other staff positions. Ruth J. Wattles' flair for dramatic production made her a well-known campus character. Another woman faculty member, Alice Curtis, impressed young students like Justus Wilkinson with her accounts of chaining herself to posts in the battle for the suffrage amendment.

A campus dormitory now bears the name of Virginia Corbett who came in 1900 to teach history and be head of the college library. In 1908 she was dean of women. Periods away broadened her horizons. In 1923 she was in Nanking, China. Her death in 1932 ended a career of leadership and dedication to the college.

Some found happiness in their families and some preferred careers. Many enjoyed volunteer services for the greatest part of the church work was carried by the women. Those with special talents and motivation developed hobbies. Lillie Nicholson was an acknowledged leader in the Riding Club and when she married E.B. Bullard in 1910 the report was that she had been offered a job "in a circus contemplating European travel, but preferred matrimonial bliss to fame in the saw dust arena." She thoroughly enjoyed ranch life and turned her hand to operating a beauty parlor for a while during a period when ranching didn't pay.

The career women were highly respected and so were those who found the social whirl to their liking. Amanda Wheat invested in considerable real estate. She was part owner of the Kissock Block. Her lawn fete at a home on Remington was a festive occasion. The hostesses spread oriental rugs under the trees. Japanese screens shielded the street view. Eight tables set for forty guests varied in arrangement. One was a rose table with a cut glass rose bowl filled with La France roses. Another table had a luncheon cloth embroidered with ferns and corresponding centerpiece. A third had forget-me-nots. The menu included sandwiches, salads, olives, salted almonds, ices, strawberries, cakes, and fruit punch. The guests included Mrs. Lee and her daughter, Rose, Mrs. Hottel, Mrs. Kissock, Mrs. Scott, and Mrs. McHugh. This was in 1895!

Another elegant party given at the Tedmon's country home

for daughter, Anna, in August, 1915 was a Chinese tea. The lawn was transformed into a Chinese tea garden, with garlands of blossoms threaded through branches. A parrot added a blaze of color. The hostess wore a Chinese robe and the food was prepared by a Chinese resident of Fort Collins. Ruth Edwards, who later taught Spanish at the college, won a contest in a struggle with the Chinese alphabet. These tidbits suggest that women found a variety of ways to contribute to life in the town and thoroughly enjoyed doing so.(66)

GRASS ROOTS DEMOCRACY: PROBLEMS IN CITY GOVERNMENT

Thirty-five mayors guided policy-making in the town between 1879 and 1975. The title of Mayor was first used after a municipal reorganization to meet state regulations. In territorial days Fort Collins operated under a Board of Trustees. The mayors were drawn from a variety of professions and included at least one rancher, sheep feeder, doctor, dentist, lawyer, merchant, psychologist, horse dealer, professor, and mortician. The budget in the 1880's was about $3,600, in 1952 $340,000, and in 1975 about $26,000,000.

Uncle Ben Whedbee did much of the work as first mayor in his store. In 1882 a real city hall with a belfry and bell was built on Walnut to house the fire station on the first floor and offices on the second. This remained the seat of government until 1957, serving a population which grew from 1300 to 25,000. The furniture in the first recorder's office consisted of some cane-bottomed arm chairs and a walnut desk. In 1888 each of the eight aldermen was provided with a solid cherry desk. From 1883, when Fort Collins became a city of second class, until 1913 the government was the mayor-aldermen type so popular then in the United States.

The work of the city officials included keeping abreast of all the new modern developments, satisfying esthetic and moral standards, and resolving personnel problems. When William Watrous was appointed night watchman in November,

Drawing city hall and fire station 1881.

City hall and station photo early 1880's.

Fire department on Walnut.

238

1882, the incumbent refused to yield and so both patrolled the streets for a time. Watrous, Loomis, and Handy went to Longmont, Denver, Pueblo, Canon City, and Salida in October, 1882, inspecting water works and studying equipment in preparation for selecting machinery for Fort Collins. In December, a representative of the Gutta Percha and Rubber Company of New York demonstrated to city officials types of hose recommended for fire protection.(67)

In 1887 the council debated the introduction of electric lights. These became a reality in 1888, the same year that the first sewer was built along Mountain Avenue from the new Franklin school to Lincoln Avenue, then northeast on Lincoln to the river. William Miner, rancher and partner of Senator

Warren in Wyoming, pushed for electricity, based on the success Warren and others were having in Cheyenne. The sewer project was the specialty of John A.C. Kissock, a Canadian who moved to Fort Collins in 1874. He was interested in cattle, real estate, merchandising, abstracting and insurance, and he used his years as alderman to further the development of sewers. There was no thought in the nineteenth century of treating the sewage before it poured into the river. However, there was an effort in 1896 to prevent sawmills, many of which used water power, from putting sawdust into the streams. In 1911 sewage lines stretched for nineteen and one quarter miles about the town.

The automobile changed traffic styles in the early 1900's. Dr. Paul McHugh signed an ordinance in 1904 permitting cars to drive twelve miles an hour on city streets, and eight miles around corners. The council watched a demonstration of Cripple Creek's new fire truck in 1912. The fire department acquired an American La France fire engine in 1914, and still used it in 1951. Members of the council authorized the first pavement construction in 1916. Their granting a franchise for the street car in 1906, buying the system in 1919, and operating it until 1951, provided mass transit.

Besides all the revolutionary changes of twentieth century technology which updated the little frontier town, there were constant minor adjustments to petty problems because of the town's rural character. No pigs could run at large after 1874, no chickens or poultry after 1910, but barns with livestock exist within the city limits even in 1975. Wagons loaded with beet pulp could not stand on the pavement according to an ordinance in 1920.

The citizens felt they could rely on the judgment of the council in April, 1885, because the eight men from the four wards were all heavy taxpayers. That group then included Bouton, Avery, Hottel, Arthur, J.C. Evans, Patterson, and Alford. They had established a reputation for leadership and frugality in government, keeping taxes low. They also had used their own money as private citizens to get many things done to improve the town. Franklin Avery, after surveying the streets, issued regulations for tree planting. In 1879 William Patterson planted trees along the whole length of College Avenue to the "college in the country," beginning the shaded avenue which was so pleasant when impressive residences were built along the street at the turn of the century.(68)

In 1887 William Miner and James Arthur, who both served as mayors in the '90's, with Loomis and Avery privately arranged for the purchase of Vescelius Grove to provide a park and pleasure ground on the river, open and free to all. Seats, benches, dancing platform, hammocks and merry-go-round were all part of the equipment. They hoped the city would arrange a foot bridge opposite Linden so the area would be a five-minute walk from the Tedmon House. The city still owns at least a portion of this area, but has not been using it as a park.

These tiny beginnings showed what people wanted in their city. As the population grew larger, the city was slow in taking over the work that a few individuals could manage privately in the early years. In 1927 an ordinance on trees and city beautification was passed but nothing was really done until the appointment of Carl Jorgensen as arborist in 1963. There was a zoning ordinance in 1929 but no board to enforce it until after the new charter of 1954.

A fortunate cooperative arrangement of the city with the Roosevelt National Forest in 1918 led to the creation of a mountain park in the Poudre Canyon. That lovely valley was rapidly becoming a private summer vacation area. The park was named for Ansel Watrous who had watched the town prosper and had worked through his newspaper and his history book to guard and improve the quality of life.

There were always complaints to the city council on the moral behavior of individuals. Dr. Ethan Allen Lee as mayor in 1890 waged a relentless war against the prostitutes. Jack Currie, who had a livery stable in the early days, was worried about the need for more lights at the corner of Remington and Mulberry in June, 1917. It was "a regular 'lovers' lane' and the occupants of frat houses do not want light there. One large porch light has been broken." But nowhere did the city get involved in social issues more complicated than the field of prohibition. This movement became such a political issue that after the women of Colorado received the vote in 1893 an alderwoman was elected to the council in 1895. The organization of the women for the vote in this area rallied around that one question. Mrs. William O. Collins, when she visited her husband at Fort Laramie in 1863, rejected eggnog at the officers' parties. Later she returned to her Ohio home where she helped found the Women's Christian Temperance Union in 1874. The men did not like the rough saloons either in the 1870's and feared they would discourage settlers from bringing families so the Board of Trustees permitted sale of liquor from May, 1873 until October, 1875 only through the one drug store operated by Whedbee. This was repealed and control of taverns planned through licensing. (69)

On Circus Day in May, 1880 "the drunks were three or four deep in the cooler floor, a disgusting mass of brutish humanity." In June, 1881 prostitutes rode through the city on horseback. A beer garden was planned and beer was sold on Sunday. One December night in 1881 James Shaw froze to death on Walnut and Linden right in front of the Presbyterian Church after drinking at Lindenmeier's saloon. The coroner's jury found it was the usual custom of that saloon owner to put intoxicated people in a rear unheated shed so there was danger that the accident might be repeated. With such incidents as background, the local chapter of the W.C.T.U. formed in August, 1880, got busy. Among the leaders was Mrs. Charlotte Calista Edwards, mother of Alfred Augustus and Robert Edwards. She had come west to keep house for Alfred till his marriage in 1883.

The first success for the ladies followed the address of Governor St. Clair of Kansas in the Fort Collins Opera House in January, 1884. A council supporting prohibition was elected in April and an ordinance prohibiting saloons passed. Its abandonment eleven months later was due to a simple reckoning of financial loss to the city treasury. The saloon keepers had been paying one-third the cost of government, $1,200. This was accepted as a temporary setback for the women and they concentrated on getting the vote to express their desire. Carrie Chapman Catt, a national figure in women's suffrage, spoke at the Opera House in October, 1893, the year the State Legislature gave women the vote.

In April, 1895 Frederick Baker and other anti-license council members won the election. Alice Edwards, whose mother-in-law worked so hard to start the W.C.T.U. in Fort Collins, received 54 votes in the second ward. Her opponent, T.H. Robertson, a successful merchant with a store on Linden and a fine house still standing at 420 Mountain got only 52. Baker appointed Alice to committees on streets, alleys and bridges and to fire protection boundaries and inspection as though her presence were not at all unusual. After all his wife was a graduate of Oberlin, the first college in the United States to adopt coeducation.(70)

Though Mrs. Edwards moved to another ward in the city and thus lost her office the following year, the platform on which she had run was adopted. The council passed an ordinance prohibiting the sale of liquor. When Frank Miller's license for his saloon on Linden expired on June 11, 1896 it ended the sale of liquor within the town. The women had used the ballot effectively.

The **Courier** noted:

**The melancholy days have come
The saddest yet, we fear,
For every man in town
Must now give up his beer.**

The men could laugh, for they fully expected the experiment would last only a year, perhaps, till the next election as the earlier two episodes had. In reality the "melancholy days" outlived even the national repeal of prohibition and endured until a city-wide vote in 1968 with strong student support for "Suds in the Center" permitted liquor sales. An all male council passed the ordinance in 1969 to carry out the decision.

When Mabel Preble was elected to the council in 1971 and became mayor in 1973 and when Nancy Gray and Peggy Reeves were added to the enlarged council in 1973, they represented broad interest in government and quite a different approach from that of the suffragists of the 1890's.

It is interesting that intellectual currents which were nationwide sometimes had repercussions in the little city council. William James' work in 1885 in psychology at Harvard University with a medium, Leonora Piper, became a topic of wide interest in the ensuing years. The council was haunted by the problem. In 1900 an ordinance prohibited mesmerism and hypnotism in Fort Collins. In 1913 fortune tellers were banned.

Some changes in voting methods for the state affected the city. The Australian or secret ballot, tested first in South Australia, was introduced into the United States in 1888 and gradually accepted. Fort Collins tried it first in 1891. Before the election there was a practice session in Denver and a diagram appeared in the paper. A few people were bewildered and their ballots had to be discarded, but the innovation was well received.(71)

Voting machines were first used here in November, 1964. Some people announced they would not participate in the election but the county Democratic chairman encouraged the public: "All should be assured that voting machines are easy to operate. The election judges have been trained." There were then 58 precincts in the county and 35 installed the machines. The local League of Women Voters got a surprise $200.00 contribution from the company manufacturing the machines for its support in training voters and in breaking down voter resistance.

The structure of city governments changed in the nation, but Fort Collins resisted early experimentation. The National Municipal League formed in 1894, studied the problem. The mayor-council type was classic and familiar. Galveston launched the commission form in 1901, and it was widely imitated, but criticized for its lack of focus on responsibility. The city manager plan was introduced in Sumter, South Carolina, in 1912, and Dayton, Ohio, in 1913 and gradually replaced the commission type. Yet Fort Collins changed to the commission structure in 1913 although its weaknesses were being acknowledged.

The **Courier** optimistically defended the idea in October, 1913: "The commission form of government has passed its experimental stage." It needed time to make a good record. Those who questioned the lack of accountability among officials were worrying needlessly. The commissioner of finance was really the old-fashioned treasurer. A.A. Edwards, accepting the office, was highly respected, a pioneer, member of the State Board of Agriculture, and neighbor and related by marriage to Franklin Avery. The fine character and reputation of the men who accepted the jobs made the system function through the '20's and '30's.

Among the distinguished residents who struggled long hours as commissioners for low salaries was Sam Clammer, who had already been both mayor and alderman under the earlier government. He was a promoter and primary owner of the new Northern Hotel which was the leading hotel after the Tedmon House on Jefferson was demolished in 1911. Fred Stover, son of a pioneer rancher, had lived north of Jefferson, then in a comfortable house on Remington, and when mayor, in one of the imposing brick homes on College. Harry Hartman, another lawyer, came to Fort Collins in 1904 and twenty-six years later became mayor. Roy Portner settled here in 1902, first doing farm work, then becoming interested in real estate, lamb-feeding, and irrigation. As commissioner he supported the project to run the old Arthur ditch underground. Burgess Coy, engineer for both the Laramie River tunnel and the Moffatt tunnel, and son of a Fort Collins pioneer, directed the construction.

Earl Douglas's parents settled in Fort Collins in 1879 and he graduated from the college in 1900. His profession was that of soil chemist. As Commissioner of Finance in 1934 he led the forces favoring municipal control of electricity. The voters had directed the council to acquire a power plant in 1932. In 1935 bonds were authorized and the plant became a reality.

In spite of some steps forward, the commission form was inadequate, but the voters resisted change which might cost more in a period of depression. They weighed the value of well-known resident amateurs against imported trained professionals and rejected the city manager form in 1938. The commissioners themselves decided to act and without a change in the charter they elevated Guy Palmes to the office of city manager in 1939. He had demonstrated ability in managing city power since coming from New Mexico in 1935 to head up the new power plant. The job description for city manager in Fort Collins was shaped around Palmes' background requiring that he must be a qualified engineer. His term in office was council-controlled and hiring and firing of key personnel required council approval.

The town was still under 14,000 in population in the '40's when reform in city government gained headway. A wearied elderly public servant once warned a young enthusiastic idealist criticizing the system: "There's **one** good thing about it, young man, it works!" That was the principle J. Morris Howell, popularly known as "Tuck", learned in serving as Commissioner of Finance from 1946 to 1952. The Junior Chamber of Commerce, then one of the community-oriented organizations, had sponsored his candidacy.

Howell, whose profession was insurance, tackled the fiscal side of city government. In the 1920's there had been one publicized case of fiscal mismanagement where an official resigned excusing his lapses by a nervous breakdown. Howell spent two years developing expertise in municipal bonding. Each of the commissioners worked on one phase of city government, so in the joint meetings, his knowledge helped in decision making. Later council people were to learn only after election the tremendous proportion of their time required to study all parts of government. The constant pressure on the Commissioners from voters emotional over trivial details or lacking in realistic business experience kept their telephones jingling. They worked hard and government experts came from many parts of the world to study the process in Fort Collins, despite its weaknesses.

There were several areas where public and private interests in city policy so overlapped that very few people really knew what was happening. The frugal system of hiring a part-time city attorney meant that this individual had to build up his private practice for a financial base, and the possibility of conflict of interest made the city's arrangement for legal advice a questionable economy.

The city thus gradually moved to the city manager type in spite of the reluctant voters. In the 1950's the women again played an important role in local politics. The national League of Women Voters was a development of the 1920's after the woman suffrage amendment to the federal constitution. Dorothy Heynau and others formed a local club in 1951. Their first task was an analysis of the local government. The need to up-date the charter to fit the actual situation was apparent. Good voter education helped win support. Would the charter pass even now? The barbers thought it would when an un-official "barber shop poll" was conducted just before the April election in 1954. The Junior Chamber of Commerce blew horns to arouse voters to go to the polls. The supporters carried the amendment and the city manager's job was form-ally recognized. He could appoint and remove all city em-ployees except the city attorney and municipal judge, so responsibility was centered.

The fact that Palmes continued in office until 1961, filling a term of twenty-two years, meant that the new charter did not seem drastic in its effect on the town. Four other men have followed Palmes in the job. The first two served less than two years each. Max Norris was appointed in 1961 and fired in 1963 because of a dispute over his management of the police department. One hundred citizens attended an open meeting on the question. Harvey Johnson was mayor and the council vote was divided 3-2 over dismissal. Ralph Boos had been assistant city manager in Las Vegas and manager in Laramie before his appointment. His period of compatibility with the council was brief, and he left in 1965.(72)

Tom Coffey made a longer record and wanted to continue in 1972 after his sixty-fifth birthday. Though he was encour-aged in this by the council, the matter was placed on the ballot. The voters decided against him and even put through an amendment making the manager responsible to the elect-orate every four years, as well as to the council. Since this changed the whole system, the constitutionality of this amend-ment is being questioned (1975).

Between 1950 and 1970 the population of Fort Collins almost tripled and planning could not keep up with the rapid development of new suburbs. In 1951 there were fourteen precincts, in 1975 forty-four. To help new and old residents understand the changes and cooperate in planning, a new organization, "Designing Tomorrow Today," popularly called DT^2 was formed in 1970 with some financial support from the city council and the Chamber of Commerce. Richard Siever,

Valeria Ogden, and Merta Cook as successive executive directors have coordinated the work of many volunteers, interested
citizens, and organizations to gather information and advise
the council in a constructive program of city improvement.

The specific projects listed in the capital improvements
program were the result of two years' study and discussions
in open forums by DT^2. The vote on February 20, 1973 for a
one cent rise in sales tax to support these passed with over
8660 voters participating. The charter election in 1954 had
brought 3000 to the polls. Dr. Karl Carson, council member
and mayor worked with the DT^2 group and drew on his experience and leadership in the state league of municipalities.
Before 1950 the council meetings could work more in the style
of old-fashioned town meetings where points were debated and
problems resolved after audience participation. The creation of
DT^2 with its committees for discussion and study prior to
council meetings encouraged citizen concentration and review
before the formal session.

Robert Brunton, trained in city planning at Cornell University and with experience as city manager in Elgin, Illinois,
was selected in 1972 to succeed Tom Coffey. He found the
participants in this new organization as well as the League
of Women Voters a core of citizens wishing to be kept
thoroughly informed on city government.

The period of growth from 1950 to 1970 so altered the city
that many who were here before that period regretted the
changes. All Colorado had moved to the excitement of growth.
One dramatic figure in the promotion program was William
B. Foshay. He built a thirty-two story tower in Minneapolis,
lost his financial empire, served a prison term, and was par-
doned by Franklin D. Roosevelt. He then turned to Chamber
of Commerce work in the west. In 1936 he began an eight year
stint in Salida where he "invented a fur-bearing trout" for
publicity. He worked in Alamosa and in Winslow, Arizona,
before coming to Fort Collins in 1951 for a short period. Here
a Nazarene church minister severely criticized his propaganda
showing a comely queen enticing tourists to Fort Collins,
the Eden of Colorado. Planning in the '70's has turned less
glamorous, but more statistical.(73)

A SENSE OF HISTORY

Very early in the town's development there was some recognition that the history of the little village was worth preserving. One method was by sharing experiences in clubs. In December, 1880 an "Oldtimer's Association" was formed with Dr. Timothy Smith, who had been doctor at the fort, as president. Auntie Stone was treasurer, and her nephew-in-law, Harris Stratton, secretary. Membership fees were three dollars a year, and eligibility depended upon residence before May 1, 1870. This barred Ansel Watrous, a rank newcomer of 1877.

The residence requirement had to be modified as the years rolled on, and many groups have organized to explore, share, or preserve Fort Collins history. Some have specific requirements like the DAR, the Pioneer Club, and the Fort Collins Westerners. Some welcome newcomers like the study group sponsored by the CSU Women's Association and the recently organized Fort Collins Historical Society.

The Pioneer Museum, completed in 1940, a federal WPA project, provides safekeeping for relics, and opportunity for the public to view them. The Landmark Commission advises the city on the status of historic buildings. Other committees are at work on the county. The Public Library with a grant for interviewing oldtimers is adding reminiscences like those collected by the Bancroft interviewers in 1886 and the CWA in the 1930's. The Archives and Special Collections in the CSU Library form a center for rare and unique material. The Heritage section of the local Centennial-Bicentennial Committee coordinates many phases. The DAR by reprinting the Watrous history and marking historic sites has stimulated interest, and many organizations not primarily formed for history are sharing in some aspects of restoration and preservation.

It sounds almost like a plethora of historical organizations but in a city of 60,000 all are useful for they provide a variety of emphasis and talent. Perhaps the multiplication of effort will preserve material which will delight the historians of the future just as the ordinary objects of one generation become the antiques of later ones.

Sometimes it seems that history is repeating itself. A piano tuner in Laramie wrote to D.M. Harris of the Commercial Hotel in February, 1895 that he was cycling to Denver. He planned to leave Laramie at 5 a.m., be in Fort Collins by 10:30, on to Loveland for lunch, and in Denver by 6. He urged Fort Collins riders to accompany him to Loveland. The introduction of the automobile dampened the cycling enthusiasm, but it was followed by a revival when smog and fuel shortages brought concern. Now he would find a bicycle campus and a bicycle town, and the counterpart of Mrs. A.W. Scott's electric car is on the way.

Square dancing, the schottische, and the polka went out about the time Auntie Stone died. The elegant Hotel Colorado in Glenwood Springs promised at its opening in 1893 there would be no square dancing. But in 1926 Henry Ford published a book and provided a teacher of old dances at Greenfield Village in Dearborn, Michigan, and in 1927 Frank Watrous, Ansel's cousin, announced a pioneer dancing club in Fort Collins to perpetuate old dances. The new wave of the old had begun.

The names of the Fort Collins pioneers themselves sometimes recalled an earlier stage of history. There were Auntie Stone's son, Washington Irving Robbins, her partner, Henry Clay Peterson, and many others: Benjamin Franklin and Andrew Jackson Hottel, Ethan Allen Lee, Bolivar Tedmon, and Montezuma Fuller. Some of these in maturity hid behind initials, but all shared in the dream of extending America to the Rockies. Plans must change directions, and much that was old must go, but as the Centennial-Bicentennial approaches, a re-evaluation of the goals of the pioneers may help in the selection.

Endnotes

Preface
(1) **Fort Collins Express**, Nov. 28, 1918, p.1.
Part I The Overview
(1) Seletha Brown, **Rivalry at the River** (Golden: The Silver State Printers, 1962), p.62.
(2) Capt. William F. Drannan, **Thirty-one Years on the Plains and in the Mountains** (Chicago: Rhodes & McClure Publishing Co., 1904, p.96.
(3) Janet Lecompte, "Antoine Janis, in LeRoy R. Hafen, **The Mountain Men and the Fur Trade of the Far West** (Glendale, Calif.: Arthur H. Clarke Co., 1971), Vol. 8, p.200.
(4) Robert L. Perkin, **The First Hundred Years** (Garden City, N.Y.: Doubleday & Co., 1959), p.42,58.
(5) Ansel Watrous, **History of Larimer County** (Fort Collins: Courier Printing & Publishing Co., 1911), p.56,86,277.
(6) **Rocky Mountain News**, Mar. 16, 1890, p.20.
(7) Elizabeth Keays Stratton, "My First Christmas in Fort Collins," **Fort Collins Evening Courier**, Jan. 27, 1910, p.4.
(8) Watrous, **History**, p.122.
(9) Watrous, **History**, p.116; family record, Margaret Isaac, 1285 S. Steele St., Denver.
(10) **Courier**, Oct. 9, 1906, p.1; **Coloradoan**, Mar. 1, 1930.
(11) Interview, Mrs. Lois Demmel McQuain, 1855 S. Lowell Boulevard, Denver, Mar. 11, 1973.
(12) **Express**, Mar. 12, 1880, p.3; **Courier**, Nov. 21, 1882; Aug. 27, 1906, p.1.
(13) **Courier**, Sept. 14, 1887; Dec. 27, 1902, p.4.
(14) **Courier**, Sept. 9, 1880; Aug. 27, 1896, p.1.
(15) **Courier**, Feb. 23, June 19, 1882; April 14, 1892, p.6; **Express**, Jan. 23, 1884, p.4.
(16) **Courier**, Feb. 17, 1881; **Express**, Aug. 27, 1914, p.6.
(17) **Courier**, Feb. 22, 1883, p.2; Sept. 10, 1885.
(18) Father Francis Byrne, Autobiography, Manuscript, Colorado Historical Society.
(19) **Courier**, Mar. 26, July 9, 1885; **Express**, April 4, 1896.
(20) Norman J. Bender, "Crusade of the Blue Banner," in **The Colorado Magazine**, Vol. 47, No. 2, spring, 1970, p.98,107.
(21) **Courier**, Aug. 6, 1885, p.6.
(22) **Courier**, Jan. 20, Feb. 20, 1879.

(23) **Courier**, Aug. 25, 1906, p.1; Mar. 25, 1908, p.1.
(24) Watrous, **History**, p.475; O. Wilford Olsen, **A history of Zoology and Entomology** (Fort Collins: Colorado State University, 1973), p.4.
(25) Cora Saxton Horsley, Scrapbook of Clippings. I, p.6, owned by Juliana Sloan Miller.
(26) Watrous, **History**, p.486.
(27) Bender, "Crusade of the Blue Banner," p.105.
(28) Fred Anderson, "Prohibition in Fort Collins 1873-1909," March, 1970, typescript, p.4,8, CSU Archives.
(29) **Courier**, May 29, 1879, p.3; Feb. 12, 1885; Philip Jordan, **Singin' Yankee** (Minneapolis: University of Minnesota Press, 1946), p.249,251,271.
(30) Fred Anderson, "Prohibition in Fort Collins 1884-1896," Dec. 1, 1970, p.15, CSU Archives.
(31) **Courier**, June 2, 1882, p.4; April 22, 1884, p.5.
(32) **Courier**, Jan. 9, 1903, p.4.
(33) **Courier**, Jan. 4, 1879; Oct. 7, 1880.
(34) Interview notes, Bernice Schultz with Mary Calloway, Feb. 1, 1934, Colorado Historical Society; **Larimer County Stockgrowers Association 1884-1956** (Fort Collins: Don-Art Printers, 1956), p.43,46,66,80.
(35) E.W. Whitcomb, "Reminiscences of a Pioneer," in Eunice G. Anderson, **First Biennial Report of the State Historian of the State of Wyoming** (Laramie: Laramie Printing Co., 1920), p.93.
(36) **Larimer County Stockgrowers' Association**, p.59.
(37) **Courier**, April 28, 1892, p.1; T.A. Larson, **History of Wyoming** (Lincoln: University of Nebraska Press, 1965), p.278.
(38) Carrie Williams Darnell, "Three Ranch Children," typescript, 1966, p.9, Fort Collins Public Library.
(39) **Larimer County Stockgrowers Association**, p.49.
(40) Amelia Buss, Diary 1866-67, Typescript, p.12,27,30,44, Special Collections, CSU Library; **Courier**, May 1, 1879, p.3.
(41) Alvin T. Steinel, **History of Agriculture in Colorado** (Fort Collins: State Agricultural College, 1926), p.592.
(42) **Express**, Oct. 14, 1881, p.3; **Courier**, Mar. 27, 1879; June 27, 1882.
(43) **Courier**, Jan. 25, 1879; Feb. 10, 1881, p.3.
(44) **Courier**, Aug. 12, 1880, p.3.
(45) **Courier**, Sept. 18, 1884, p.5.
(46) **Courier**, June 29, 1893, p.1.
(47) **Courier**, April 9, 1885; **Express**, April 8, 1915.
(48) **Courier**, Feb. 20, 1879, p.3.
(49) **Express**, Oct. 14, 1881, p.3.
(50) Horsley, Scrapbook I, p.14.
(51) **Coloradoan**, Nov. 5, 1930, p.2.
(52) **Fort Collins Standard**, May 6, 1874; **Courier**, Aug. 26, 1880.
(53) **Courier**, May 31, June 6,7, 1882.
(54) **Courier**, June 8, 1882.
(55) **Courier**, Nov. 9, 1882, p.4.
(56) **Express**, Jan. 12, 1884, p.4; **Courier**, Oct. 22, 1885; July 12, 1888.
(57) **Courier**, Sept. 10, 1891; Aug. 10, 1893, p.1.
(58) **Courier**, Nov. 4, 1880, p.3; Sept. 25, 1882; July 9, 1885.
(59) **Courier**, May 20, 1897, p.1.
(60) **Express-Courier**, Jan. 4, 1932, p.6.
(61) Horsley, Scrapbook II, p.21.
(62) Benjamin P. Draper, Colorado Manuscripts in the Bancroft Library, Colorado Dictations, Larimer County, 1886, manuscript, 1946, unpaged, in the Denver Public Library.
(63) **Rocky Mountain News**, Mar. 16, 1890, p.20; **Colorado Graphics**, Aug. 6, 1892, p.3.
(64) **Rocky Mountain News**, Dec. 27, 1906.
(65) **Courier**, Oct. 12, 1903, p.1; Paul C. Huszar, D.W. Seckler, D.D. Rohdy, **Economics of Irrigation System Consolidation** (Fort Collins: Colorado State University Experiment Station, Technical Bulletin 105, 1969), p.2; Robert G. Dunbar, "Water Conflicts and Controls," in Carl Ubbelohde, ed., **A Colorado Reader** (Boulder: Pruett Press, Inc., 1962), p.225.
(66) Steinel, **History of Agriculture**, p.297; R.J. Wattles, "Mile High College: History of Colorado Agricultural and Mechanical College," 1946, p.266,339, typescript, CSU Archives.
(67) **Courier**, Oct. 17, 1903, p.1; Aug. 3, 1911, p.1; Steinel, **History of Agriculture**, p.473.
(68) **Courier**, June 30, 1904.
(69) **Express**, April 7, 1918, p.1.
(70) **Courier**, Dec. 19, Dec. 30, 1902; **Express**, Mar. 21, 1915, p.1.
(71) **Courier**, Feb. 22, May 23, May 26, 1904.
(72) **Courier**, April 1, 1905.
(73) **Express-Courier**, Nov. 24, 1930, p.1.
(74) **Courier**, Oct. 9, 1907, p.7, Edith E. Bucco, "Founded on Rock: Colorado's Stout Stone Industry," in **The Colorado Magazine**, Vol.51, Fall, 1974, p.325.
(75) C.V. Maddux, "Soliciting Beet Labor," in **Through The Leaves**, October, 1922, p.4, Great Western Sugar Company Library.
(76) Robert N. McLean, Charles A. Thomson, **Spanish and Mexican in Colorado** (New York: Board of National Missions, Presbyterian Church, Aug., 1924), p.34,37; Wayne Moquin, Charles Van Doren, ed., **A Documentary History of the Mexican Americans** (New York: Praeger, 1971), p.258.
(77) Copies of these issues, Special Collections, CSU.
(78) The Alonzo Martinez Post 187 now uses Peter Anderson's old farm home as their headquarters.

Part II

(1) Donald Jackson, Mary Lee Spence, ed., **The Expeditions of John Charles Fremont** (Urbana: University of Illinois Press, 1970) p.723.
(2) Charles H. Carey, ed., **Journals of Theodore Talbot** (Portland, Oregon: Metropolitan Press, 1931), p.20.
(3) Gertrude Barnes, "Following Fremont's Trail Through Northern Colorado," in **The Colorado Magazine**, Vol. 19, No. 5, Sept. 1942, p.185; Watrous, **History**, p.25.
(4) **Coloradoan**, Nov. 10, 1930, p.8.
(5) Watrous, **History**, p.84; Virginia Trenholm, **The Arapahoes, Our People** (Norman: University of Oklahoma Press, 1970), p.150.
(6) Watrous, **History**, p.47; C.A. Duncan, **Memories of Early Days in the Cache la Poudre Valley**, p.24, undated pamphlet, Fort Collins Public Library; Interview notes, Bernice Schultz with Mr. and Mrs. Frank Chaffee, 1933-34, p.198, Colorado Historical Society; Eugene Smith, ed., **Pioneer Epic-Sarah Ann Milner Smith: 1844-1939** (Boulder: Johnson Publishing Co., 1951), p.42.
(7) **Report of the Commissioner of Indian Affairs**, 1863, p.125,131,136; 1864, p.235-237.
(8) **Courier**, Jan. 27, 1910, p.4.
(9) **Colorado Transcript**, Golden, Jan. 9, 1867, p.4.
(10) Evadene Burris Swanson, "Friday: Roving Arapaho," in **Annals of Wyoming**, spring, 1975.
(11) Draper, Colorado Manuscripts, biographies, Buss Harrington, Hallowell.
(12) Janis letters, Pioneer Museum; **Courier**, Jan. 27, 1887, p.1.
(13) Robert O. Rupp, "Fort Collins Military Reservation," p.33, typescript in Fort Collins Public Library.
(14) **Rocky Mountain News**, Mar. 16, 1890, p.20; Indenture record, No. 99, Oct. 18, 1863, Larimer County Courthouse.
(15) Harold M. Dunning, **The Overland Trail North** (Boulder: Johnson Publishing Co., 1969), p.40.
(16) Catharine Wever Collins, "An Army Wife Comes West," Letters of Mrs. Collins 1863-64 in **The Colorado Magazine**, Vol. 31, No. 4, Oct., 1954, p.241 ff.
(17) W.O. Collins, Order Book, Oct. 27-April 8, 1863, p.4,30,33,49. Special Collections, CSU; Smith, **Pioneer Epic**, p.36.
(18) Mrs. J.W. Hanna, "My Pioneer Home on the Cache la Poudre," in **The Colorado Magazine**, Vol. 15, Nov., 1938, p.223,228; Eugene F. Ware, **The Indian Wars of 1864** (Lincoln: University of Nebraska Press, 1965), p.74,82,255; Merrill J. Mattes, **The Great Platte River Road** (Lincoln: Nebraska State Historical Society, 1965), Vol. 25, p.479.
(19) **Courier**, Oct. 16, 1884, p.4; **Express**, Mar. 12, 1887, p.1; **Denver Times**, Jan. 11, 1901, p.7.
(20) **Denver Post**, Mar. 4, 1911; Military record, George W. Pingree, National Archives; Norman Fry, **Cache la Poudre, The River** (Fort Collins, 1954), p.11; R.E. Ford, "Pingree in Park," in **Colorado Forester**, 1930, p.37 ff; W.H. Wroten, Jr. "Railroad Tie Industry in the Central Rocky Mountain Region 1867-1900," PhD. thesis, Dept. of History, U. of Co., 1956.
(21) **Courier**, Jan. 15, 1885. The tower was used later for drying hose, but the date "1914" was marked on the bell.
(22) **Courier**, June 18, 1896, p.1; Interviews, Carl Strauch, Harold Johnson, Ranch-Way Feeds.
(23) Bert Nelson, Edward Willis, Fort Collins Factory 1903-1955, typescript, p.25 in Great Western Sugar Company Library.
(24) **Courier**, April 13, 1899, p.3.
(25) **Courier**, Jan. 2, 1904, p.4; Jan. 22, 1904, p.4.
(26) **Express**, Jan. 3, 1884, p.4; Jan. 22, 1884, p.4; Interview Alice Swinscoe Pike, June 12, 1973.
(27) **Courier**, May 14, 1917, p.6.
(28) **Courier**, Aug. 29, 1895, p.1.
(29) **Courier**, Jan. 6, 1881, p.3.
(30) John Hartman, "A History of the Poudre Valley National Bank of Fort Collins," June 1, 1950, typescript, p.46 ff., United Bank Trust Dept.
(31) **Courier**, June 18, p.1; Aug. 6, p.1, 1896; **Express-Courier**, April 22, 1934.
(32) Clyde McIntyre, "Start and Development of the Presbyterian Church," p.84, undated reminiscences, Colorado Historical Society.
(33) Father Byrne, Autobiography; J.W. Lawrence, St. Luke's History 1875-1925,p.6.
(34) Allen Breck, **The Centennial History of the Jews of Colorado: 1859-1959** (Denver: Hirschfeld Press, 1960), p.75; **Courier**, March 19, 1904, p.1; Interview with Clarinda Lane, May, 1975.
(35) **Courier**, Nov. 5, 1891, p.1.
(36) **Express**, Dec. 30, 1880, p.2; Sept. 1, 1910, p.1; **Courier**, Jan. 22, 1885, p.1; Jan. 7, 1892; June 14, 1888.
(37) Wesley Swan, **Memoirs of an Old Timer** (Fort Collins: Don-Art Printers, 1972), p.75; Sylvester Birdsall Papers, Pioneer Museum.
(38) Interview, Herbert and Julia Damm.
(39) **Courier**, Dec. 29, 1888, p.4.
(40) **Courier**, Mar. 6, 1879, p.3.
(41) **Courier**, Oct. 2, 1879, p.3; Dec. 24, 1891, p.1; Oct. 9, 1907, p.4; **Express**, Sept. 9, 1880; **Express-Courier**, Sept. 18, 1927, p.1; Jessie Kissock Clark, "Pioneer Hotels in Larimer County," in **The Colorado Magazine**, Vol. 31, April, 1954.
(42) **Courier**, Oct. 19, 1893, p.1; Horsley, Scrapbook I, p.6.
(43) **Courier**, Feb. 23, June 15, 1882; June 18, 1896; **Express**, Jan. 23, 1884, p.4.
(44) **Courier**, April 5, 1883; Jan. 5, 1899; **Express**, Jan. 11, 1890; Interview with Kenneth Fuller.
(45) **Courier**, Jan. 11; April 10, 1879; Jan. 8, 1880.
(46) **Courier**, Aug. 31, 1893; Aug. 1, 1895; June 10, 1908, p.16; **Express**, Aug. 20, 1914, p.2.
(47) **Western Architect & Building News**, May, 1891, p.1; Harlan Thomas, Autobiographical Sketch c. 1941, College of Architecture and Urban Planning, U. of Wash., Seattle.
(48) Richard Brettell, **Historic Denver** (Denver: Historic Denver, 1973): Louise Ward Arps, **Denver in Slices** (Denver: Sage Books, 1959), p.169,171.
(49) **Courier**, Nov. 27, 1890, p.1.

(50) **Courier**, Nov. 26, Dec. 17, 1885; June 14, 1888, p.1; Dec. 21, 1893; Jan. 12, April 13, 1899.
(51) **Express**, June 4, 1914, p.5; **Courier**, Dec. 20, 1894, p.1; Jan. 3, 1895, p.3; April 18, 1895, p.1.
(52) Fry, **Cache la Poudre**, p.21.
(53) **Courier**, Jan. 3, 1895, p.3; June 24, 1908, p.4; Oct. 23, 1913, p.6.
(54) **Courier**, April 10, 1879, p.3.
(55) George S. Bobinski, **Carnegie Libraries** (Chicago: American Library Association, 1969), p.36; copies of correspondence on the library grant, Fort Collins Public Library.
(56) W.J. Morrill, "Birth of the Roosevelt National Forest," in **The Colorado Magazine**, Vol. 20, No. 5, Sept., 1943, p.178.
(57) Enos A. Mills, **Early Estes Park** (Big Mountain Press, 1963), p.XIV.
(58) **Express**, Mar. 6, 1908, p.5; **Courier**, Mar. 12, 1909, p.3.
(59) **Courier**, Oct. 27, 1916, **Express**, Oct. 15, 1914, p.6.
(60) **Courier**, Dec. 6, 1884, p.4; Horsley, Scrapbook II, p.5.
(61) **Express**, Aug. 22, 1915, p.1; E.S. Peyton, R.A. Moorman, "Last of the Birneys," in **American Railroad Journal** (San Marino: Golden West Books, 1965), p.66; "Some of My Best Friends are Streetcars," in **Saturday Evening Post**, Vol. 220, Dec. 6, 1947, p.42.
(62) **Courier**, April 12, 1883; Sept. 3, 1885; Mar. 17, 1892; **Express**, Oct. 8, 1887, p.1.
(63) Frank C. Miller Papers, Pioneer Museum.
(64) Fancher Sarchet, **Murder and Mirth: The Story of a Colorado Trial Lawyer** (Denver: Sage Books, Alan Swallow, 1956), p.27,145.
(65) Talk, W. Charles and Helen Graves to Western History Interest Group, Jan. 25, 1971.
(66) **Express**, Mar. 28, 1896, p.1; Aug. 6, 1915, p.5; **Courier**, June 27, 1895; April 4, 1910.
(67) **Courier**, Nov. 16, Dec. 4, 1882.
(68) **Courier**, June 18, 1896, p.1.
(69) **Courier**, April 9, 1885; June 5, 1917, p.3.
(70) **Courier**, Dec. 8, 1881, supplement, p.2; April 4, 1895, p.5.
(71) **Courier**, Oct. 15, 1891; Oct. 26, 1893; April 5, 1894.
(72) **Denver Post**, June 13, 1965, p.7.
(73) **Rocky Mountain News**, July 25, 1952, p.26.

Colorado State University Dates

1862   Congress passed Morrill Act authorizing land grant colleges

1870   Territorial Legislature established Agricultural College of Colorado to be located in Fort Collins

1876   Colorado's constitution included provision for "the Agricultural College at Fort Collins"

1877   First General Assembly of Colorado created State Board of Agriculture to administer the college

1879   Old Main completed; college opens for 19 students in September

1903   Name changed to Colorado State College of Agriculture and Mechanic Arts

1944   Name changed to Colorado Agricultural and Mechanical College

1957   Becomes Colorado State University

Early Key Dates

1836	Probable date of hiding of powder
1843	Fremont's second expedition
1854	Part of Nebraska Territory
1861	Colorado Territory organized; Larimer County established, including modern Jackson County, with Laporte as county seat
1862	Overland Stage route established through Laporte
1864	County government becomes active
1864-67	Military fort at Fort Collins
1867	Cheyenne is "end of track"
1868	Fort Collins becomes county seat
1869	Union Pacific line completed across nation
1872	Agricultural Colony organized to promote settlement at Fort Collins
1873	Town government for Fort Collins granted by County Board of Commissioners
1877	Fort Collins gets railroad connection "with the outside world"
1883	Fort Collins becomes city of the second class by state proclamation
1896-1969	Prohibition in Fort Collins
1907-1951	Streetcar system in operation
1911	Watrous' **History of Larimer County** published

Population Growth

Census of	Town or City	County
1870	—	838
1875	400-500?	—
1880	1,356	4,844
1890	2,011	9,712
1900	3,053	12,168
1910	8,210	25,270
1920	8,755	27,872
1930	11,489	33,137
1940	12,251	35,539
1950	14,937	43,554
1960	25,027	53,343
1970	43,377	89,900
1973	55,375	114,000

Mayors of Fort Collins

1. 1873-1879 Benjamin Whedbee President of Town Board, first official mayor
2. 1880 David Patton
3. 1881 Jacob Welch
4. 1882 George B. Brown
5. **1883 Abraham L. Emigh**; Fort Collins became a city of the second class
6. 1884 John M. Davidson
7. 1885-87 George Bristol
8. 1888 James C. Evans
9. 1889 Dr. E.A. Lee
10. 1890 Henry H. Hall
11. 1891-92 William B. Miner
12. 1893-94 James B. Arthur
13. 1895-1902 Frederick R. Baker
14. 1903-04 Dr. P.J. McHugh
15. 1905-08 Sam H. Clammer
16. 1909-10 Myron H. Akin
17. 1911-12 Jesse Harris
18. 1913 H.M. Balmer
    1913-18 Sam H. Clammer 1st mayor elected under the commission form of government provided by the 1913 charter; city gets home rule
19. 1918-24 Fred W. Stover
20. 1924-30 Frank R. Montgomery
21. 1930-36 Harry H. Hartman
22. 1936-42 Ray R. Mathews
23. 1942-48 William M. Bevington
24. 1948-54 Robert W. Hays
25. 1954-55 C.H. Alford
26. **1955-57 William H. Allen** 1st mayor under council-manager form of government provided by the 1954 charter
27. 1957-59 Robert W. Sears
28. 1959-61 Jack A. Harvey
29. 1961-63 Eugene H. Frink
30. 1963-67 Harvey J. Johnson
31. 1967-68 Dr. Thomas Bennett
32. 1968-73 Dr. Karl Carson
33. 1973-74 Ms. Mabel Preble
34. 1974-75 Dr. J.W.N. Fead
35. 1975- Jack Russell

City Managers

Mar. 1, 1939-Sept. 15, 1961 Guy Palmes
Sept. 15, 1961-June 17, 1963 Max Norris
June 17, 1963-Sept. 1, 1963 William Widdows
Sept. 1, 1963-June 19, 1965 Robert Boos
June 19, 1965-Sept. 30, 1965 Stanley Case (acting)
Oct. 1, 1965-June 12, 1972 Tom Coffey
June 13, 1972-October, 1972 Michael Di Tullio (acting)
October, 1972— Robert Brunton